Investing in Stocks: Between Growth and Value

Long Term Wealth Creation with Low Risk and Low Cost

Jean-Pierre Winandy, PhD

Limit of Liability/Disclaimer of Warranty

While the author has used his best efforts in preparing this book, he make no representation or warranties with respect to the accuracy or completeness of the contents of this book and specifically disclaim any implied warranties of merchantability or fitness for a particular purpose. No warranty may be created or extended by sales representatives or written sales materials.

This book is sold with the understanding that neither the author nor the publisher are engaged in rendering legal, accounting, investment advice or other professional services. The advice contained herein may not be suitable for your situation. You should consult with a professional where appropriate. Neither the publisher nor author shall be liable for any loss of profit or any commercial damages, including but not limited to special, incidental, consequential or other damages.

Table of Contents

About the Author

Jean-Pierre Winandy, a trained economist and lawyer with a PhD in tax law (University Panthéon-Assas, Paris II) has been investing in stocks for more than 40 years managing his own funds. In his professional life he has been an equity partner of several professional services firms ultimately with a large international law firm. He has been on the board of directors of several mostly financial companies. He is an assistant Professor at the University of Luxembourg. He has published 7 books on legal subjects (tax laws, corporate law and accounting) and more than 130 articles. This is his first book on investing.

Preface

The attention of the reader is drawn to the point that in the present book a number of concepts are described which are not necessarily endorsed by the author. Any work on the functioning of financial markets is based on such concepts which need to be understood by any investors regardless to which "school" or "church" they belong in this field. Criticism of such concepts or theories has to be allowed: this is the essence of any scientific approach. Departing from such objective and fact-based approach is nothing else than abandoning the field to some extremist anti-scientific forces, like conspirationists which believe that the financial crisis of 2008-2009 or the Covid-19 crisis have been the result of some individuals or other dark forces. As the Unesco states on its website on Covid-19:

"Conspiracy theories undermine science, facts and trust in institutions, and pose an immediate threat to individuals and communities.

There have always been conspiracy theories, but the pandemic underway has proved to be a particularly fertile ground for their spread. They are part of a wider trend of increasing hate speech, and increased racist, xenophobic, and anti-Semitic attacks, which also target LGBTQ communities."

It doesn't matter much who the individuals and groups behind these theories are exactly; what is for certain is that their objectives are to divide society, increase hate speech and physical violence against minorities and ultimately weaken liberal democracy as it still exists in most Western countries.

Introduction

As indicated by its title, this book deals with investing with a long term view in shareholders' equity (that is in common stocks of publicly traded companies).

In the first place this means that this book is about 'investing' which means it is not about 'speculation'. This distinction is nowadays viewed as old-school but the only reason to discard it is that this fits Wall Street's purposes. The term "trader" is nowadays favored over the term "speculator." Wall Street adores speculators, or traders, even more than long-term investors as what it likes above all is a lot of activity which translates into fees which go straight into their pockets. The difference between investments and speculations is that whereas the first generate cash flows the second do not. Whereas investors select stocks based on fundamentals, speculators buy and sell securities based on their assessment whether these securities will next rise or fall which means they do guess what the market will do next, or in other words they base their buy and sell decisions on the likely behavior of others.

In the absence of cash flows the returns generated by speculative operations depend exclusively on the future behavior of markets. Accordingly, precious metals, collectibles, works of art, antiques, etc. as they do not generate any cash flows are out of the scope of the present book. They can only generate cash by their sale and the future buyer is dependent on being able to find another buyer later on: this is relying on the "Greater Fool Theory", namely that even an overvalued asset may be sold with a profit provided ... the holder is able to find a greater fool than themselves.

Obviously, there are many asset classes other than common stocks which are available for investment and each of these have their supporters who will claim they bring superior yields either in the short term or in the long run.

Why do I exclude asset classes generating cash flows other than stocks? The main reason is that stock investments have, over the long run, (the hundred and twenty years starting with the beginning of the twentieth century) and on average proven by far superior to these other asset classes and the recent past seems to confirm that tendency in a convincing way. (This discrepancy existing between stocks and other asset classes is evidenced by the so-called "equity premium" which is treated in Chapter 2 hereafter). Skeptical readers may say "every dog has his day" and that the fact that during a given period a certain asset class is superior to others does not prove it will be so forever. That is true; however it should be pointed out that firstly this superiority covers the whole period during which reliable data is available (in other words, it is not based on a more or less artificially delimited period) and secondly corporations are at the heart of the capitalistic system (which itself has proven its efficiency compared to alternative economic systems) and as such they will most certainly still be around and prospering for a very long time.

Full disclosure requires that this outperformance of stocks (compared to fixed income securities) seems to not have existed over the period 1831-1861.

In the first place, fixed income investment (principally bonds, Treasuries and other debt obligations of all kinds) have historically been dismal investments. Touted as "widows-and-orphans" investments they are nowadays, in times of extremely low interest rates (and even "negative

12

interest rates"), to be viewed more like a "return-free risk" than a "risk-free return", certainly so if inflation and taxes are taken into consideration, although this is only rarely done in practice.

Other reasons for concentrating on stocks are that these markets, despite their huge diversity, offer investors a liquidity which is simply breath-taking in addition to having extremely low transaction costs.

The present book is not about how to get rich in 6 weeks or any other short period. The perspective here is a long-term one, that means of at least a period of 10 to 20 years, preferably a lot longer. Going for the long term is the only way to profit from the magic of compounding (Einstein's eighth wonder of the world) which is the principal engine of building wealth in a legal way. As John D. Rockefeller had already noted, to become really wealthy you have to have your money work for you. The money you may earn by selling your work force is very small in comparison.

The different asset classes producing cash flows are not generating the same returns and as shown by long term series of data (covering more than a century of financial markets history) these returns are fluctuating widely from one asset class to the next. The classical distinction made in financial theory consists in opposing stock investing to fixed-income investing. Stock investors incur higher risks than their colleagues purchasing bonds, Treasury notes, commercial paper or depositing money in a bank account: all these are creditors and as such are ranked senior (which means they have priority over stockholders). Even if creditors do incur risks in their investments (in addition to default risk which means that their debtor may go bankrupt, they suffer the risk of inflation) their future nominal returns may be calculated with precision as of the day of their initial investment. For equity investors (stockholders) the different scenarios they may experience are a lot more diverse. The stock may be a star, the new Amazon, or it may be a dog and no dividend may be paid for years before the investor sells at a severe loss. If the company goes bankrupt this loss my even reach 100% of the investment made.

In other words, stock investors do incur higher risks than so-called "fixed-income investors": according to finance theory they are compensated for assuming these higher risks by higher returns: this difference in return is named "equity premium" (or "equity risk premium") and it simply means that equity investments have higher returns than risk-free assets (or close to risk-free assets), the prototype of which category are government bonds. The existence of the so-called equity premium is important and its high level persisting over a very long time is a mystery.

How are value stocks and growth stocks defined? The definition of both types of stocks is not extremely clear-cut. Value stocks are those traded at a rather low ratio compared to fundamental characteristics like earnings (or dividends), or even book value (even if that last value is nowadays increasingly neglected). Growth stocks are generally defined as those which given their growth perspectives are traded at "high" multiples compared to earnings, dividends or book value.

Edge of the Individual Investor

One of Wall Street's most favored ideas is that individual investors would have no chance against institutional investors with their huge amounts of capital, their far superior knowledge about financial markets in addition to being better connected. This arrogance is reflected in the concepts of "smart money" and its opposite "dumb money." If "smart money" refers to those investors who are anticipating trends better than others whereas "dumb money" refers to those who are following the trends and invest once the smart money sold after having made all of the easy profits then this distinction has its justification. However, very often the distinction made tends to equate smart money with the money managed by institutional investors whereas dumb money is handled by individual

14

investors. This may have been true at the beginning of the 20th centuries when market manipulation and insider trading (in addition to insider tips) were the name of the game (as related in Edwin Lefèvre's classic book "Reminisces of a Stock Market Operator" in which the investment strategies of the famous speculator Jesse Livermore were described). Since those days the world has changed a lot and the playing field did become a lot more level.

Another obvious advantage of individual self-managing investors is that they are able to save the cost of intermediaries of all kinds (managers of investment funds, hedge funds, etc.) except for those of a low-cost internet broker (which in the meantime are mostly free for not charging any transaction fees anymore)[1]. This will give them a very substantial advantage (when compared to investors purchasing shares of investment funds) which in most cases of discretionary managed funds will amount to 1 to 2 per cent of their invested capital per year. Over the long run, this point is of extreme importance (as we shall see later on).

A third advantage, (although apparently less obvious than the preceding ones, it may at the end of the day be even more important), is that they, unlike Wall Street, do have time and hence may adopt a long-term approach which nowadays has nearly totally disappeared on Wall Street.

Professional money managers, in the first place need to attract investors able and willing to entrust huge amounts of capital funds to them. This is a salesman's task which unavoidably leads those managers to exaggerate their skills and their performances, in this way substantially raising their clients' expectations. These clients to whom they have promised solemnly, in exchange for their high fees, to each year "beat the market" by a wide margin will constantly check their managers' results compared to the chosen benchmark: investors might very well vote with their feet in case those results are not up to their professional

15

managers' lofty promises. This constant pressure leads these managers to adopt only one strategy, namely make sure to not be left behind by too much compared to the market at large: in other words, professional money managers (once they have attracted a substantial amount of capital) do not even try to "beat the market." Their only objective is to not be beaten by the market by a too-wide margin which would in all likelihood expose them to the risk of losing a very substantial amount of their managed funds and with it the fat fees which go with these capital amounts. This leads those managers to adopt so-called "closet indexing" (as we shall see in Chapter 2.) meaning that they will tend to have broadly diversified portfolios.

The ability to ignore short-term stock price fluctuations, is a tremendous advantage of individual investors compared to institutional investors.

This kind of short-term bias creates significant opportunities for the long-term investor who will be able to purchase at reduced prices first class stocks with temporary problems or even without problems, but fallen into disgrace. This kind of situation occurs all the time, for example Wal-Mart with corruption probe in Mexico, JP Morgan with the London Whale issue or Target with the steal of client credit card data, Facebook with the Cambridge Analytica data scandal, Apple and its alleged excessive dependence on China or on the iPhone. Whereas such issues may have serious implications on the quarterly or even annual results of the company concerned, it is beyond doubt that, generally speaking, markets tend to exaggerate the long-term effect of such issues (the so-called "recency bias" is at play here). In general, such scandals create interesting buying opportunities and experience proves that the markets do have a very short memory and several months after the issue has popped up and has made the headlines in the media, stock prices do recover and often they promptly revert to their pre-crisis levels.

This cautious approach of investors is not new: a traditional Wall Street rule is: "do not buy into a law suit." Such rule is debatable as it risks to confuse uncertainty with genuine risk. Whereas the latter is something to seriously monitor, the former is something which may be used by investors to their own profit as will be explained in Chapter 2.

A final advantage of self-managed individual investors is that they are able to have a far more concentrated portfolio than the professional investors will be allowed (or willing) to have. Investment funds, like public mutual funds, are not allowed to have shares of one company exceeding a certain percentage (5%) of the total NAV (net asset value) of the fund. Furthermore, even if regulations do allow for a highly concentrated portfolio, the funds would probably not want to have them and this for a number of reasons: in the first place, professional managers do want to avoid above all to seriously <u>underperform</u> the market. Such marked underperformance, will translate into trouble: a direct loss of job and/or loss of a substantial portion of their client base which as a minimum will deeply hurt compensation of the manager involved. Secondly, clients, risk averse as they are, will react aggressively if losses are high and, beyond "voting with their feet" they may sue the fund and/or its manager for not having acted in a prudent and professional way.

Granted that a more concentrated (a less diversified) portfolio will inevitable have higher fluctuations than one having 20 to 40 shares: the manager of such a concentrated portfolio assumes high "benchmark risk" meaning that their performance compared to the declared benchmark (the standard or point of reference for measuring the performance, for instance the S&P 500) might significantly deviate from this benchmark. As said here above, if there is one thing that the professional investor does have to avoid it is to seriouFsly underperform the market, for instance to have a down-year when the market is up by, say 10-15%.

If that happens, many of their clients will forget that their money manager has beaten that same benchmark (meaning. the market) during the three preceding years and they will move their account to a competing fund (with a manager who recently has shown a "hot" hand). This erratic behavior which is called chasing performance is highly counter-productive as it has disastrous consequences for investors who, while aiming for returns beating their benchmark, do in reality reach the exact opposite, they miss the benchmark by a wide margin. It is a fact which is confirmed by many empirical studies that asset managers which make the top of the lists are unable to repeat their standings for many years. The reason of this undeniable fact is probably to be found in the circumstance that in addition to the manager's competence, luck is involved for a large part which means that those managers at the top of the lists tend to do less well in the following years in order to be replaced by those who got lucky and improved their performance significantly: the well-known phenomenon of regression to the mean is at play here.

The individual investor, unlike the professional investor, does not get fired for underperforming the market and the only thing they have to take care of is to make sure that the fundamentals of the investments do not deteriorate, and just sitting out the market crunch. This behavior will have the additional benefit to save trading costs and taxes. If the decrease is due to market moods, then the investor can be sure that these moods will change again over a very short time (although nobody is able to set a date on the precise moment this will happen) and their shareholdings will again be valued according to the traditional criteria.

On the other hand, individual investors do also have some disadvantages compared to institutional investors which are full-time professionals and have a multiple of their resources. This means for instance these actors may react a lot quicker to market news than the individual investor. Investors should adapt their investment approach accordingly and not try to beat institutional investors at a game where speed is of importance.

One undeniable advantage of the individual investor (concept which is identical to saying a person self-managing their assets) is that it eliminates the risk of getting involved with a fraudulent professional, à la Madoff or other Ponzi scheme operators. Madoff's fraudulent activities translated into investors losses of some $65 billion, $36 billion came from 25 investors—including large institutional investors like hedge funds, charities, and some very rich and sophisticated billionaires: so much for the concept of "smart money." At the occasion of the internet bubble as at the occasion of the Great Recession institutional investors as well as individual investors eagerly bought shares as long as stock prices increased just before they started to sell in panic as soon as stock prices headed in the other direction.

Ponzi Scheme

This type of scheme has been named after Charles Ponzi, an Italian immigrant to the US, who in 1920 had designed an ingenious scheme in order to make money *from* (not *for*) gullible investors. In a newspaper ad he promised a return of 50% (!) in 45 days by allegedly trading International Postage Union reply coupons. The whole scheme broke down when Boston Post investigations showed that only $75,000 reply coupons were issued annually, not enough by a long shot to allow the investment of the millions he had collected from the naïve public. Ponzi made believe he had found a waterproof way to invest his investors' funds whereas no money was really invested: the system, consisted in paying the yields supposedly realized by the first investors with the funds collected from later investors. It is obvious that such scheme will break down rather quickly once the stream of new victims comes to slow down, as happened to Madoff during the Great Recession when some investors asked Madoff for repayment of their funds in order to compensate for their losses on their publicly traded stocks. Thousands of such schemes have been set up worldwide since the days of Charles Ponzi for shorter or longer time periods. It is a testament to human nature (human greed) that they work again and again.

It is also striking that many of the victims of such schemes initially were extremely skeptical and even have admonished others to avoid this opportunity like the plague. However, when they saw their peers cashing in their first juicy "interest" payments they suspended their disbelief and healthy skepticism and they also invested. A similar pattern of human behavior could be seen during the internet bubble of 1999-2000 when some investors were very critical initially on the perspectives of the many internet stocks but finally changed their mind when they saw that prices did not stop increasing relentlessly, they finally took the price hikes as a convincing argument for the value of those shares. Instead of using the market exclusively for its liquidity they made the gross mistake to take it for its alleged wisdom (whereas that precise period of 1999-2000 was the worst period for doing so).

Paradoxes of Stock Markets

In many respects stock markets are fundamentally different from other sectors. Accordingly, many people who are successful in their own profession and who want to take the same approach on the stock markets find out that this is exactly the wrong thing to do. Hereafter I will only mention some of the differences compared to other sectors, most of these points will be treated in more detail in the following chapters.

"Action may not always bring happiness, but there is no happiness without action." — Benjamin Disraeli

Whereas school children are already told to embrace a high level of activity and approach any task with enthusiasm this is actually the wrong mindset in the stock market:

unexcited inactivity is the behavior which over the medium term and the long term is remunerated.

If we often hear : "you get what you pay for" or "if you pay peanuts you get monkeys" these rules are not valid in the fields of money management (say hedge funds with their outrageous 2%/20%-rule or actively managed fund compared to index funds) where the rule is in fact the more you pay in fees, the less you get (certainly if they take those fees into consideration, as they should).

In their personal life people normally do experience that there is a rather strict relationship between results and efforts put in - take for instance the student preparing for an exam - that again is not what you should expect in stock markets. By doubling your efforts to research things you can in no way expect to double your results from your investment activities. Often another rule kicks in, namely that half-knowledge is worse than no knowledge at all, be it only for the reason that to have some knowledge is prone to lead to overconfidence. Overconfidence paired with some knowledge is a dangerous combination. As George Bernard Shaw warned "Beware of false knowledge; it is more dangerous than ignorance."

Sometimes stock markets behave differently from other markets: this means that participants in stock markets adopt behaviors which are totally different than those they adopt in other markets. It is quite familiar that if prices increase shares will be more eagerly demanded than if prices linger. As examples just look at the FAANG stocks or TESLA.

As Warren Buffett has stressed many times, most people who are investing in shares all over their lifetime should rejoice when markets are depressed. This is not a kind of masochism in the mind of the Oracle of Omaha but simply good sense. If markets are depressed investors are able to buy additional stocks at low prices or in other words to get more stocks for the same amount of money. Even if they are not buying stocks themselves, they may still profit indirectly as the companies who have issued these stocks may repurchase stocks also at lower prices which means that, all things equal, the present shareholder will get a proportionally higher claim on a share of the future profits of the company. Ideally both investors and the company will profit simultaneously from these lower stock prices by actively purchasing additional stocks.

Many investors do shun volatile stocks and prefer those stocks whose prices do not fluctuate too much: in Wall Street speak, they prefer low-beta stocks (if beta of a given stock is lower than 1, stock prices will fluctuate less than the market average). Again, investors should look for high-beta stocks as this means that they may profit from those fluctuations by loading up stocks if prices are low and sell when prices are high. Provided investors have a clear idea of the actual value of their stocks and that they are not influenced by wild stock market gyrations, volatile prices can only be beneficial for them.

Bad news for the company may be good news for investors. The reason for this apparent paradox is that any news pertaining to the company will trigger reactions from shareholders and will directly affect stock prices. As financial markets, which hate uncertainty, tend to exaggerate, it may be that the loss in stock prices will by far exceed the actual impact of those bad news. As an example for such bad news which translate into a blessing for stockholders it suffices to have a look at the tobacco industry: despite the fact that the whole industry was heavily under attack from health agencies in all developed countries and despite countless law suits filed against them, these headwinds did not prevent Philip Morris from being the company with the highest return over the whole period from 1925 to 2003 (under the assumption that all dividends were reinvested).

It is paradoxical but true: by avoiding to take any risk inherent in equity investing an investor frequently takes the biggest risks of all, namely they accept the *certainty* of permanent capital loss, at least in real terms, even if this loss is only slow and rather linear. After having suffered two stock meltdowns in less than a decade – the internet bubble of 2000-2002 and the financial crisis of 2008-2009 (also called the Great Recession) – many investors avoid common stocks like the plague. Instead, they place their funds in fixed-interest assets, in the form of bank deposits, Treasuries, shares of money market funds, or corporate bonds, arguing that these investments are "safe" or "not risky." Unfortunately, over-cautiousness in 2020 and later on, far from bringing back the funds lost in 2000 and 2008 will just make the problem worse: it is a fact that the current period is a period of historically very low interest rates and the presently applicable rates (after taxes) do not allow to compensate for inflation. Why do investors not apply the P/E ratio to bonds? If they did so they would conclude that a ten-year Treasury bond with a nominal 1.% coupon corresponds to a P/E ratio of 100 which might strike this cautious investor as very high even, for a "risk-free" asset. Even worse, the measly 1% yield of the investment translates into real and far from uncertain losses if we take taxes and inflation of, say, 2% per annum in consideration.

What makes things even worse is that the opportunity costs of such fixed interest income have been extremely high over recent years. Measured in terms of the S&P 500, an investor could have earned 8.5% annually by investing in an S&P index fund from 2008 to 2019. Sadly enough, investors will most certainly give up their risk aversion only when the markets will have climbed a lot more and just shortly before they correct heavily.

Diverging Views

It is an undeniable fact that each and every securities transaction requires a buyer and a seller who, as they take divergent positions at the trade, to have diametrically opposed views on the stock concerned. It is a curious reality that if everybody had the same assessment on the merits

23

of a given stock no single trade would happen. It is also a reminder for any investor who have very strong feelings on a given stock (either positive or negative ones) that if they are able to find a counterpart for their trade, the opposing thesis must also be defendable, otherwise how would they find a counterpart making the said trade possible at all? This point should have a humbling effect on our investor and induce them to second-guess their opinion.

It needs to be said that if this statement that different views are needed for any stock transaction to occur, is generally true it is not true in all the cases: Take for example the case of an investor who has purchased Apple stocks at a price of $120 per share and who when the price reached $350 sold a substantial part of their Apple shares in the process of rebalancing their portfolio. This sale does not mean the seller is bearish on Apple. Another case where diverging views are not required is given in the area of the rapidly growing index funds: these funds do buy and sell shares without having any views on their value at all. They have to do that just in order to mirror image the benchmark index (the S&P 500 for example) they have set out to follow. More generally, any investor who urgently needs money for reason of unexpected expenses sell their shares without that one could infer from that decision that the seller views its shares to be clear sales.

Relationships Between Business Value and Stock Price

Investors in common stocks should always bear in mind that by buying stocks, which represent securities issued by a legal entity, they are economically (even if not legally) becoming co-owners of a business and they should decide to purchase the stocks only if they believe in the future of the underlying business and not for the reason that the stock price could increase another 10-15% over the next weeks or months (or even worse for the reason that the stock price has increased by 50% over the last year).

Any investor following this last approach is in fact a speculator. It is for good reasons that Benjamin Graham insisted on the fact that the investment should be "businesslike." "Investment is most intelligent when it is most *businesslike*" (of The Intelligent Investor, p. 286). Graham then elaborates on what exactly he means to say with this statement.

This means that an investor selecting a securities portfolio in order to make money from buying and selling stocks is engaged in a business of its own and may expect to be successful only if he follows business principles. Just as any shop-owner prefers to be themselves at the head of their business as opposed to mandate someone else to manage the portfolio.

If we assimilate self-managing one's securities portfolio to running a business this also means that leverage is not as such excluded: any regular business has outstanding debt, be it only for the reason that their suppliers are only paid with some delay. However, the level of indebtedness has to be in line with the business realities, the risk of the portfolio, the interest rates charged, etc. It should not be forgotten that the business of self-managing a portfolio of common stocks is not, per se, a risky activity: there are no meaningful fixed costs and if one avoids short selling, losses are limited to the amount invested (due to the limited liability incurred by stockholders). Accordingly, taking up some leverage may be a perfectly a sound business decision, improving investment yields without meaningfully increase riskiness of the portfolio.

As investing in a company's stock is akin to being a partner in a business the direct consequence for the long-term investor is that the business, as a living organism, will evolve. If the fundamentals of the business improve (or deteriorate) over time, then stock prices will follow and increase (or decrease) somewhere in line with the changes

25

in fundamentals. However, it should not be lost of sight that normally, financial markets do anticipate future changes in fundamentals but the future being by definition uncertain there is no guarantee that these anticipated changes will actually realize in the way they have been forecast. Anyway, if over time the earnings of the business increase, stock prices will most certainly follow (except if the acquisition price was already anticipating those future increases in profits).

Changes in earnings are not the only parameter to influence stock prices: a second variable is the P/E ratio which is applied to these earnings: the P/E ratio represents the multiplier which the market, at a given moment, applies to the earnings flows of a company. This P/E ratio is influenced by a lot of macroeconomic factors (in the first place interest rates which are heavily influenced by the FED decisions and actions) but is also specific to the sector to which the company belongs and to the specific company concerned. All these P/E ratios fluctuate over time.

If business fundamentals have an impact on stock prices, there are relationships also the other way round in the sense that stock prices influence underlying values. Those changes are due to the so-called 'theory of reflexivity' of stock prices developed by George Soros. As a general rule, it may be said that a company may totally ignore its stock price, but this is fully the case only if it has a very solid financial position, meaning it has sufficient capital. However, if additional capital is needed, the price of the company's stock tends to get important and depressed stock prices will considerably increase the cost of capital to be paid by the company. Depressed stock prices may also trigger take-overs by other companies (which obviously contains certain career risks for members of the incumbent management up to and including the CEO level), especially if the state of the company's business is not a good one for being mismanaged.

The Impact of Ideology in Business

Most people have a rather high opinion of themselves which tendency is furthermore reinforced if they are successful in their domain of activity, say, a renowned physician or a world-class electronic engineer: their success breeds complacency and overconfidence. Accordingly, if you ask any academician whether they are rational, objective, scientifically directed individuals the answer will not be really doubtful.

However, it appears that this optimism is not really warranted if we just look at what the British economist John Maynard Keynes wrote on this subject: "The ideas of economists and political philosophers, both when they are right and when they are wrong, are more powerful than is commonly understood. Indeed, the world is ruled by little else. Practical men, who believe themselves to be quite exempt from any intellectual influences, are usually the slaves of some defunct economist."

It seems that this "stickiness" of old theories and conceptions do not only apply to the "dismal science" but do even apply in the hard sciences like physics are concerned. The German physicist Max Planck commenting on his own career in his Scientific Autobiography, sadly remarked that "a new scientific truth does not triumph by convincing its opponents and making them see the light, but rather because its opponents eventually die, and a new generation grows up that is familiar with it." Later on Paul Samuelson expressed this same idea concisely by the following phrase: "science progresses funeral by funeral."

In finance, this preeminence of ideology can also be observed. As an example take the case of Enron, the fraudulent disaster based on a dangerous cocktail of hubris, managerial incompetence and greed all stacked together by the dogmas that deregulation and free markets, in that case applied to the field of energy, will miraculously solve all the problems of mankind. Those dogmas were also at the roots of the financial crisis of 2008-2009.

Among the most cherished beliefs held nowadays on Wall Street and Main Street are the following ones which are of neo-liberal descent as revived by the Chicago School of Economics: "markets know better", meaning competition will create the most efficient outcome for society and "government interference is not the solution, it is the problem", hence laissez-faire beats regulation.

In practice, major disasters, as the one of the Great Recession, are often followed by a new wave of regulation, as it is politically acceptable to do so, which some years later on will give rise to another round of deregulation as the memory of the disaster fades and as lobbyists have been able to weigh on the political process. Generally speaking this cycle is totally inappropriate. Overall it may be said that very often and in most areas there are enough regulations meaning enough laws, especially criminal laws, to sanction inappropriate behavior: the problem is that they are often not applied in fact: if existing laws are not applied; new laws will not change anything because they will not be applied either.

This enforcement deficit, in no small part due to the fact that those in charge of enforcement, under ongoing austerity measures, which are a consequence of another neo-liberal tenet, lean budgets, do often not have the resources in money and personnel to efficiently enforce the applicable legislation.

The dominant ideology of today, in the US at least, is that free markets, altgough they gave as the Great Recession of 2008-2009, are the solution to all of mankind's problems and many very influential people are prisoners to that ideology. So far, the evidence that the undeniably biggest problem of mankind, which is climate change (and which unfortunately does not go away by denying its existence), will be solved by free-markets: unregulated free markets will just make the problem bigger.

Chapter 1: Asset Allocation

"People tend to complicate something in direct proportion to its importance."

Anonymous

The first decision investors have to take is actually the most important one: it concerns the so-called "asset allocation", meaning the asset classes they choose to hold and which proportion of the total portfolio each of these classes will represent, for instance, say, 40 per cent stocks, 50 per cent bonds and 10 per cent cash. The classic composition of a securities portfolio has been 60% stocks and 40% bonds. Obviously, these proportions are not cast in stone and they will inevitably fluctuate over time. In case such changes of the proportions of these respective asset classes occur, the question is whether the portfolio should be rebalanced (in order not to deviate much from the chosen allocation) or not.

This asset allocation decision is important for the reason that the different asset classes in which funds may be invested are not created equal, far from it. As mentioned in the Introduction, the present book is based on the premise that stocks are by far the most interesting asset class which does of course not mean that other asset classes do not also have their *raison d'être*.

The differences between these asset classes are mind-blowing: 1$ invested in stocks in 1802 would have produced about $600,000 in 2003 (inflation adjusted) compared to $1,072 in bonds and $ 301 in treasury bills. (Treasury bills are non-interest-paying discount bonds where the implied interest rate is given by the difference between purchase price and maturity value). Compared to these huge differences the effects of which type of stocks (bonds) precisely have been picked appear very incidental. Some money managers consider that at least about 75% of the long-term rate of return is due to asset allocation (for instance and most importantly the allocation of assets between stocks, bond and cash) and 25% on the selection of the individual securities, bonds or stocks (reference is made to the so-called "stock-picking") as well as the investment of the cash. These percentages confirm the validity of the statement that asset allocation is the most important decision to be made by the investor.

Securities and No-Income-Producing Assets

Investors are not limited to only invest in securities or in cash and in cash equivalent assets. Beyond these assets there is large family of asset classes composed of commodities, precious metals, paintings, antiques, etc. which have in common that these assets, regardless of how long the investor will keep them, will never produce any income and the assets concerned will be the same as long as the investor is willing to keep them (and beyond!). Let's take gold as a typical and very prominent representative of this asset category. Over the centuries gold has had some mythical aspects, and it has had and still has its adepts (also known as "gold gurus") who generally react quite aggressively if someone dares to say something negative about its qualities as an investment.

However, regardless of what the gold gurus may say, gold is an extremely poor investment. At best it is an inflation hedge. Let's also mention that it was illegal for US citizens to own gold, with the exception of jewelry and collectors' items since 1935 (based on the Gold Reserve Act of 1934) to 1975 (which in fact was a blessing for them because over that period as over most other periods of human history gold has been a poor investment). Furthermore it is noteworthy that the Gold Reserve Act of 1934 was followed by a revaluation of the gold price from $20.67 to $35 per ounce which represented a steep devaluation of the US $, which paved the way for a large increase of the GDP from 1933 to 1941. Nowadays, some people would call such action "currency manipulation."

According to one long-term study[2] one dollar invested in U.S. stocks in 1802 would have been worth (in real terms) $597,485 in 2004, compared to $1,090 for a dollar invested in bonds $301 in treasury bills but only $1.39 in gold.[3]

In the Middle Ages one ounce of gold bought its owner a man's wear of the highest quality. Currently, at a price of some $2,000 per ounce this is still the case. In other words, over the last 700 years, gold has maintained its purchasing power but nothing more. This is not what, by anybody's standards, may be viewed as a terrific result.

For those not yet convinced and who may consider that this time period of more than 700 hundred years is too short to draw a clear-cut conclusion, here is another one: Barton Biggs in his book Hedgehogging points out that in the Old Testament an ounce of gold could buy 350 loaves of bread, which is roughly what it will buy today in most developed countries. In other words, over some 2000 years, gold has just maintained its purchasing power without any increase in value.

By comparison, from 1802 to 2004, the <u>real</u> return of stocks was 6.8% a year with reinvested dividends.

At this point some comments are needed on the issue of calculating the yields of different assets classes over long periods. In the first place such long-term studies are needed as any studies over short periods like a decade for instance are exposed to criticism as by determining the period of analysis it is easy to show just any asset class in a favorable light which the author of the study wants to promote.

If such long-term studies are needed they are awfully difficult as over the past, financial data were not a the level of quality they have nowadays and large generally recognized market indices were not known yet to the same degree as they are now. Hence, researchers doing such studies have to do a lot of gap-filling for data and have to make countless assumptions which again are not necessarily neutral meaning whether one thing is assumed instead of another one, the outcome of the study will be different and the yield of one asset class will be increased or decreased. The difficulties of this task are described in detail in a seminal study of Elroy Dimson, Paul Marsh, and Mike Staunton, authors of "Triumph of the Optimists: 101 Years of Global Investment Returns", from 1900 to 2000 included, published in 2002. The difficulty of this task was that in many of the countries object of their survey, comprehensive market indices did not exist at the beginning of the 20th century. Accordingly, such indices had to be constructed retrospectively. For instance, the Financial Times Index (FTSE) did only come into existence in 1935. The tendency then is to rely too heavily on companies and sectors which at the moment the reconstructive work is done were important which result in overweighting of companies or sectors which became important later on, whereas such evolution was not foreseeable in 1900. The principal tasks of the authors was to avoid several common biases, namely survivorship bias and success bias, which if uncontrolled lead to an increase in returns of one or the other percentage points per year. All these problems also mean that the results of such long term studies may validly be exposed to some criticism.

Asset Allocation and Age

According to conventional wisdom, the older you are the lower the proportion of stocks you hold in your portfolio should be. As an implementation of this rule, the proportion of shares is given by the following formula:

100 – age = proportion of assets to be held in stocks.

This means that if a 30-year old person should have 70% of their assets in shares, which proportion should decrease to 25% once they have reached 75 years. This is pretty much a nonsensical rule as it is only referring to age without any consideration to other more relevant factors. Why should a 90-year old person shift their securities from stocks to bonds (except for 10% which could be invested in stocks according to the above rule) if they have a comfortable income from pensions, good medical insurance and some rental income just because they are advancing in age? In fact, more relevant than the investor's age is the fact for how long they can survive without the funds blocked in their investment portfolio; if no large withdrawals from the investment portfolio are foreseeable, the funds may well be fully invested in stocks.

Contrary to what many advisors may claim, an investor's time horizon is not necessarily limited by their life expectancy but it might well be longer. The time horizon is the time during which one's assets need to last. It is not the time until the investor retires or the time when they start withdrawing funds.

The issue of the investment time horizon is of crucial importance as it is directly connected to the problem of investment risk, which any cautious investor would view as the most important (and the most challenging concept) in investing. As we will see in Chapter 2., risk depends to a very large extent on the long-term (or short-term) approach adopted. If the time horizon is one year (meaning the investor will need the investment funds in one year's time), then they should not invest in stocks as these are a lot more risky, and definitely more volatile, than most other assets classes. As the time horizon extends to 10 years, the situation improves a lot and most annual comparative results are in favor of stock investments. With a time horizon of 20 years or more, substantially all results are positive and approximate the long-term average rate of return.

The lesson from this is that, unlike what many advisors may recommend, a mix of assets from different classes is in no way required, provided that first the time horizon is long enough (say a minimum of 20 years) and of course that the investor has the emotional stability not to change strategy in case of a long-lasting bear market. A crucial requirement here is of course that the entry price into the investment is low, meaning especially that the equity investment was not made at a time of record stock prices.

Different Types of Investments

Never in the past, have the investment opportunities offered to investors been as manifold as nowadays. They may buy securities (stocks, common or preferred), bonds (regular or convertible ones) which again may be corporate bonds, municipal bonds (which have a preferential tax treatment) or Treasuries (if their maturity is at least two years, but not greater than ten, they are called notes whereas if their maturity exceeds ten years they are called bonds), derivatives (of all kinds, most importantly, options like calls and puts), real estate (residential or office buildings, or participate in such real estate assets in the form of REITs), foreign currencies, commodities, futures, investment funds (in the form of mutual funds or under corporate structures, index funds, equity funds, money market funds, ETFs), gold, silver, commodities, collectibles, cyber currencies, etc. For some of these asset classes the investor has the choice of being long or short; being short means the investor sells assets they do not own and in this way they speculate on a decline of the asset price. Furthermore any investor may be active in different markets, in different time zones, starting with the Asian markets, which open shortly after the New York markets have closed, and once the Asian markets have closed, the European markets open and during the afternoon the US markets open again, etc.

Although it may be tempting to believe that by participating in a number of these markets at the same time in view of diversification (erroneously thinking that in this way you may make money "all the time", in a way "around the clock"), investors should be aware that this looks more like a strategy for losing money "all around the clock." Each of these markets have their own rules and any individual, even working full time as an investor, is unlikely to trade efficiently more than one or two markets at the time.

That being said, it remains to be decided what kind of market (s) the investor should act in. Again, it has to be stressed that these markets are not created equal, no more than the different asset classes. These markets may be divided in different classes, most importantly in local markets and in foreign markets. A very cautious approach is advisable in case an investor opts in favor of foreign markets with which they are unfamiliar. The level of corporate governance may be extremely different compared to the one they may be used to on their home market and the degree to which stockholders may have legal recourses might not be adequate. In case of doubts on these issues investors should refrain from their plan to invest on these markets. Another choice open to investors is to decide whether to invest in developed markets or in emerging markets. In finance theory, investing in foreign markets, in addition to the home market, represents a welcome occasion to decrease risk by diversification. However, this advice is hardly followed by investors who denote a marked "home bias" in their investing behavior shunning all foreign markets. Studies show that the very large majority of investors do not have any exposure to securities of other markets than their home market.

Traditionally the asset-allocation decision is in practice simplified in the following way: what is the proportion between bonds and stocks? This apportionment is obviously paramount for those investors who use their investment income to pay for their living expenses. They will first be required to determine how much income they need now and in the foreseeable future, which will determine, on the basis of the currently applicable interest rates, what percentage of their assets should be held in bonds.

However, the need for income (in fact this means a steady slightly growing flow of income at least in nominal terms) may also be satisfied through dividend-paying stocks: some companies are reliable dividend payers and in this respect their shares may be viewed as a bond with, however, two distinctive features: the annual coupon is normally increasing (although without any guarantee this will actually be the case) and the security does not have a maturity. Even if in practice such stocks may be an extremely reliable income source, the investor should never forget that a dividend payment (unlike a coupon of a corporate bond) is not a contractual commitment of the issuing company and it may easily be reduced or even cancelled by the issuing company; although companies are very reluctant to reduce their quarterly dividend coupons, it will be reduced/cancelled if the profits of the company break away. Examples for such reductions are numerous: let it suffice to mention General Electric which when it was one of stocks part of the Dogs of the Dow group, reduced its dividend by half (to 12 cents) as of the first quarter of 2018 before reducing it a second time to just one penny as of the first quarter of 2019. Also, in the current Covid-19 crisis many companies in the especially hurt sectors, like Macy or Nordstrom in the retail sector for instance, either reduced or cancelled their dividend payments altogether.

The asset allocation decision has, in recent years (meaning the period following the financial crisis of 2008-2009, also called the Great Recession), received a different meaning due to the Federal Reserve's interest rate policies (followed or preceded by many other central banks all over the world): since the said crisis years, the US and for that matter the rest of the developed world, has known very low interest rates: this is good news for all businesses with a high debt to equity ratio (in addition to being good news for over-indebted countries, qualification which nowadays may be applied to all countries...) having large amounts of debt outstanding which only require modest interest payments but is not beneficial to fixed-income investors who will note that once they have to reinvest the capital of their bond coupons and of their redeemed bonds (by assumption issued before 2008) they will receive substantially lower coupons on the reinvested amounts.

More important in the present context is that the dividend yields of a number of high capitalization so-called "dividend aristocrats" is substantially higher than the rate of interest which may be obtained on corporate bonds issued by the same corporations. This situation is totally different than the one prevailing during the second half of the 20th century during which bonds had the higher yields compared to dividend-paying stocks.

However, during the decades preceding the Great Depression of 1929-1932, dividend rates were higher than corporate bond coupons. This shows again that in the world of finance (just as in other areas) no tendency is going on for ever: as the saying goes, history does not repeat itself but it rhymes.

The comparison with respect to yields with US Treasury is even more striking: comparing the 10-year Treasury yield (a risk-free asset) with corporate dividends the conclusion over the last century are as follows: during the 19th century and the first half of the 20th century, the dividend yield of US stocks exceeded the average bond yield as investors assumed that riskier assets should yield more than secure bonds. However, that situation changed as of the late 1950's when the 10-year Treasury yield exceeded the yield of the S&P 500 dividend yield. This situation, although considered abnormal, did lasted for more than 50 years and only changed recently. Did investors behave irrationally when during more than 50 years they accepted to hold risky stocks with a dividend yield lower than the risk free yield on 10-year Treasury bonds? Such conclusion is far from sure. In fact, comparing dividends and bond coupons is an odd comparison. It is comparing apples to pears for the following fundamental difference between the two: whereas the only income the bond investor will cash in on their investment is their bond coupon, corporations do not pay out all their profits as dividends, far from it. Many companies, especially those with strong growth prospects, do not pay any dividends at all (e.g. Amazon, Alphabet, Facebook).Stockholders in addition to their dividend cheques have justified expectations to realize a capital gain on selling their stocks years after having purchased them. For bond investors such capital gains are in fact excluded, at least if the bonds are held until maturity.

When taking the asset-allocation decision, investors, especially individual investors, should never forget to keep things as simple as possible which would militate for a very limited number of asset classes: for instance say 10-15 per cent of cash and the balance in stocks, say half of which are high dividend payers and which are meant to satisfy their needs for current income flows. As these needs for income are variable from one investor to the next one, just as the amounts of capital available to them, capital allocations will have to be tailor-made for each investor: there cannot be any one-size-fits-all approach.

Convertible bonds have an undeniable appeal for investors due to the conversion feature which does allow them to abandon the position of a creditor and to take the one of a shareholder. If investors are able to get a conversion feature, all things equal, that is on top of all other features, then they make a good deal. Unfortunately the conversion feature is often meant to render a bad common bond eligible for investment. If so, then the conclusion that a convertible bond is a safe investment may be totally erroneous.

The old adage, "Never convert a convertible bond" which consists in profiting as long as possible from the privileged position of a creditor is not always respected in practice.

Derivatives

"Financial-market innovations are good for Wall Street but not for clients."

Seth Klarman

Paul Volcker, Fed chairman during the years 1979-1987, expressed a similar idea when he famously said that the most important innovation in finance of the 20th century has been the ATM.

Derivatives, by definition, are contracts between two parties deriving its value from an underlying asset. For example, a stock options contract on 100 Apple shares is priced according to the price fluctuations of Apple stocks. It goes without saying that such contracts are zero-sum operations (as mentioned before). However, such derivative contracts in addition to that feature, have another characteristic which increases the level of risk beyond that involved with, say, a straight forward purchase of shares namely an additional form of risk: counterparty risk. This is the reason why Warren Buffett referred to these contracts as "weapons of mass destruction" (chairman's letter to shareholders, 2008, p. 17). Derivative contracts as those concluded for instance by AIG before the financial crisis are concluded for very long durations, up to several decades, consist in an exchange of funds by which party A pays money at the beginning provided that B pays money back (either the same amount or a different amount) if the price of the underlying asset reaches certain thresholds.

Under this scenario, A (in addition to the risk on the underlying assets) assumes a counterparty risk in the sense that if B goes bankrupt, A's claim on B will be worthless. Such long-term contracts as they appear in the books of A and B (either as claims or as debts) have to be evaluated in the books of both parties concerned. If both parties use valuation models with different assumptions it cannot be excluded that both will show a profit, or a loss on the same transaction.

As for such contracts there are no real markets (hence the so-called mark-to-market valuation method cannot be used and the door is open to mark-to-model) and also given the fact that these contracts mature only in 10, 15 or 25 years (at a time when present management will long be retired...) the temptation for companies which are in a dire financial situation is high to come up with fancy valuations, which lead to questioning directly the reliability of the earnings declared by large banks and other institutional investors. Another reason explaining why overoptimistic assumptions may be used at the occasion of the valuation of these contracts in the annual financial statements is that these valuations will have a direct impact on the compensation of the management of the company.

Although Buffett has qualified these derivative contracts as "time bombs" or "weapons of mass destruction" (both for the participants in these contracts and the economic system in general) it is a fact that Berkshire Hathaway does regularly enter into such derivative contracts which led some commentators to the conclusion that Buffett is hypocritical by doing what he apparently condemns. These comments are not justified as they overlook one important point: as explained here above, counterparty risk is only suffered by one of the parties to the derivative contract namely the one which pays the funds at the beginning (let's call it A) and which holds a claim on B who has to repay the funds at the term of the contract. As explained by Warren Buffett in the chairman's letter to shareholders, 2008, p. 18,

Berkshire Hathaway does only participate in contracts where Berkshire receive the money upfront and in this way will not assume counterparty risk. (Incidentally, given the fortress balance sheet of Berkshire Hathaway, the other party to these contracts does not assume any such risk either as Berkshire will still be there the day these contracts reach maturity). As also mentioned by Buffett in the mentioned chairman's letter to shareholders these transactions do also generate significant float (similar to its famous insurance float) that is low or no-cost capital which may be invested profitably.

By the way, such counterparty risk is not a matter of concern for those standardized derivative contracts which are settled through organized exchanges assuming that clearing house systems are used and where counterparty risks are taken over by the clearing system.

Stocks, Real Estate, etc.

Stocks represent a participation in a company which means that the holder of shares (economically) is a co-owner of the assets of a company even if the running of that company is entrusted to the managers who may or may not be shareholders as well. These shares participate in a company which, provided it is prosperous, grows and develops: each and every year it produces income and this income will make that the value of the shares after 10 or 15 years have nothing to do with their value at the moment of purchase of these shares.

This increase in value is not dependent only on market fads, general price inflation (although this element makes that these gains are partially only nominal) but essentially have to do with the increased earnings power of the shares. An example which is very often given in this respect is the one of Coca Cola shares, also for the reason that these shares are around for more than a century already. The company has existed since 1884 but it went public only in 1919. In 1984 the average sale per day was 9 glasses (the sale in bottles only happened later on). In 2019 according to the Annual Report of the Company the average daily sale is 2 billion. When The Coca Cola Company went public in 1919 the shares were offered at $40 per share. One year later, they had fallen to $19, meaning that they had fallen by more than 50% (which was surprising because its perspectives should have been far from bad for the reason that in 1920 started the period of Prohibition, which is good news for any soft drink company). The same share in 2006 counted for more than $5.6 million (assuming the reinvestment of all dividends paid since 1919). Given this exponential evolution, successive investors could actually buy and sell the shares making a more than handsome profit.

Recently I came across a book on investing published in 2019 by two British authors, [4] who overall did a lot of promotion for investing in gold (especially over the period 2000 until 2019). This point is not commented further here but it clearly relies on excellent timing. Comparing the price of an ounce of gold to the DJIA over a long period of time the author argued that the ratio DJIA/price of gold has substantially increased over time. This is true but the comparison is pointless. Whereas an ounce of gold is something which materially does not change over time, the DJIA (as it represents stock prices of 30 big companies which participate in a continuously increasing economy) logically increases over time (beyond the devaluation of the currency which affects both parts of the ratio). Hence, it is entirely justified that the DJIA increases in real terms (somewhere in line with the growing US economy and also with the world economy given the worldwide operations of the major US companies) this is not the case for gold, an asset which, unlike the stocks included in the DJIA, does not produce any income and accordingly the ratio DJIA/gold price logically increases over time: thinking this ratio should be stable over time is wishful thinking by gold gurus.

At another place of their book the same authors hypothesize why Warren Buffett does not invest in gold and he explains that as follows: as investment in gold was illegal for US citizens up to the year 1975 his mentor, Benjamin Graham, from whom allegedly Warren Buffett has taken over his investment models (sic!) this would explain why he does not invest in gold. This convoluted explanation does not hold water: in the first place, Warren Buffett has not overtaken blindly investment models from anybody else and furthermore he has on multiple occasions expressed his views on that subject. At the 2005 Berkshire shareholders meeting he said: "I would say that gold is way down on my list as a store of value. I mean I would prefer owning a hundred acres of land near hear in Nebraska, or an apartment house, or an index fund."[5] In his chairman's letter to shareholders (in the issue concerning the year 2017) explained his position on investing in no-income producing assets in general and specifically in gold. After noting that all the gold of the world would fit into a cube of 68 feet per side with a price tag of $9.6 trillion Buffett goes on explaining that with that price one could buy all U.S. cropland (400 million acres with output of about $200 billion annually), plus 16 Exxon Mobils (the world's most profitable company, at that time, one Exxon Mobil earning more than $40 billion annually) and still have $1 trillion left over for walking-around money. Then Buffett asked the rhetorical question: "Can you imagine an investor with $9.6 trillion selecting pile A over pile B?" Clearly, Buffett is not a gold fan.

Many investors in all parts of the world consider the direct investment in "stone" to be the summum of risk-free inflation-proof investment for which there may only be one direction, namely up. This conception is supported by the fact that typically real estate is an asset which is difficult, time-consuming and expensive to trade (fees of intermediaries, transaction taxes, capital gains taxes) so that this asset class, contrary to stocks, is held for extremely long periods . When the owner of such real estate assets disposes of the asset 30 or 40 years later they are amazed to see they have realized a huge capital gain which unfortunately is due to "money illusion" for the larger part of it. Another point which is ignored as well is the fact that over such long periods of time many improvements have been made to the property: although each of these improvements may have been relatively small, on aggregate the total amount of these would strike the sellers as surprisingly high.

Generally there are no cases where statistical data relative to the evolution of sales prices for buildings extending over several centuries would exist. The reasons is that the technical standards prevailing for such buildings are evolving rather quickly with the consequences that it is less expensive to tear down buildings which are more than say fifty years old than to renovate them. Just think of residential buildings dating back to the end of the 19th century, when they did not have electric cabling, no running hot and cold water, no separate bathrooms, no central heating. By exception, in some city centers of old historical towns, especially in Europe, zoning laws will not allow for such solution of rebuilding such century-old buildings as they are placed under monument-protection rules.

A case in point are the price evolution of houses of a prime location of Amsterdam, the so-called Herengracht from 1628 to 1973, (in Dutch gracht means canal), to this day a prime location on one of the still existing canals of the city of Amsterdam in the Netherlands. Over the said period of 345 years the annual inflation-corrected price increase was only 0.2%, meaning just a doubling of prices.[6]

In July 2005, CNBC interviewed Ben Bernanke, and he was asked what would happen if house prices dropped across the country? 'It's a pretty unlikely possibility,' Bernanke responded. 'We've never had a decline in house prices on a nationwide basis.'" (from "The Rules of Contagion: Why Things Spread - and Why They Stop (Wellcome Collection) (English Edition)" by Adam

Kucharski).This statement reflects the widely-held view that real estate prices do never fall, at least not on a US-wide level. However, this view is also incorrect as also shown by numerous studies.[7]

This erroneous belief that real estate prices do never fall has also been at the origin of the Great Depression: the computer-based models used were based on incomplete historical data.

Cyber currencies

A short comment on cyber currencies. It might well be that a cyber currency, based on the block chain technology, is in itself a good idea. Honestly, I do know that and I am not competent to write on that subject. However, what I do know is that the way cyber currencies are nowadays offered to the public as a means of speculation, the value of which will increase tremendously is inherently incompatible with the character of a currency: although currencies nowadays are traded daily in huge volumes and their relative prices (their exchange rates) vary continuously according to supply and demand, the world's major currencies are fundamentally stable over the short and medium terms. This is not a coincidence which might change anytime but an indispensable requirement of the globalized business world and so much so that if free-floating currencies do start to fluctuate strongly, central banks will intervene in order to reduce that volatility. If a given cyber currency, say, Bitcoin, is used in the most frequent business transaction which exist, namely in a sale of any type of goods, say, cars or timber, by way of example, the payment of this transaction will be done with a certain delay only, let's say within 2 months following the day the sales contract was signed and maybe 1 week after the supply of the good. If during that time period the price of that currency increases by 20%, then the bill for the buyer will increase by 20% which in all likelihood will mean that the buyer will suffer huge losses on that transaction. This issue is even considerably magnified in case of pure financial transactions: assume a corporation issues a bond with 10-year maturity (any anticipated redemption is excluded) expressed in Bitcoins. If Bitcoins increases significantly compared to the $ the corporation incurs substantial risks of bankruptcy. As the strong volatility of Bitcoin and by extension of all cyber currencies is known by all business operators, this means that Bitcoin, as long as it will be as volatile as it has been over the past, will not be suitable for genuine business transactions and will remain, probably forever, another game in the Wall Street casino, without any meaningful economic function as a currency used in financial operations or as a means of payment in international trade.

Cash Reserves or Not?

Investors should only invest those funds which they are sure they will not need within the foreseeable future, say within 3 to 5 years. Funds which are needed to cover expenses coming due over that period should be parked in fixed-income securities with a corresponding maturity in order to avoid interest rate risk.

This being said, the question debated here is a different one, namely whether the funds dedicated to the investment portfolio,(meaning funds which precisely are not needed for covering living expenses) should at all times be fully invested in securities or not (even if the investor does not forecast their funds invested could be needed in the near future). In a bull market the investor should be fully invested and if they are not, their overall performance will suffer; any substantial cash holding means assuming "benchmark risk" as the investor's portfolio becomes substantially unlike their benchmark. This is especially so if interest rates are at historically low rates, as is currently the case.

Obviously, this works both ways: in a bear market, it is advantageous for the investor (and their performance metrics) not to be fully invested in securities. If we assume that overall the tendency of common stock markets is upwards (which is actually the case), what is then the argument to keep a cash cushion? The answer is that such cash reserves may be helpful to profit from the opportunities which are periodically left open by irrational market fluctuations.

It is beyond any doubt that the fact to have liquidities available at the moment of the worst market crashes happening in a generation is a tremendous advantage, provided that (and this is a very big caveat) the investors having this dry powder at their disposal are actually in a position to really profit therefrom. It is extremely easy in 2020 to have a look at the 2009 stock charts (with the full visibility the rear-view mirror offers) and to imagine what a killing one could have made in 2009 by buying the market bottoms. Each and every one has to ask themselves whether they would really have had the guts to invest their available funds in those shares which at that moment were offered at fire sale prices. All those who have been around during those periods (where doom and gloom are pervasive and daily reinforced by the media) do know that the honest answer to that question is not a clear and loud, "yes."

Probably the only one whose clairvoyance over that period cannot be challenged was Warren Buffett. Under his chairmanship Berkshire Hathaway did invest some US $20 billion into the markets at a moment when elsewhere people either did not react under *rigor mortis* or if they acted at all they did sell in panic further contributing to the meltdown. Those of the two last mentioned categories subdued by panic are the same who consider that Buffett benefits from a special bonus because he is able to get "sweetheart deals" which will be offered to nobody else. The simple truth is as follows: at the beginning of 2009 when the stocks of all US, European, Japanese, etc. companies were beaten down to extremely low prices just anybody was welcome to buy those shares on the stock market, the shareholders could just not be stopped from selling them. Nobody cared whether the name of those potential investors was Warren

Buffett or John Doe. Truth is that there were very few buyers around (the low prices prevailing can only be explained that way…) because everybody was totally unsure about the future of the world economy and of capitalism in general. In this environment, very few (as well individuals as institutional investors) had the courage to actually buy shares. The so-called "smart money" did not live up to its reputation.

For normal investors it is less certain whether at the occasion of huge market disruptions, as in 2008-2009, they would have the cold blood to really invest at down-beat prices or whether they would remain on the sidelines until uncertainty (and with it the fire-sale prices) would disappear.

John Templeton, guessing that sooner or later the US would enter the war and considering that many of the companies suffering from the Great Depression would recover in a wartime economy doubting whether he would have the right reactions when the going gets really tough, used to place orders at very low prices and he decided in September 1939, just after WWII had broken out in Europe, to buy $100 worth of every stock on the stock exchanges that was selling under a dollar per share.[8]

Every investor has to answer the question whether they will keep their composure in a market crash for themselves, being understood that investors will most certainly overrate their capacities to overcome the ambient morosity. In other words, if any investor, from the start, has serious doubts whether they will be able to buy if the market has lost 30-40 per cent and the media only have bad (really bad) news to offer, then any cash reserve will be of no use in those extreme circumstances. It is true however that such cash reserves could still be useful in case of relatively minor market corrections of say, 5-10 per cent, which happen more or less every year and which are not necessarily accompanied by extremely negative market assessments.

Anyway, and given the above remarks, it is probably advisable to keep the cash reserves of the investment portfolio at low levels, say 5-10 per cent at a maximum, especially if interest rates are at historically low rates which means that the opportunity costs of holding such cash balances are relatively low.

Furthermore, assuming that the investment opportunities detected are extremely promising, investors have the possibility to leverage their portfolio. Any internet broker will allow the purchase of a certain amount of stocks on loans (provided the shares held are of sufficient quality). In this way investors, confronted with suddenly appearing excellent investment opportunities will be in a position to invest their cash reserves of 5 to 10 per cent increased by borrowed funds from the internet broker of say 20 to 30 per cent, with the clear objective to reduce or even eliminate this debt over a relatively short period of say 12 to 18 months: this reduction may occur through the dividend payments cashed in on their portfolio, but more importantly, through sales of shares and from new funds (e.g. income from their professional activity).

Under no condition ("no" has to be taken literally here) should the investor leverage to the limits of what is allowed by the broker. If they do so, the slightest decrease in stock prices will trigger margin calls, meaning they will have to sell shares at a particularly bad moment that is when record low prices dominate. Furthermore, interest rates charged by internet brokers are typically very high; financing an investment portfolio for a significant part by this type of debt will seriously impact the investment returns and will be bearable only under very favorable market conditions.

In case of a market crash what is even more important than investing at down-beat prices is the resolution not to sell in panic.

Bond Investing

Ironically the "widow-and-orphan investment" par excellence, which is sovereign debt, and which is virtually risk free (at least if the bonds are issued by triple-A borrowers, especially countries), in the present low-interest environment of the third decade of the 21st century, does not show any reasonable chance of a positive return at least not after inflation and taxes.

Even when disregarding the present low-interest period bond investors have over the whole 20th century not been in an enviable position: the average long-term real return (below 2% in the US) on government bonds was negative in money countries: a case in point here is Germany, a country where criticism of the interest policy of the ECB is pervasive and where a view widely held by the public is that the low interest-policy is intended to support the highly indebted states of southern Europe at the expense of the German savers who do not receive adequate returns on their savings.

When compared to the US treasury bond rates, interest rates have been seriously negative for one or several annual periods during nearly each decade (with the exception of the 1920s) of the 20th century: the high inflation rate of an average of 16% from 1916 to 1919 led to strongly negative bond returns. In substance, the same thing happened during WWII although with lower inflation rates. The 1960s and 1970s where marked by ever increasing inflation rates which lead to consistently negative real returns in excess to minus 2% until inflation was finally tamed by Fed policies under chairman Paul Volcker at the beginning of the 1980s.

On the other hand, the chances of losses, even substantial losses, are real. In the first place, sovereign debtors (not to talk about corporate debtors), all over the world, historically have defaulted many, many times over the last centuries. Astonishing as it may seem one country which is part of the serial defaulters, namely Argentina, with so far 8 defaults it is one of the most default-prone countries in history, in 2017, has been able to float a loan amounting to $2.75 billion with a 100-year maturity.

Currently on a worldwide basis there are some $15 trillion debt (mostly sovereign bonds) with negative returns meaning that the creditor pays the debtor to accept his money and to (hopefully…) repay him a somewhat lower amount than the one he received years before. This is Alice in Wonderland.

It is perfectly understandable that investors have a strong predilection for triple A bonds which means that these bonds have a very low default risk. However, this does not allow them to conclude that these bonds are "risk-free." Beyond the risk of such default, there are still many remaining risks: the interest rate risk, incurred by bond investors means that any slight increase in market interest rates applicable to long-term bond obligations will lead to a significant loss in value of the bonds issued , meaning the risk that if an investor who purchased a 30 year Treasury bond newly issued at the then prevailing nominal rate of 4% and if shortly afterwards the market interest rate increases to 5% then the price at which the old bonds are traded will sharply correct downwards to a level which makes sure that the bond yield is equal to the now higher interest rates. For a long term bond (a 30-year bond) that price correction will be rather hefty. It is true that the long-term investor holding the bond to maturity may ignore such temporary impairment of the bond.

These price corrections, induced by interest rate fluctuations, obviously work both ways: if after a certain bond has been issued interest rates decrease (say from 4% to 3% in the preceding example) then bond prices will increase significantly which will please the existing investors. However in that case these investors will be confronted with another type of risk called reinvestment risk which means that the investor periodically receives an interest payment which they want to reinvest in bonds again. However, as the market interest rates have steeply decreased it will not be possible to reinvest these interest proceeds at the initially prevailing interest rates and the yield of the fixed-income portfolio will decrease.

Our bond investor is not yet done: they still suffer inflation risk, the risk that the coupon on the moment it is paid and the redemption proceeds when the bonds mature, will have a purchasing power which is lower than the one prevailing when the bonds were purchased. This risk increases with inflation rates and is especially dangerous if interest rates are low when even a benign inflation rate may absorb a high proportion of the nominal return the bonds offer and they may even exceed that rate.

In fact, investing in bonds is part of those bets which anybody should avoid at all cost, namely lopsided bets where the odds are distributed in an unfavorable way: a small upside and a big downside. Any investor may buy bonds issued by an extremely prosperous company and they still will only receive a relatively modest interest rate in addition to the repayment of the principal amount on redemption date. In fact, this is only the best-case scenario: default risk is a reality for bonds, especially for corporate bonds. This is the reason why corporate bonds sell at lower prices which means they offer higher yields than government bonds, in fact assuming this concept refers to governments with a triple A rating, meaning they are in a superb financial standing.

In times of low interest rates investors in their chase of yields do often take foolish risks by investing in weak companies oftentimes offering higher interest rates than those obtainable on the best bonds. However, in this way investors do considerably increase their risk of not being reimbursed on the principal amount. The point is that this increased risk is not at all compensated by the slight increase in the interest rate. In fact, in a specific case the compensation might be adequate but to really be covered the investor would need to hold a very diversified portfolio of bonds of the same risk class. If the investor only holds bonds of one issuer, say General Electric, the outcome will be an unmitigated one: in case GE goes bankrupt the bondholder will most certainly (but not necessarily) suffer a severe loss of capital more than outweighing the delta yield they received by investing in a less than triple-A company. If on the other hand GE does not get in serious trouble the delta yield will be a compensation for assuming a somewhat higher risk which in fact did not materialize.

For these reasons most experienced advisors recommend to only invest in a diversified portfolio of bonds other than sovereign bonds of the highest ratings or corporate bonds of triple-A borrowers (which largely avoids the risk of investing in the only company going bankrupt) or to invest in deep-discount bonds: this last category of bonds, may grant an adequate protection in terms of yield for the risks assumed: suppose our bond investor buys a bond for 75% of its par value on the secondary market. In case the bond will be redeemed (at par, as usual), then they will in addition to their regular yield realize a capital gain of 33.34%. The classical advice given by bond specialists is to buy only either the best bonds or the worst bonds and to avoid everything in between.

It is important to underline that the investment analysis to be made by bond investors and stock investors is fundamentally different: corporate bond investors will only ask whether the issuer company will survive long enough to be still in business on maturity of the bond in question; equity investors will ask a more difficult question namely in how far the issuing company will prosper. Confronted with the choice of buying Apple bonds or Coca Cola bonds, with a 10-year maturity, assuming they both carry the same yields, the investor may safely conclude that fundamentally they do not care as both companies will survive the next 10 years. For equity investors the choice is way more difficult as they have to do an educated guess (not just on the solvency of these companies) but on their future growth and profitability: In this respect Apple and Coca Cola will doubtlessly have very different perspectives.

The question we may ask at this point is whether bond investing is preferable to stock investing from a risk-return point of view. In his book Stock for the Long Run, Jeremy Siegel in the 1994 edition had pointed out that over a thirty-year period stocks have always outperformed bonds. Robert Shiller in his book "Irrational Exuberance, the third edition (2016), argues that this is not entirely true for the reason that as Siegel would have admitted himself there is at least one period, namely the period 1831-1860, where bonds have outperformed stocks.

The practical impact of this discussion is rather low. The two said authors seem to agree that in all independent 30-year periods (except one: from 1831-1860) stocks have outperformed bonds. Even if that exception did not exist then it would still not be proof that such underperformance could not happen in the future: remember the standard warning: "past performance does not guarantee future returns." On the other hand, outperformance over the overwhelming majority of periods is still a very solid argument for most investors: this past performance, even if not guaranteeing future returns gives the base rate for our future investments.

Bond investing is an area which is also not immune to innovation. In 2017 the World Bank issued a $320 million catastrophe bond meant to back its Pandemic Emergency Financing Facility. [9] Although called "bonds" in fact they represent a kind of insurance coverage which would be triggered if the Ebola epidemic spread from the Democratic Republic of Congo to neighboring countries: if that happened the principal value of the bonds is payable to the World Bank's accounts. The interest rate on the bonds which were paid by rich-country donors varied, according to the riskiness of the tranche concerned from 11.5% to 6.9% over LIBOR. Although when the bonds were issued nobody thought of Covid-19 those deaths count when the bond triggers are calculated.

Low-Interest Environment

The trend of very low and even negative interest rates seems to be here to stay. The beginning of that period was the Great Recession of 2008-2009; whereas up to the year 2016 included the FED prime rate was constantly below 1%, rates increased cautiously as of 2017 to reach the 2.25-2.50% level but those timid increases were again cancelled out at the end of 2019 and in 2020. At the beginning of 2020 it appears that worldwide funds amounting to some $15 trillion do carry negative interest rates which means nothing less than borrowers (not lenders!) are being paid for accepting the funds put at their disposal by lenders. Even going back to the Antiquity it will be difficult to find a precedent for such anomalous situation. This very exceptional environment has led to surprising situations: in 2017 Austria has issued a €3.5 billion Loan with an interest rate of 2.1% and a maturity of 100 years. In August 2019 the bond hit a top of 210 cents to the euro falling down to 178 cents in September 2019. On an annual basis this would come to an *annualized* gain of 87%. The rise in price has reduced the yield to maturity to just 0.9%. [10] This example shows how volatile such long-maturity bonds are reacting to relatively small variations in interest rates in absolute terms even if in relative terms a change from 2.1% to 0.9% is of course substantial.

It has to be stressed that even over the 20th century negative real interest rates (meaning after taking inflation into account) were not that uncommon. For instance, over the whole period 1900-2000 the average annual real bond return have been negative in five countries (out of the 16 countries under review), namely Germany, Italy, Japan, France and Belgium[11]. What is new is that nominal interest rates are negative (which means in fact that real interest rates are even more negative (by the inflation rate which in

56

most of the Western countries is currently measured at roughly 2% on average).

Zero-Sum Game

Buying the above various assets available to investors frequently results in zero-sum games, concept which refers to a mathematical representation of a situation in which each participant's gain or loss is exactly balanced by the losses or gains of the other participants. This means either that the assets concerned are speculations or that they involve contractual agreements between a buyer and a seller taking opposite positions. In this second case the gain of the one is the loss of the counter-part (if we disregard transaction costs). If those transaction costs are taken into account, it is a "negative-result game" for the traders as a group (and hence for the very large majority of individual traders).

All options (and generally speaking all derivatives) fall into this category of zero-sum investments. Investors should avoid these markets as the chances to come about as a winner over the long run are close to zero: this has more to do with gambling than with investing. It is a lot easier to make money in stocks where the base rate (some 10 percent of yield per year on average before inflation and taxes) is clearly in the investor's favor, especially if they are minimizing their costs, as they should.

On the other hand, stock markets and bond markets are are not places where mathematically one side's wins are the other side's losses. In strong bull markets close to everybody wins whereas in bear markets (nearly) everybody loses. In the long run markets go up so that theoretically everybody may win.

Stock Markets and Inflation

The conventional wisdom in finance has always been that investments in stocks, as they represent a share of the

57

assets of a company, are good inflation hedges, meaning that it was assumed that if inflation goes up the same would happen to stock markets. As such, stocks were always supposed to favorably compare to bonds which pay constant annual coupons and reimburse the principal amount years (sometimes decades later on) without any compensation for the loss of purchasing power the funds invested have suffered in the meantime. It is true that bonds are dismal investments in times of strong inflation. But that does not mean that stocks would necessarily represent a good or even only a decent inflation hedge. This is not the case, at least not generally speaking.

Let's first point out that recently there have not been any periods where price levels decreased on an annual basis and furthermore that nobody currently forecast a deflation period. Although this is far from sure, this might be recency bias at work, because as now living economists have never experienced an extended period of deflation they consider this an impossible scenario. It should not be forgotten that in the US the price level reached in 1920 had decreased by nearly a third in 1933 and it was not until 1947 that the 1920-level was reached again.[12]

Inflation, at least beyond a very low level, has several negative impacts on business income of companies which are often not in a position to increase prices sufficiently quickly in order to keep up with increasing costs. This is certainly the case for companies selling commodity products, less so for franchises. Especially hurt by inflation are those companies having high requirements for equipments. These companies do write off the costs of their fixed assets over their useful lifetime and in this way they obtain the tax deduction for the capital invested. However, given the constant price increases for capital goods the cash flow generated by the old equipment will be insufficient to allow for a replacement of the existing capital equipments which need to be replaced. Finally, investors have learned that high inflation periods will often end in a recession, as was the case in 1974. Investors anticipate such downturns and they do so by moving out of stocks.

It is difficult, especially for younger investors, to position themselves back into the 1970s and the climate of rampant inflation then prevailing. In the U.S., consumer prices were up 6.7 % in 1977, 9% in 1978, 13.34% in 1979, 12.5 in 1980 and 8.9 in 1981 before flattening down significantly in to 3.8 in 1982 and 1983 and 3.9 in 1984: the high inflation spiral was finally broken.

Stock market indices are always quoted in non-inflation-adjusted amounts which grossly overstates the actual progression of stock prices over time. The Dow Jones Industrial Average has first reached the 1,000-points limit in 1965 but thereafter, during 16 years it did not durably cross this highly symbolic threshold. Finally, once inflation was defeated through the Fed actions with Paul Volcker at the helm, the DJIA durably crossed that threshold only in 1983. However, in real terms (meaning inflation corrected) the index would not have exceeded the level of 1,000 points before 1995: In that year the DJIA crossed the threshold of 4838 for the first time which rate corresponded to 1,000 in 1965, given that over the said period 1965-1995 the cumulated inflation rated reached 383.8%.

Another ongoing debate in most of the countries is if and in how far price indices (the Consumer Price Index, CPI) truly reflect the real depreciation of money. Consumers, when shopping in their local supermarket, will assure you that the real price inflation is way higher than the official statistics show it to be. This might however not necessarily be the ultimate truth. Consumers just as any human being, are subject to cognitive biases as explained in Chapter 5.

Furthermore, the opinion of consumers are predominantly shaped by their ongoing purchases of foods and staples. They may not take into account the fact that PCs, TV flat screens, smartphones and other electronic products in general do decrease in price and at the same time substantially increase in quality.

Index (or Passive) Investing

Investment funds come in different shapes and colors. The principal idea behind an investment fund is to group the investing power of a large number of investors in order to obtain economies of scale and diversification of risk to a degree which no individual investor acting alone would be able to achieve. Such economies of scale may be attained at different levels: The research expenses to be made by a given investment fund are what they are whether the fund has $50 million, $500 million or $5 billion under management.

Investment funds do also largely vary with respect to the asset classes they invest in. Some are concentrating on equity investments, others do limit themselves to fixed-interest securities, monetary assets, real estate assets, etc. Others are allowed to hold different asset classes at the same time.

Funds also differ heavily with respect to their legal and tax structure: some are corporations other undivided ownerships of assets, some are taxable entities *per se*, for others taxation only occurs on the level of the fund investors. These aspects are not further belabored here.

Another distinction is between funds which are actively managed whereas others are passively managed: funds of that last category do simply mirror the large market indices like the Dow Jones Industrial Average, the S&P 500, the Russell 3000 or the Russell 2000 (small caps). These index funds, unlike actively managed funds, do not search to beat the market, they *are* the market (or by investing in a large number of securities they aim to be as close as possible to the market which they use as benchmark, for instance the S&P 500). The implication of this choice to mirror a large index is that managing such a fund is literally a no-brainer. No investment decisions have to be taken other than following the decisions of the institutions which operate the namesake index: if company A is kicked out of the Dow

Jones Industrial Average (DJIA), (as has happened with General Electric (GE) on June 26th 2018 when it was replaced by Walgreens Boots Alliance, WBA) time has come to sell the shares held by the DJIA Index Fund in GE and to have them replaced by the shares of WBA. Since the Dow Jones Industrial Index was launched in 1896 the composition of the index has changed 54 times or roughly each two years. However changes of the composition of the investments are a lot more frequent than biennial. Arguably the composition of the index changes on a daily basis: this is the case for asset-weighted indices like the S&P 500 for example but also for price-weighted indices like the DJIA for which a stock with a price range of $40-50 (say Cisco) has a lower weight than a stock with a price range of $450-500 (take Apple as an example).

Obviously, the cost of managing such an Index Fund are far lower than that of a so-called "actively-managed fund": no research whatsoever is needed. The difference in costs is substantial and at the end of the day this difference in cost is the principal reason why actively managed funds currently do suffer huge net outflows of capital. Index funds only have to hug their benchmark index in order to make sure they will continuously show a performance as close as possible to that of their benchmark index.

By investing in an index fund mirroring the S&P 500 stock index the investor is assured to obtain the market yield of the said index (minus fees) during his period of investment. In other words, an investor holding a DJIA Index Fund during the period 2019-2025 will receive roughly the same yield as the DJIA, decreased by the management expenses of this fund.

Typically such management expenses of index funds are very low and they vary between 5 and 20 basis points (or between 0.05% and 0.2%). By comparison, actively managed funds do incur considerably higher costs which typically range between 1 and 2 per cent. These costs are substantial and they are the single most important reason

61

why actively managed funds, although at the outset claiming that they beat the market, only very rarely do so in practice. Roughly 80 per cent of actively managed funds, far from beating their benchmark index, underperform the same index, often by a substantial margin.

One or two per cent may not sound a lot but this is not the correct way to look at things. Investors should bear in mind that the percentage rate applies refers to the capital invested and not to income generated only. It is a fact that the historically best performing asset class, that is equities, does generate pre-inflation yields of 9 to 10 per cent. If we deduct inflation of say 2-3 per cent we have a net yield of 7%. This is the amount an actively managed fund performing at market level may reasonably earn by investing in the stock market. If the investor decides to realize their investment via an index fund, they will actually get this yield (minus the operating costs of the fund reflected by the so-called "expense ratio" of, say, 0.1 per cent per annum). However, if the investment is realized via an actively managed fund the costs of 1-2 per cent per year are far from being incidental as they represent between 14.3% and 28.5% of gross income of the fund. If in absolutely terms such fees may not end up to much for the average investor, we will see in Chapter 3. how much of a difference 1 or 2 per cent make over a long period of say 30 years and more.

According to a study covering the years 2010 to 2015 by Russel Kinnel of Morningstar on the merits of the firm's expense ratios it appeared that it indeed paid off to select the lowest-cost funds available which across the board beat their high-cost competition, which rule held true in all asset classes for all periods: this result was due to a combination of two factors: not only did paying lower fees directly boost the bottom-line of the fund but in addition the low amount of fees guaranteed that the asset managers were not interested in doing a lot of trading, with the result that their pre-cost returns was higher than the one of the high-cost rival funds. The final advice of the report was that: investors should make expense ratios a primary test in fund selection.

However, actively managed mutual funds are not the undisputed stars when it comes to investment management fees. Hedge funds are doing a lot "better" in this respect by typically charging according to the "2-20 model" which means that at the beginning of any year the investor is charged 2% on his capital (called "Asset Under Management", AUM) as an annual fee and a performance fee of 20% on profits of the fund during the year.

If that is still not enough in terms of fees payable, the investor instead of investing in a regular hedge fund may choose to invest in a "Fund of Funds" which in the hedge fund environment means that the hedge fund issuing the shares to the investor will only select other hedge funds for investing its clients' funds. The obvious effect will be that the ultimate investor will suffer not only one level of fees (the hefty 2-20 regime) but they may suffer another layer of fees of typically 1.5% and 10% respectively. If that is still not enough they may even opt for a hedge fund of Hedge Fund of Funds, which means that there are 3 layers of investment and as many levels of fees involved…

Needless to say that with such a structure chances to generate a positive result for the investor are slim, in fact zero: this outcome should not come as a surprise for the reason that such solutions are not designed to make money for the investor but only to make money from the investor.

In 2007 Warren Buffett had entered into a $1 million wager with Protégé Partners ("a specialized asset management and advisory firm that was founded in 2002 to focus exclusively on investing in established smaller hedge funds and select emerging managers") that a selected basket of 5 funds of funds to be selected by Protégé Partners would not be able to beat a regular index fund over a 10 year period. In his chairman's letter to shareholders for 2007 (p. 11), Warren Buffett announced the final outcome of the wager. Whereas the S&P Index Fund delivered an annual yield of 8.5% (for a total gain of 125.8%) beating each of the hedge funds (whose names were not disclosed to the public). The only year when the hedge funds were beating the S&P Index fund was the first year covered by the wager (namely 2008) when the S&P Index Fund lost 37.0% whereas the funds-of-funds' losses ranged from 16.5 to 30.1%. In all the following 9 years the funds-of-funds, as a group, trailed the Index Fund.

Fund A: 2.0% (on average)

Fund B: 3.6%

Fund C: 6.5%

Fund D: 0.3%

Fund E: 2.4%

Accordingly none of those funds-of-funds did come close to the Index Fund.

Just as no stock is a good investment at any price, no investment manager is a good manager at any level of fees and just as the price paid for a stock matters, the costs incurred for managing a portfolio greatly matter as well.

Incidentally it would appear that the fees accepted by markets are coming down rapidly: In November 24, 2019 the Financial Times reported that the performance fee for equity hedge funds has dropped from 19.1% at the start of 2008 to 16.4% in 2019, according to HFR (data group).

The huge inflow of funds which currently benefit index funds come from the millions of disappointed investors which year in and year out do just have to note that far from the "beat-the-market" promises, they are recording yields which are miles away from only remotely *reaching* the market results (let alone from beating them).

In September 2019 Bloomberg reported that in August 2019 assets in index-tracking U.S. equity funds amounted to $4.271 trillion, exceeded for the first time assets managed by actively managed funds (amounting to $4.246 trillion run by stock pickers), according to estimates from

Morningstar Inc. Roughly speaking, about 25% of assets are managed passively. Cyrus Taraporevala, CEO of State Street Global Advisors in the Financial Times of October 15, 2019 forecast that this ratio of 25% passive versus 75% active would flip by the end of the 2020s.

Index fund investing is a completely different ball game from actively management funds. In the first place the selection criterion is as simple as it can be: as it does not really matter who manages the fund, it is enough to select the fund with the lowest fees. Chasing performance is not of relevance here as all index funds will have about the same results (for the reason they have the same assets in their portfolio). Nevertheless this extremely simple method of investing will outperform some 80% of all investors. In purely quantitative terms this method gives by far the best return on effort put in: there is basically no competition I know of where you may pretend to be in the top two-deciles of all competitors whereas doing basically nothing. As indicated in the Introduction, stock investments is not a place where one may observe a tight connection between efforts put in and results.

This being said, index fund investing as any other form of investing (or as any other human activity, for that matter), does not just have advantages. Critics of this investing method put forward the following two principal arguments:

Mindless investing. The manager of an index fund does not do any research, and they may not know and even less care what the companies they have invested in are actually doing. In a way they rely on the organization which takes care to identify the benchmark index and to do the corresponding buy and sell operations in order to mirror as closely as possible the benchmark index. The said fund manager should not be blamed for doing this but that is the only thing they are supposed to do: by doing anything else, they would certainly run into serious problems.

Market cap weighting leads to overpaying for stocks. At any moment in time companies which have done very well over the last 2 to 3 years with high P/E ratios will represent a sizable proportion of the total assets. Conversely, stocks which are beaten down for whatever reason do only represent a small fraction of what they used to be worth several years ago. An index investor buying the shares of the S&P 500 Index Fund XYZ on a given date will buy for about 5 cent on the dollar of Apple Inc. (On March 31, 2020 the highest weighted float-adjusted company of the S&P 500 was Microsoft 5,12% of the index). This percentage is so high for the reason that Microsoft did extremely will over the last years (at least until the coronavirus crisis). Because they did so well it is rather likely that they will do less good over the following annual period(s). If this prediction realizes, the weight of these shares in the index will decrease and maybe Microsoft will only represent 4% of the index fund. This means indirectly the investor disposes of more than a fifth of their position and they do so at prices lower than those they bought them at. For investors market-cap weighting indices involves the risk to buying high and selling low.

The relatively recent concept of "smart beta" is based on the shortcomings of the traditional equity index construction which are generally based on market capitalization. The objective is to produce alpha at a cost lower than those involved by traditional active investing. The shortcoming of this type of index is that the index investor in such a market capitalization fund (say the S&P 500) will at the moment they buy into the fund have a large proportion of their funds invested in stocks which have already had a good run and a very small proportion in those stocks which may be the FAANG stocks of tomorrow. In order to avoid such risk of buying the winner of yesteryear a simple remedy is to design an equal weight index. But other alternatives are available as well: for instance indices are constructed by using factors which have made their proves, like momentum, value, growth, size, etc. Stocks are then bought and portfolios are rebalanced in a transparent way according to these indices used.

Smart beta as a kind of hybrid between active and passive investing, has become very popular over the last 5 years as they have doubled to reach $1.1 trillion. Recent research however shows that over the period 2009 to 2018 smart beta funds have underperformed their benchmark by 3.83 and 4.48 % respectively over the 5 and 10 year periods.[13] In the US multi-factor funds lost 2.55% over 5 years and 1.92% over 10 years.

Investors might consider index funds based on market cap weighting and opt in favor of so-called equal-weighted funds. They may for instance compare the performance of the equal-weighted S&P 500 ETF (RSP) versus the market cap weighted S&P 500 ETF (SPY). RSP apportions an equal dollar amount to each of the 500 companies of the S&P index with the obligation to rebalance each quarter. These two features mean not only that mid-cap companies are way heavier represented in the portfolio but also that, through rebalancing, the winners of the quarter will be sold in order to add to the decliners of the latest three months. Over the period 2009-2017 RSP gained 345% compared to 246% for SPY despite a higher expense ratio of 0.40% versus 0.09% for SPY.[14] The above mentioned study warns that smart beta investing, may very well underperform for a long time span. This is especially so in a long bull market were value investing is doing relatively poorly (as it did over the said period).

Biased composition of the indices

Numerous studies have shown that the composition of the large Stock Market indices is heavily biased in favor of shares showing important growth rates. In itself this does not need to be a bad thing but the problem is that these shares tend to be overpriced: the simple announcement that a share will soon be part of a given market index will increase its price, whereas a price decrease occurs if deletion from an index is announced. Both these types of fluctuations are disadvantageous for index investors: they receive less than fair value if a new company is admitted to the index and on leaving the index they suffer a loss in value on the shares concerned. This phenomenon is reinforced due to the great success of the benchmark index, the S&P 500 for instance: if a company is announced to be admitted to the said index the automatic consequence is that the shares of the company get pushed up as soon as the announcement is made. An extreme example is the case of Yahoo! which on November 30th 1999 was announced to be admitted to the S&P Index as of December 8[th,] 1999. On December 7th, the shares had increased by 64 percent above the level they had reached on the day the announcement was made. The stock was selling at more than 500 times earnings.

In 2016, a company is a member of the S&P 500 Index during 20 years on average, whereas the corresponding number was 61 years in 1958.

The reader may ask: does all this really matter or is it just an incidental phenomenon with just a marginal impact at best. It seems that it does actually matter and this for the reason that when comparing the stock price evolution of those shares newly entered into the index to those deleted from the indices the second group performed better than the first one!

Any general stock index cannot remain unchanged during decades but it has to adapt, be it only for the simple reason that companies are not eternal but some disappear, either because they go bankrupt, they get absorbed (which means they disappear as a legal entity) or they are taken private (they go on to exist as legal entities but their stocks will no longer be publicly traded).

Beyond those radical changes, a general stock index by its very nature tries to be as representative as possible when compared to the economic activity of the country. Again, the huge economic transformations of the last decades and the corresponding changes in people's lifestyles (e.g. computers, smartphones, internet, social media, etc.) mean that some companies have fallen into irrelevance whereas others have stormed ahead to become among the most valuable companies (in terms of market capitalization) on the market. All this means that changes to the index are unavoidable and in fact are relatively frequent. Unfortunately these changes are not always to the benefit of the index investor. Let's have a look at the one index which is generally considered to be by far the best-constructed and the most representative of the general activity of the economy, namely the S&P 500.

Construction of the Indices

The S&P 500 Index was set up for the first time in 1957 and it contained exactly 425 industrials, 50 utilities and 25 railroads. Hence, this single index was a mirror of the total economy whereas the Dow Jones since its inception has been composed of three different indices: DJ Industrial Average (DJI) for industrial companies (in the broad sense of this word), the DJ Transportation Average (DJT) and the DJ Utilities Average (DJU).

In 1988 the S&P abandoned these fixed numbers in favor of a more flexible approach but still aiming at building a representative index through 500 companies "in leading industries of the economy." From 1957 to 2003, 917 companies have been added to the Index. Forty years later only 74 were still part of the S&P 500, the other 426 having been replaced and in some cases the replacements have themselves already been replaced a second time. Strangely enough the additions to the index did not add to propel the index to higher levels: to the contrary! The new additions did underperform the index whereas those companies deleted from the index outperformed not only the companies which replaced them but also the benchmark index! The reason for this surprising result was that although the newly added firms grew sales and earnings faster than those they replaced, the problem was that the prices at which these stocks traded when they entered into the index were too high. Prices paid always matter and they do so big time. Investors tend to overrate growth and they pay a high price for that mistake.

The Dow Jones is a much more concentrated index and also far more simplistic in its construction. It is not weighted by capitalization of the participating company but … price-weighted which means that a stock with a price of $480 (Apple for instance) will have 8 times the weight of a stock having a price of $60 (Intel for instance). When the DJ Index was first calculated in the year 1884 the calculation of the index simply required the adding-up of the prices of all the stocks composing the index and the total was divided by the number of companies composing the DJ Index. In the meantime the divisor, which changes continually in order to take into account the effects of certain corporate actions like stock splits or spin-offs for instance, it is no longer 30 but a number smaller than one, meaning that in fact the number is divided by the divisor of 0.14602128057775. A change of $1 in price in any particular stock within the average, equates to a 6.87 (or $1 \div 0.14602128057775$) point movement.

The most recent adjustment to the composition of the DJIA has occurred on August 31, 2020 and it concerned 10% of the stocks of the DJIA: the stocks of Exxon Mobil, Pfizer and Raytheon were replaced by those of Amgen, Honeywell and Salesforce. This change was signicantly influenced by one of the most salient shortcomings of the DJIA, namely the one of being a price-weighted index. At a moment when Apple the most highly priced stock, with a price of some $500 making it the highest priced stock of the DJIA, split its stock into 4 on August 31, 2019 it was the moment to eliminate some low priced stocks (Exxon Mobil and Pfizer) of the said index and to replace them by higher priced ones (the 3 new entrants).

Similarly, if the S&P Index 500 would have been equal weighted instead of being capital-weighted between March 24, 2000 and December 2, 2010 it would have shown a return of 66% instead of a loss of -19% in its capital-weighted form.[15]

Investors would be wrong to think that the technicalities of construction of the indices are of little practical interest. The contrary is true. As shown by a November 2011 article on Bloomberg by John Steele Gordon the fact that in 1939 IBM was replaced by AT&T as a component of the Dow Jones Industrial Index did have as a consequence to severely dampen the progression of the DJIA as the stock price of AT&T increased only by 300% from 1939 to 1979 whereas the stock price of IBM increased by 22,000%. As a consequence without this change the pre-Depression highest level of the DJIA would not only have been reached on November 23, 1954 (closing at 383) but many years before already.

Passive investing is a currently ongoing trend with far-reaching consequences for the entire wealth management industry including the business model of hedge funds with its ridiculous fee structure. On October 25, 2019 the Financial Times reported that according to former Fidelity Investment's star investor Jeff Vinik (who formerly managed the famous Magellan fund) institutional investors are no longer looking for stock pickers with the consequence that he has decided to close down the hedge fund bearing his name just 8 months after relaunching it. According to Jeff Vinik, institutional investors are looking for outperformance of index products over a long period of time with respect to equity products whereas hedge funds have underperformed the indices in prior years. Concerning the 9 first months of the year 2019 the average hedge funds returned 8% compared to the S&P 500 yielding 19% over the same period.

When long-term indices are used how should stock returns be averaged: by a geometric or arithmetic average? Arguing that arithmetic averages reflect the actual changes in their portfolios which investors actually experience Dimson, Marsh and Staunton use arithmetic averages. This reason does not appear particularly convincing especially so if very long term studies are concerned (101 years for the case in point). In 1990 it does not matter anymore which annual returns the investor of the 1920s actually experienced over the years of the Great Depression. Only geometric mean rates guarantee comparability of the results with those of other studies.

Diversification

This subject will be introduced by several quotations.

"Because we cannot know the future, we diversify", Paul Samuelson.

Sir John Templeton says exactly the same thing: "Only those who know the future do not have to diversify."

"In order not to be killed we accept to not make a killing and diversify", Anonymous.

Blamed for making too large a bet on one stock Lord Keynes reacted sarcastically: "Sorry to have gone too large on Elder Dempster. I was suffering from my chronic delusion that one good share is safer than 10 bad ones."

"Diversification is a protection against ignorance, a confession that you do not know the businesses you own", Warren Buffett.

"Diversification is the enemy of performance. Accept volatility and concentration", Barton Biggs, p. 97.

"The greatest safety lies in putting all your eggs in one basket and watching the basket. You simply cannot afford to be careless or wrong. Hence, you act with much more deliberation." G.M. Loeb.

These various contradictory quotations, which are made by equally qualified and respectable persons, are meant to show that this subject is one of those where a consensus cannot be reached.

Academic theory insists on the paramount importance of diversification, that is that an investor should have a carefully chosen portfolio composed of stocks of different companies, belonging to different sectors, and possibly to different countries. The objective pursued by such diversification is to avoid that the investor by being unlucky and having chosen one company in the sector (maybe the only one) that gets hurt by unforeseen difficulties which may even lead to bankruptcy will suffer a severe damage to their portfolio from which they will possibly never recover. This is sound advice and it should be followed by the average investor (especially the inexperienced one).

However, the impact of such diversification must be put into perspective. Indeed, whereas it makes sense to protect against cases of major financial difficulties, including bankruptcy, by having a large number of shares in the portfolio, such diversification will in the first place increase the probability that such calamity will affect one of the stocks owned, although it will obviously decrease the financial damage (the amount of the loss) in case such disaster actually occurs.

In this debate over whether the investor should privilege diversification or selectivity it should be stressed that diversification is in fact the negation of the possibility of selectivity. If it were possible to always choose the best stock, diversification could only be harmful.

Diversification is however not that surely a means to efficiently reduce the risks of the portfolio. Indeed, it is undeniable that financial markets are increasingly interconnected with the consequence that it is not very likely that the losses of some common stocks could be eliminated by the gains realized on other common stocks. Implementing a successful strategy with that objective would probably require to take either short positions on some common stocks and/or to follow option strategies. As mentioned in Chapter 3. these are not strategies which I consider advisable and hence investors who see things differently will have to look elsewhere if they want to pursue such alternative strategies.

At first glance, these widely varying views on the merits of diversification seem to be totally incompatible. However this is not the case. In reality, diversification is either advisable or not so depending on the investor and on the stocks they invest in.

Any investor who does not do serious research, who has little experience, who is emotional, who frequently follows analysts' advice, should diversify. In this way they will at least be protected against catastrophic losses and they have some chances to receive market returns. The best solution for them is probably to diversify to the extreme, that is to buy into an index fund which means that they simply "own the market."

At the other extreme, we have the experienced, analytical investors who will do thorough research before buying any stock. They will only buy if there is an adequate margin of safety and will not sell if for some unimportant reason the shares of their company will do poorly, and as long as the fundamentals of the company are fine. Concentrated portfolios also require that the investor is able to emotionally stand that their results will be very volatile which means that they may strongly deviate from market indices (for being lower as well as higher) over long periods of time: in other words, they suffer high benchmark risk

Concentration of portfolios on a very small number of shares assumes that the investment is made in companies which have a predictable business, in other words mostly outside of the high tech area, which cannot be disrupted in a very short period of time by the internet or technological breakthroughs.

In summary, the investor holding a very concentrated portfolio invests in a way that the future is not that unknown as the preceding quotations seemed to suggest it is (cf. those of Paul Samuelson and John Templeton).

Of course, this does not mean that concentrated portfolio investors will be able to predict the next Pearl Harbor, the next 9/11 or the next meteorite that will hit the earth and maybe extinguish all life on it. But then, even diversified portfolios will be of little help if such extreme events occur. The only thing concentrated-portfolio investors do pretend to know better than most people is how their investments will fare relatively to others over the long term. The fact that they are investing in a small number of shares only forces them to be particularly thorough in research and in their selection: they cannot afford to be mistaken (and they have to react aggressively if they are actually mistaken).

For the regular investor who does not have the experience and the time (or both) to do concentrated investing there is one interesting mind game to play. When constructing their portfolio and assuming they have selected one stock in which they want to invest 3-4% of their total portfolio, they should always ask themselves the question whether they would be willing to invest a sizable chunk of their portfolio into this same company. "Would I be willing to invest 30-50% in this stock?" If the answer is a clear no they should ask whether they should at all invest in that stock. By carelessly selecting companies (implicitly on the basis of the argument that it is "only" a small position which does not hurt even if things go wrong) one ends up with a portfolio of very low quality. The whole idea of diversification is that losses on some positions will be more than compensated by profits on other positions. This is however not a law of nature (like gravitation) and if sufficient care has not been taken when selecting the various investments, it might well be that a large majority of shares will go down and some even substantially without losses being wiped out by gains from other positions.

This means that diversification should not be a substitute for analysis (except for the index-investor). During the 1980s promoters of junk bonds claimed that a diversified portfolio of junk bonds would carry low risk only. This conclusion was based on statistical evidence of prior years when companies in good financial standings issued bonds of investment grade but which were later on downgraded by the rating agencies when they incurred financial problems. Statistics showed that these "fallen angels" represented only a very small fraction of the total amount of bonds issued. This fact was then used as an argument when in the 1980s bonds were issued which were below investment grade on the moment they were issued: the argument was then made that based on the past experience with fallen angels the difference in interest rate would more than compensate for the rare default of the issuing company. Obviously the assumption that the past experience with fallen angels would be relevant for assessing the ratio of defaults of companies which were over-leveraged from the start was severely flawed as consecutive events would prove in a rather convincing way.

However, the fact to hold low quality bonds of corporate borrowers belonging to different industries did not protect investors against economic recession or increasing interest rates. Diversification will be a protection only if all assets are of sound quality and furthermore they are not affected in the same way if certain risks materialize.

Apparently, and perhaps surprisingly, it appears that individual investors do not diversify. A study of 1974 made by Blume, Crocket and Friend shows that 50% of investors do hold no more than 2 stocks and only 10,7% held more than 10 stocks. Another study dating back to 1974 shows that the average number of stocks in the portfolio was 3.41.

Diversification is not a panacea. The basic idea is that out of a population of suitable investments, carefully sorted out and all having an appropriate margin of safety, you choose a certain number because you can never be sure that one or the other of these stocks do not get hurt by unforeseen events. If, however, the shares chosen for investment are all over-valued (as is usually the case for growth stocks especially of the high-tech field) then diversification cannot help or at least not help sufficiently to render the investment worthwhile.

As a last point on this subject it is my view that investors who opt for having a diversified portfolio should not be obsessed by the wish to have a portfolio according to preset proportions: say a portfolio of 30 shares belonging to 10 different sectors. Diversification, except for index investors, is of secondary importance when compared to the most important element which is the quality of the individual stocks: if the investor finds 4 absolutely world class stocks in one sector they should not hesitate to overweight that sector compared to the other 9 sectors of their portfolios and also not shy away from giving more weight to the best of those 4 companies compared to the other 3. If one or the other of the 10 predetermined sectors does not show promising investment targets then that sector should not be represented at all in the portfolio. It would be a grave mistake to invest in a mediocre company just for the purpose that such investment would fit the diversification objective. In other words, the dominant objective should be selection of first-class companies and diversification is far less important. By analogy to the statement once made by Akio Morita, co-founder of SONY, a company renowned for the quality of its products: "Look after the components and the products will look after themselves" one could say here: "Look after the individual stocks and the portfolios will look after themselves."

Giving more importance to the precise proportions of a portfolio compared to the quality of the stocks composing that portfolio is not having the right priorities.

Another related issue is the question of rebalancing of the portfolio if, due to different rates of stock price fluctuations, some stocks represent a far higher share than the initially determined average amount. Such unbalances are not something which *per se* should trigger investor activity: selling the strong performers and investing the

77

proceeds in the low performers would be "like cutting the flowers and watering the weeds." as Peter Lynch famously wrote in his book "One up on Wall Street." Instead of doing so, investors should sell their losers and let their winners run.

Whether rebalancing action is required is to be decided on the basis of the generally applicable rules of fundamental value and the margin of safety. Assuming the winners have outgrown their intrinsic value a sale might be envisaged but whether the proceeds will be reinvested in the losers is a totally different question which has to be answered separately following a valuation of the concerned companies but after taking into consideration the relative attractiveness of all other investment opportunities.

Modern Portfolio Theory

The so-called "Modern Portfolio Theory" (MPT) may be traced back to Harry Markowitz's article "Portfolio Selection" published in The Journal of Finance in March 1952. This article is based on the Efficient Market Hypothesis which is the object of Chapter 3. According to the MPT, whereas asset classes produce returns corresponding to their risk level, diversification into different asset classes allows to increase returns for a given risk level (or to decrease risk for a given level of return). When it comes to selecting one portfolio over the next one, Markowitz took the reasonable position that a portfolio offering the same level of risk for a lower level of return has to be eliminated as being non-efficient. After eliminating those non-efficient portfolios what remains is an arch of portfolios which are all efficient which is why Markowitz called this curve "the efficient frontier."

The MPT offers the possibility to compose a certain number of diversified portfolios offering the highest possible returns at a given risk level (or alternatively the lowest possible risks at a given level of return). Which of these portfolios figuring on the efficient frontier is the preferred one? The MPT does not answer this question. It is up to the individual investor to decide, based on their risk tolerance, which portfolio composition they prefer: If Portfolio X offers a return of 10%, Portfolio Y a return of 11% and Z a return of 12%, whereas the risk level of Y is 8% and the one of Z is 18% higher than the one of X, the choice of each investor for one of these three portfolio compositions will be different from one investor to the next and MPT is unable to give the answer to this question.

The CAPM (Capital Asset Pricing Model) has introduced the distinction between systematic and unsystematic risk.

Systematic risk means risk which cannot be connected to individual investments and which, by definition, cannot be diversified away. Such risk may originate from macroeconomic factors, like interest rates, currency exchange rates, tariffs, economic recessions, wars, etc. To a certain extent these risks may be mitigated by asset allocation decisions in the sense that different asset classes, uncorrelated or only lowly correlated, do not react in the same ways to changes in such macroeconomic factors.

As opposed to systematic risks, unsystematic risks are risks which are specific to one company or one industry. They are sometimes also called specific, idiosyncratic or residual risks. These risks, which vary from one company to the next, may be managed by individual companies, and they may be eliminated through diversification. They may be financing risks, legal risks (think of litigation risks for Uber, tobacco companies, herbicide producers), product risks (coal and oil industry in a world transiting to renewable energies), etc. This type of risk is not correlated to market risk.

By referring to investing it may be said that instead of choosing either Intel or Nvidia (assumed that both have a similar expected return) it may be advisable to invest in both, which if the forecasts are correct, would not harm the return but reduce the risks of the portfolio. One step further in reducing non-systematic risk would lead our investor to buying the whole semiconductor sector, for instance by purchasing the corresponding sector ETF. By doing so the investor would still assume unsystematic risk in the form of risk of the semiconductor sector. That risk may also be diversified away by buying the whole stock market via for instance a suitable Index Fund, the S&P 500 or the Russell 3000.

Sometimes it is said that diversification is the only free lunch in investing. The reason is, so the argument goes, that without harming expected returns, risk can be reduced.

Chapter 2: Return and Risk

Any investment in stocks (or in any other category of assets for that matter) represents an arbitrage between risk and return. A commonly used statement is that risk and return are positively correlated: high return requires the assumption of high risks. Low returns can be obtained at a low risk level. This general statement is flawed as we will see somewhat later.

Risk is by its very nature an elusive concept, unlike return. It is not uncommon to read, even in books or articles authored by academician's statements like the following one: "On Black Monday, October 19, 1987 US investors lost 23% in one single day..."[16] Such a statement is inherently problematic as it is arguably not true: only those investors who sold in panic lost anything. All the others swiftly recovered their book losses over the following weeks. This is the difference between volatility and risk. Whereas those who sold, suffered risk (a permanent loss of capital) the others only suffered short-term volatility.

Risk may be defined as the probability of suffering a loss multiplied by the potential amount of a loss.

Let's first concentrate on returns.

Stock Market Returns

Stock market returns are composed of two elements: earnings growth (part of which may be paid out year in and year out in the form of dividends) and changes to the P/E ratio; this second part of the shareholders' return is sometimes called "speculative return", although the term "speculate" is no longer faddish. Over the entire twentieth century, the 10.4 percent average annual return of US equities was composed of 5% from dividends, 4.8 from earnings growth, and 0.6 percentage points from P/E changes (speculative return). In other words, over a long time span, the impact of investment returns by far trumps the impact of speculative returns.

However the picture is much different when we look at it over shorter periods. From 1980 to 2000, the period of the greatest bull market of the 20th century for example, the market's approximately 17 percent annual return was composed of 4 percentage points of dividends, 6 percentage points of earnings growth and a massive 7 percentage points per year due to the increase in the P/E ratios.

Earnings

There is no question that the principal driver of the value of stocks is the evolution of earnings: said differently, if earnings double the price of stocks should roughly also double (and conversely in case of a decrease in earnings). There is no guarantee that they always should correlate in such a mathematical way but it is a fact that over the long run this should broadly and on average be the case. In fact there is a second element in this equation: investors are in a first step looking at the current earnings of a given company but in fact in order to assess whether the stock of Apple, for instance, is a buy they have to make an educated guess of the future earnings of that company. In other words, they have to estimate in how far future earnings will be different than current earnings. This assessment of the future evolution of earnings is reflected in the current P/E ratio of the company. In other words, the P/E ratio will fluctuate which means that the multiple to be applied on current income will change over time so that the earnings per share amount will either be multiplied by a higher or a lower multiple depending on the future perspectives investors see in the business prospects of Apple. Due to these fluctuations of the P/E ratio the "earnings effect" will be impacted in most cases: it will be increased if the PE ratio increases and decreased in the opposite case. For instance, if the earnings of Apple increase by 10% the stock price will increase by 10% if the PE ratio remains stable; however if the said ratio increases from 25 to 30 (that is 20%) then the earnings effect will be increased by a speculative return of 20% to reach 30%.

Such changes in the PE ratio are difficult to predict and they depend on a lot of factors which are totally out of control of the company under review: for instance, interest rates, general economic outlook, etc.

The performance of stocks can only be appreciated accurately by total return measures which includes not only capital gains but also dividends. When referring to stock market indices this condition is only rarely fulfilled. None of the leading US indices (DJ, S&P, Russell) is a full performance index. Internationally only the German Dax and the FTSE 100 (as of 1993) are so-called performance indices meaning that it takes the periodic dividends into account (with the consequence that the DAX Index increases even in a year where stock prices would not move at all).

When assessing the multiple to apply to the present earnings of a company, investors should be aware of a certain number of concepts which companies use in their presentations of things and which they are (for understandable reasons) not utterly eager to explain in detail to their shareholders or to the general public. Reference is made here to the concept of earnings based on GAAP rules and alternative concepts.

GAAP Rules

GAAP stands for "Generally Accepted Accounting Principles" which means principles laid down by the Financial Accounting Standards Board (FASB), grouping a number of accountants mandated by the SEC to set binding rules on corporate accounting matters. These GAAP rules are not cast in stone and they evolve over time as new issues come up giving rise to public controversy as to the proper accounting treatment to adopt.

The currently applicable GAAP have some shortcomings which investors have to be fully aware of in order to be able to critically assess the picture which is given by the financial statements any company has to publish at least on an annual basis. According to the facts of the concrete case, earnings as shown by GAAP rules either understate or overstate the real earnings of the company.

Here are some of the most important shortcomings of GAAP accounting:

1)Capital expenditure (investment in fixed capital) is not recorded as an expense the moment the expenses are incurred but they are taken care of over the useful lifetime of the assets acquired under the form of depreciation (tangible assets) or amortization (intangible assets).

2)Investments in working capital (for instance in inventories and receivables) are not shown in the income statement. They are only shown in the balance sheet and the reader of this document has to compare the closing date balance sheet of several consecutive years in order to assess whether the business requires additional investments in working capital.

3)Intangible items (advertising costs and R&D outlays) unless purchased on the market are immediately expensed although they are meant to increase income over a number of years; in other words the accounting treatment applicable here is totally different than the one described sub 1 above and applicable to tangible fixed assets. Arguably, a more accurate approach would be to also capitalize these costs and depreciate them over a certain number of years (as such is the case for fixed assets).

4)Shareholders' equity, under GAAP is free, meaning that no deduction may be taken in the P&L account for earnings reinvested in the business.

5)Stock options granted to employees. This controversial subject with very substantial financial implications on companies' results is treated in detail later on in this Chapter 2.

6)Advertising expenses of companies selling consumer staples like Coca Cola which have huge advertising budgets: although allowing the company to increase its competitive position are fully expensed the year they are incurred.

7)Interest expenses are fully expensed the year they are incurred although inflation will in fact reduce the real value of corporate debt.

Investors should correct GAAP figures in order to come to a more accurate view on the earnings situation. Such adjustment may allow them to come to the conclusion that although GAAP earnings may be growing, adjusted earnings are actually deteriorating: such an insight may allow the investor to get out of an investment ahead of the pack and to avoid disastrous losses.

An alternative way to calculate earnings are operating earnings which represent ongoing revenues and expenses, omitting unusual non recurrent items. Operating earnings usually exclude investment gains or losses, impairment charges on inventory, fixed assets or goodwill, restructuring charges (for instance closure of a plant or of a division). Operating earnings are forecast by analysts and scrutinized on a quarterly basis.

The relatively unclear rules concerning the definition of operating earnings are often used by management to exclude from operating income a number of expenses which should be included there.

Sometimes management will take care to book these costs for periods where earnings are anyway depressed (this is the so-called kitchen sink approach and which is justified by the argument that these costs are non-recurrent and consequently should simply be ignored) which will work its magic in future periods where investors will have the impression earnings have made a huge jump and they will tend to believe that these earnings reflect the new earnings power of the company, in this way significantly increasing the stock price.

Accounting rules are what they are and the careful reader should be in a position to critically analyze the figures produced by the company's management. Some rules applicable lead to overstated earnings whereas others imply understated figures.

In the first category we find rules on corporate pensions. Whereas companies are required to set up a fund for retirement income benefits, this is not the case for other pension-related benefits, for instance health benefits. Accordingly, the provisions set up for these health care benefits are often understated.

An Alternative Earnings Concept: EBITDA

Whereas the concept of earnings is very old and goes certainly back to the 19th century already, an alternative concept measuring the performance of companies has been developed by scholars and eagerly adopted by practicians namely EBITDA, acronym standing for "Earnings Before Interest, Taxes, Depreciation and Amortization." Allegedly this notion does better reflect the company's operating performance by disregarding financing structure (interest), the tax environment, accounting decisions (amortization and depreciation). Another non negligible fact is that EBITDA will show a higher amount of earnings than the traditional measures which is always useful if one wants to convince someone a stock is a bargain.

EBITDA leads to wrong conclusions as may be shown by a simplified example on two companies respective earnings situations.

Company A (service company)

Revenue: 100

Cash expenses 80

Depreciation and amortization: 0

EBIT: 20

EBITDA: 20

Company B (manufacturing company)

Revenue: 100

Cash expenses: 80

D&A: 20

EBIT: 0

EBITDA: 20

Although these 2 companies have the same EBITDA, company A is clearly more valuable. Whereas A does have income and cash flow of 20, B does not have any income; although it does have cash flow it will have to reinvest its depreciation allowances as capital expenditure in order to replace its worn-out machinery. It does not have free cash flow over time.

One of the major adjustments to GAAP earnings in order to get to EBITDA or adjusted earnings is the adding back of stock based employee compensation, based on the reasoning that it is a non-cash expense. Such adjustments are especially frequent with young high-growth companies which are generally very cash-poor. The on-going argument which was always pushed forward by these companies was that this is a non-cash expense. If it is true that the company will not have to write a cheque the moment these options are granted, they do have a very real cost for which the bill is footed by the shareholders: any increase in the number of shares of the company will, all things equal, translate into shareholder dilution which means that the per share earnings will decrease correspondingly: the cost for shareholder is undeniable and cannot be discussed away.[17]

Return

Return can easily be measured: such is at least the case for past (or historic) returns but obviously not for future or expected returns which can only be estimated or guessed on the basis of, yes ..., past data (if any). As the standard warning goes: past performance does not guarantee future returns. When estimating future returns the concept of Expected Value (or long-term average value of the variable) is used: it is calculated by adding together all possible returns multiplied by the probability of each of these returns to occur. For instance investment A is expected to deliver a return of 7% (with a probability of 30%, or 0.3) and a return of 10% (probability of 70%, 0.7), the expected value would be 7x0.3 + 10x0.7= 9.1%.

With respect to common stock investing, returns consist in the first place of the ordinary dividend, generally paid on a quarterly basis (this is the case in the US). By adding the difference in the share price from the beginning of the year compared to the one of the year end to the dividend income, total annual return is obtained, being understood that this return is only partly realized yet, only the dividend part being actually paid out to the stockholder. These return figures may then be used to easily compare securities among themselves, for instance ranking them by increasing or decreasing returns.

Alpha

In investing, alpha (the first letter of the Greek alphabet), represented by α, measures the performance of a certain strategy, investment method, portfolio (or of the portfolio manager) on a risk adjusted basis against a benchmark and as such it measures the ability of the portfolio (or of its manager) to beat the market (as measured by a certain benchmark), the excess return the investor may obtain by entrusting their funds to that specific manager. Alpha allows for the rating of managers and shows whether their active management has actually added something to (or subtracted from) the market's performance. It is then up to the investor to check whether the amount of alpha is sufficient and compare it to the amount of fees charged to him for this additional return.

The question any investor should ask is whether they are looking to generate beta[18], which is the market return, or alpha, which represents the deviation from market return, in fact a positive deviation from that market return. If the investor, in an environment of low returns, aims for beta, fees charged by most active managers are too high in comparison to the alpha they in fact (and on average) are able to generate (after deduction of the fees collected from the investors). After all, average returns, minus fees, equates below average returns.

Alpha is meant to identify whether the actual performance of a portfolio is in line (or lower or higher) than the expected performance based on the risks incurred. The objective is to find out whether the investor has been compensated for the risk (or better volatility) they have assumed.

Alpha is the difference between Actual Return and the Expected Return. The expected rate of return is relatively easy to calculate. The following ingredients are required:

1)The risk-free rate of return (the Long Term Treasury rate)

2)The long term rate of return of the benchmark index

3)Beta, which is easily available for any publicly traded stock, for instance on Value Line, Yahoo Finance, etc.

If we assume the Risk Free Rate of Return (RFR) to be 2%, the Market Return (MR) to be 8%, beta to be 1,3, then the Expected Return (ER) will be the result of the following formula:

ER = RFR + β* (MR – RFR)

Concretely: ER = 2 + 1.3 * (8 – 2) = 9.8%. This rate is the return, on a risk-adjusted basis, which an investor may expect annually from their portfolio and the performance of the benchmark.

A portfolio manager has generated Alpha only in as far as they exceed the ER (9.8% in our example). Managers of a fund may only brag about their performance if they exceeded this rate: if not then they did not produce any Alpha which means that they did not deserve any fee beyond the low fees of a passive index fund.

With respect to the performance of active fund managers, various studies confirmed without little room for doubt that the traditional warning, "past performance does not guarantee future returns", is normally highly justified in this area. Very, very few fund managers, are able to confirm consistently that they are able to beat the benchmark index and this even without taking their fees into account. Even if Wall Street does not want to hear it, the unavoidable conclusion from this stubborn fact is that the art of asset management does not exclusively involve skill of the manager but other factors, such as luck for instance, certainly play a dominant role. In any given year the number of active fund managers who are able to beat the benchmark index are only 10 to 20%, the precise rate varying according to the study to which reference is made. In fact, it is nowhere surprising that some managers show performances above the benchmark indices. This happens even when pure chance is involved, like the roulette game in casinos, or a coin-tossing competition. If such games are played many times some players will have better results than others, just as in a casino some gamblers might even be able to temporarily 'beat the House'. However, such outperformance does not mean anything, the more so that the outperformers will not be the same over time. Hence, it is a fool's game to change the fund manager from one year to the next as it might well be that the best rated manager of last year may not be able to confirm this favorable rating.

This situation leads many asset managers to adopt so-called "closet indexing" which describes the behavior of professionals who claim to actively manage the capital amounts entrusted to them, although in reality their actual choices of investments guarantee that their results will not deviate much from their benchmark index.

There are some notable exceptions to this tendency. Some asset managers do in fact have very concentrated portfolios with the result that they have extremely volatile results.

Bill Ackmann with his hedge fund Pershing Square Capital Management is one of the very few renowned asset managers who do have a very concentrated portfolio. As a result, he heavily underperformed the benchmark for a number of years before showing an outstanding 2019 with a blockbuster result of 58%.

This behavior of most asset managers is certainly also one explanation why so few fund managers do succeed in beating the market: the reason is that very few actually try to do so! If they have a concentrated portfolio with a reasonable chance of beating the market they know that such option will lead to a certain risk of missing the benchmark. In order to avoid such possibility with the potential risk of losing clients who in their chase of performance will switch over to other managers with better recent performance.

One of the side aspects of such intriguing behavior of managers is the so-called window dressing by which, shortly before the end of the quarter (or of the year) fund managers dispose of their losing stocks to replace them by stocks which recently did well: the Apple, Facebook, Tesla *du jour*. Such behavior should be a huge red flag for investors.

Individual investors, self-managing their funds, do not have to play such games. Once we are referring not to returns recorded by the fund managers but move over to the returns of the investors (the after-management-fees returns) the situation is even significantly more pronounced and the results shown by investors do even less allow for any market outperformance. What is the reason for this situation of the investors being worse thant that obtained by their own fund managers? The answer is simple and it is the erratic behavior of most investors which consist in dancing in and out of the funds at precisely the wrong moments, in this way honoring the old rule, "buy high, sell low", which generate investors returns which are even lower than the after-fee results which the funds record.

For investors, the lessons of all this are easy to draw and they may be summarized as follows: in the first place they should avoid to pay high fees (which would be justified if "alpha" were actually delivered but are totally ludicrous if not even the full amount of beta is actually obtained). In the second place, investors should not time the market by entering and leaving it at the worst possible moments: they should remain invested all the time by selecting passive funds (with very low fees) either investing in the whole market or in substantial chunks of it. In order to avoid entering the market at precisely the wrong moments, care should be taken to not enter when market indices (or, where relevant, sector indices) are at record highs, but the purchases should be spaced over a certain period of time, of several months at least, where cost-average techniques could also be considered.

The Sharpe ratio, as designed by the 1990 Nobel Prize winning economist William Sharpe, indicates the risk adjusted performance of a stock or of an investment portfolio by comparing the said return to the return of a risk-free investment, such as US Treasuries.

The Sharpe Ratio

After deducting the risk-free return from the expected return of a stock investment the resulting figure is divided by the standard deviation of that same investment. The higher the ratio (2, or 3 at least) the better, a ratio below one is not satisfactory.

This ratio is attributed to Nobel Prize laureate William F. Sharpe and it is reflected by the following formula:

$$SR = \frac{Rp - Rf}{\sigma}$$

Rp: the expected or prospective return on an asset (portfolio);

Rf: the risk-free rateof return (generally the rate of one month Treasury bills);

σ:the standard deviation of returns (the risk) of the asset orportfolio.

The Sharpe Ratio SR in other words is equivalent to the equity premium (see below) divided by the standard deviation of the portfolio (assumed to measure risk). The higher SR, the better it is, which means we are looking for a portfolio with a high equity premium and a low σ.

The Equity Premium

This concept (also called the "equity risk premium") refers to the excess return that investing in the stock market provides over a risk-free rate of return.

Although the exact amount of the equity premium strongly varies from one author to the next one, this point is not of major importance. The equity risk premium is generally calculated as the geometric mean which represents the performance over a longer period by an annualized rate of return. The calculation of that rate is made by adding 1 to the first rate of return, multiplied by 1 + second rate of return multiplied by 1 + third rate of return, etc. until the nth rate of return. Then the nth root of this product is calculated and 1 is deducted.

The geometric mean depicts reality as if the rate of return were constant over the whole period for which the geometric mean is calculated. Of course, any investor knows that this is not the case and that the actual rates experienced fluctuate wildly. To show this volatility a different representation is needed in which different rates of positive rates of growth are depicted in columns of identical width. For instance, if the mean rate (of annual rates shown over the whole period) is 10% we may group in one column all the years which show growth of 5 to 10%, to the left all the years with growth from -5 to +5, then even more to the left all years with negative growth of -5 to -15 etc. To the right of the column 5-10% we will show another column 10-15% growth, followed by a column of 15-20% growth, etc.

If the existence of such a risk premium may easily be explained by the fact that over the short term stocks are doubtlessly riskier assets than, say, government bonds, the question which was also addressed by a number of studies was whether the level of the risk premium was justified as well. On this point some authors have concluded that they could at justify only a relatively small part of the premium.

How can that be? An element of response is probably to be found in the concept of "myopic risk aversion." Later on in the book we shall see that risk aversion means that confronted with an equal chance to earn $100 and to lose $100, most people will turn down the bet. Hence, people are risk averse and furthermore they are myopically so for the reason they concentrate excessively on the short term which of course does favor bonds in comparison to stocks: over the short term stocks are substantially more risky than bonds; the reason lies in the volatility of stocks which, as it is a lot higher than for bonds, leads many investors to the conclusion that stocks are risky and should be avoided altogether whereas bonds would be less risky and would be suitable for "widows and orphans."

It is a fact that over the 20th century (including the two first decades of the 21st century) the equity risk premium has been very high. The reason for this high level was that in many countries things worked out in a positive way: the end of the Cold War (which did never degenerate into a nuclear disaster), the impact of globalization, the rapid development of China and a number of emerging economies led to an enormous development of international trade. These positive developments explained higher returns than those which could reasonably be expected in the 1970s and 1980s and may explain a high equity risk premium.

Factor Investing

Factor investing is a method used to enhance returns, decrease risk and improve diversification by selecting stocks on criteria associated with higher returns, like for instance value (as measured by a low ratio price to book value, or price to sales), size (small-capitalization stocks have higher returns than large-capitalization stocks[19], quality (low debt to equity, stable earnings, a strong moat), or beta (low-beta stocks, associated with less volatility). These different factors, like size or beta are easily available on the most popular finance websites.

R-squared (R2)

The so-called R2, also called the coefficient of determination, measures in how far the variance for a dependent variable is explained by the variance of independent variable(s). The formula for R-Squared Is R2= 1- Unexplained variation/ Total variation. When applied to stock investing it represents the percentage of a stock's movement which may be attributed to the movement of the benchmark index. For instance, R-squared tells us what is the part of any movement of the stock price of Apple which is explained by fluctuations of the S&P 500, the benchmark index. R-squared may not exceed 1, unlike beta. Whereas R-squared measures the degree of correlation between stock movements and the benchmark, beta measures the amplitude of such movements.

Dividend Policy

First things first: what is a dividend? In fact there are two types of dividends: cash dividends and stock dividends. Cash dividends are by far the most frequent in current practice as stock dividends have practically disappeared. Stock dividends consist in the increase of the number of shares issued by a company incorporating thesaurised (undistributed) profits into the corporation's share capital. In essence, if a 4% stock dividend is declared, the number of shares issued by the company will increase by 4% meaning that a shareholder having owned 1,000 shares before the increase will now hold 1,040 shares. The effect of this stock dividend is similar to the one of a cash dividend followed by a reinvestment of these dividends in the stocks of the company issuing the shares. There is however a difference in outcome of these two alternatives: In case of a cash payment with reinvesting of dividends there is a tax leakage of, say, 15% which means that by reinvesting the 4% cash dividend the investor will not own 1,040 stocks of the company, but only 1,034 stocks, the difference between those two figures having been paid in taxes.

A cash dividend is a payment decided by the board of directors of a company (in other countries, for instance in continental Europe, the shareholders' meeting generally decides on distribution of dividends) by which the company decides to allocate the profit partially or totally to its shareholders. Such payments are not mandatory which means that a company despite realizing a high ROE

(Return on Equity) for many years is not obliged to pay out any dividend at all. Conversely, a company which in a given year suffers losses may still pay out dividends (up to the amount of profits accumulated over the past).

Any profitable company has to decide whether it is paying out dividends or not. The first condition to do so is precisely that the company is profitable. For corporate law purposes, only positive results may be distributed. It is a fact that such distributions are generally viewed favorably by shareholders (even if this view is not necessarily always justified rationally and it might even be a poor capital allocation decision). If such a decision normally has a positive effect, it has to be noted that once a dividend is paid out, it will be viewed extremely badly if some time later the dividend is reduced or even entirely cancelled. Companies tend to have a profit payout ratio which is fairly low, say not more than 50% (although this ratio is much higher in mature industries especially if they have low needs for capital expenditure, like the tobacco industry). In other words, a small drop in annual profits will not jeopardize the dividend payment to which investors have become accustomed.

The extent to which companies pay dividends is highly variable according to the business sector of which they are a part. Typically, high technology companies do not pay dividends except if they are relatively mature companies which are not assume to experience exponential growth rates anymore (e.g. Microsoft, IBM, Apple or Intel). Utility companies, whose capital investment requirements are limited, do pay high dividend rates. The same is true for cyclical companies and for most consumer staples.

The dividend policy adopted by a company has a direct influence on the shareholders it attracts. Companies who have paid dividends over decades (without ever dropping it for any given year), are quite attractive for investors who need this income for a living (e.g. retired persons). From this perspective, companies which have consistently increased their dividend for a long period of time are especially interesting, which explains why a number of companies do exactly that, namely increase the dividend year in, year out even if only lightly and far less than they could actually afford to do.

Some companies are renowned for not paying any dividends for decades. This is for instance the case in the high-technology area where it is assumed that a company with a strong growth record has numerous investment opportunities so that when they start paying a dividend this is viewed as a confirmation that management does not see any growth opportunities anymore and it will probably see its stock price tank as soon as the dividend announcement is made.

In fact, it has to be observed that the decision to pay a dividend is an important one which is not only a consequence of the business fundamentals of the company but it has a bearing on other strategic decisions, namely what are the intentions of the company with respect to future investments, to mergers and acquisitions, expansion of its markets, etc.? In other words, the dividend policy of any company has to be decided on the basis of a number of strategically important elements: it needs to be thoroughly thought over for the reason that dividend announcements send important signals to financial markets. A company which has paid a certain quarterly dividend for a number of years and which increases this dividend by a substantial amount will generally see its stock price increase significantly. Such significant increase of the share price is explainable by the fact that investors consider that this dividend increase means that the company is bullish on the future perspectives of the company not just for the current quarter or year but well beyond as it would probably not increase its dividends in the absence of a lasting profit increase of the company. Sometimes there is a considerable overreaction to such announcements which is easy to identify. If the announcement of a dividend increase from $2 to $2.25 is followed by a share price increase of $3 this means that the buyer at the higher price will pay in advance all the additional dividends which he will receive at the new rate over the next 12 years, which is clearly excessive.

Dividends are sticky: once a company pays a dividend and assuming it has done so for a number of years, the financial markets do expect these payments to go on and in practice the company will not be able to easily cancel these dividends in the future (except if the financial position of the company gets really bad as was the case for General Electric in 2018 and 2019 when its dividend per share was reduced in two steps from 24 to 1 cent). The same thing happened to Boeing which came under serious pressure with the crashes of two Boeing 737 MAX aircraft which led the company into serious financial problems followed by the Covid-19 pandemic triggering the cancellation of dividends as of March 20, 2020.

Shareholders, many of which have precisely chosen these shares for their dividend-paying feature, do generally react quite negatively and dump their shares. Any omission of the dividend payment will be viewed as a sign the company is in deep trouble and that doubtlessly it tries to hide very negative details of its situation. For these reasons, dividend policy requires a thoughtful and to-the-future-oriented approach allowing the company to adopt a policy of consistent dividend payments, with moderate annual growth rates which will make sure that the dividend policy is sustainable. Such policy, over time, will attract precisely those dividend investors who look for this type of companies and who count on these dividend cheques for their living expenses (and which might not expect a phenomenal share price growth over the medium).

A large proportion of investors, predominantly elderly persons, live at least partly from their dividend cheques and the payment of periodical dividends has been the principal reason these investors have bought those stocks in the first place. Companies will increase dividends only if they can be reasonably sure that the new level of quarterly payments can be upheld in future, in other words that the increased dividend is sustainable. The exact amount of this ratio which should not be exceeded varies from company to company. A company like Altria (MO) does have a payout ratio of around 80% and still increases the dividend every year. This rate is testimony for at least two fundamental characteristics of this company and to a certain extent of the industry of which it is a part: net income of the company is stable and capital expenditure requirements are very low. Dividend paying companies of other industries blessed with less favorable economics (for instance cyclical companies) will normally take care that the payout ratio does not exceed 50 to 60%.

What has been said in the preceding paragraphs with respect to dividends relates to common stocks of companies and not to so-called preferred stocks. Such preferred stocks deserve their epitaph of being preferred for the double reason that in case of liquidation of the company their holders get paid by preference to common shareholders (meaning before these common stockholders) and for the reason that no dividends may be paid on common stocks if the preferred dividend has not been paid. Preferred dividends have to be paid on the dates foreseen, whereas common dividends are voluntary payments of the company. On the other hand, preferred dividends, just like bond coupons, will not increase over the years. They are fixed payments whereas common stock dividends typically do increase and investors expect them to do so over time.

Which shareholder precisely is entitled to a dividend payment? The so-called "ex-dividend date" helps to answer that question.

Ex-Dividend Date

All those shareholders who own shares on "record day" are entitled to the dividend decided by the board of the company for a specific period (in US this means generally the latest quarter). Since 2017 the process of stock trading is made on the basis of the T+2 (or "trade date + 2 days") rule which means that it takes 2 days from the day a transaction is made until it is entered in the company's records. Before 2017 the settlement process took 3 days (hence the T+3 rule applied). If someone buys 1,000 shares on Monday, this transaction will be recorded on the books of the company on Wednesday of the same week (or two business days later). The ex-dividend day is the first business day preceding the date of record.

If a company declares a dividend (for instance on August 28, 2020 this date is the declaration date), which will be payable on, say, September 30 and which will accrue to all shareholder of record on the company's books on or before Monday September 16 ("record date") with the ex-dividend date being the first business date before that record date, i.e. Friday September 13. In order to being able to cash in the dividend a shareholder needs to buy the shares before the ex-dividend date, at the latest on Thursday September 12. Buying on that day will under the T+2 rule allow the buyer to be on record on Monday September 16. On the ex-dividend day (Friday) the shares trade at an amount lower by roughly the amount of the dividend.

Do Dividends Matter?

The age-old question debated among finance scholars is whether the payment of dividends is or is not beneficial to shareholders. Under the so-called "irrelevance theorem" as developed in a paper published in 1961 by Modigliani-Miller (according to which it is irrelevant whether a corporation pays out its profits as dividends, repurchases shares or redeems its outstanding debt) these questions don't matter at all. This irrelevance would however only be given if there were no taxes discriminating against one or the other of these options. At the time the Modigliani-Miller paper was drafted, the tax treatment of dividends and capital gains was far from neutral. Whereas dividends were taxed at 50% or more, capital gains were tax favored and were taxed at 25% (in addition, this lower tax is only levied at a later stage, that is on realization of the taxable gain). In the meantime these rules have changed but neutrality does still not exist, neither in the US nor in the overwhelming majority of the other countries.

Taxwise, dividends are not treated well by the lawmakers of most countries and this in two ways: firstly dividends are taxed at higher rates than capital gains (at least for long-term capital gains, meaning those which are realized only after a certain minimum holding period) and taxation of dividends cannot be deferred (unlike the one of capital gains: it suffices not to sell the shares and taxation of latent capital gains can be postponed, possibly even "forever").

The predilection of many investors (especially of retirees) for dividend stocks has deep psychological roots. Dividends are to stocks what apples are to the apple-tree: a recurrent fruit which will be produced at least annually and which may be consumed without regret and without doing any harm to the source of the fruit. You might as well refer to John Burr Williams classic book The Theory of Investment Value who wrote in 1938:

"*A cow for her milk,*

A hen for her eggs,

And a stock by heck,

For her dividends."

In substance this means that many investors endeavor in mental accounting: consumption expenses should be financed by current income (of which dividends are a part) and not out of capital: the rule being, don't dip into capital. This conception, although wide-spread, is often misguided: if a company earns 6% on its equity of which it pays out two thirds (which corresponds to the traditional

103

recommendations as traditionally favored by academicians) as a dividend then the fruit of this source of income is not limited to the 4% dividend actually paid out but it also includes the other part of income which was thesaurised. Hence, the shareholder may sell roughly 2% of their shares annually without jeopardizing their future dividends (assuming of course that the earnings situation of the company does not deteriorate).

Dividend-Paying Stocks or Not?

As it is often the case, there seems to be a quite significant gap between the analysis made by Academia of dividend payments and the way investors view them. If Academia considers this question as irrelevant (see here above) investors do seem to highly appreciate periodic payments from their company.

The question addressed here is whether investors should privilege dividend paying stocks or avoid them. Dividends, or more precisely cash dividends, represent a distribution of profits realized by the company. In theory, a company should pay dividends only if it is unable to invest its profits at rates higher than those the investor could achieve. In other words, the dividend decision is a capital allocation question. This is for instance the view defended by Warren Buffett whose Berkshire Hathaway has never paid a dividend (if we disregard one exception which occurred in 1967 when a minuscule dividend was actually paid). This point of view makes sense for the reason that in actual life, Buffett has consistently been able to invest Berkshire's profits at rates higher than the average investor would have been able to do it, although this has no longer been the case recently, as is demonstrated by the ever-increasing cash pile which has accumulated since at least 2016 when the last major acquisition has been done by Berkshire Hathaway.

The problem with dividends is actually that shareholders do not always look at the whole picture. This means that they give the impression a dividend would be something new, out of the blue. A dividend payment is viewed as something positive whereas a dividend reduction or even a cancellation of a dividend is hugely negative. Reality is somewhat different: arguably a dividend payment does not give the shareholder anything they would not already own (at least potentially). In fact, a shareholder is entitled to a proportionate share on all future claims on the company's profits which means ultimately they may expect to receive the full earnings attributable to their shares. By paying out part of this profit, the company does nothing else than paying out part of their profit share, whereas the remainder will be kept by the company and be paid to them later on, either as a dividend or as a liquidation proceed on winding up of the company. If the company pays out profits entirely, then the book value of the company will not grow. If, on the other hand, the company does retain all its profits, then the company's book value will increase (and the share price should eventually follow) unless the company buys back shares which is in fact an alternative way of paying out profits to the shareholders.

Might there be any benefit in selecting companies with a record of paying substantial annual dividends? Many studies seem to indicate this is actually the case.

Graham, The Intelligent Investor, already concluded that a dollar paid out had as much as a four times higher effect on the share price as a dollar booked to undistributed earnings.

Tax aspects do also have to be considered. Any distributions of dividends attract a substantial tax levy withheld at source by the paying company (of currently 15%) and in this way represents a tax leakage which, at least for the time being, is avoided by a non-dividend-paying company.

Even if logically there should not have been any dividend distributions at that time when the tax code heavily discriminated against such dividend payments, reality was very different and corporations regularly paid dividends. How can such behavior be explained?

Although nowadays the tax treatment of dividends and of (long-term) capital gains is basically the same for individuals, it is interesting to note that the debate between dividend payments and capital gains is still alive. As is well known, Berkshire Hathaway Inc. does not pay any dividends (although it is certainly not a quickly-growing tech stock like Alphabet or Amazon). To a minority of its shareholders requiring the payment of a substantial dividend, Buffett suggests to sell part of their shares and in this way triggering capital gains taxation. The said proposal does not satisfy many of the shareholders who go on to require dividend payments.

Over recent decades a growing number of companies (especially of so-called growth companies) have abandoned the formerly standard policy of paying out at least 60% of earnings as dividends based on the reasoning that reinvesting earnings would better serve stockholders' interests.

Many growth companies nowadays either pay no dividend or a rather small dividend only and reinvest the remainder of profits and at the same time explain that by doing so they act to the best interests of their shareholders. In this way the continuance of the current dividend is assured and a gradual and slow future increase is rendered possible. Those growth companies that do not pay any dividend consider that their first priority consists in financing their growth opportunities which at the end do provide a better return than those which the shareholder could obtain if the profits were paid out.

Many studies have shown that practice is not in line with these theories and that if two companies having the same earning power are in the same position, then the one paying the highest dividend will sell at a higher price.

It is true, however, that there is a strange paradox here: value is increased by withdrawing value. The more equity the shareholder withdraws from the company the more they value the remainder.

Upsides for dividend investors

Dividend paying companies offer a number of advantages for investors which I will try to outline on the following pages.

Show me the money

Finance scholars underline the fact that accounting rules offer many possibilities to show a profit whereas in reality the company does not earn any money. "Dividends don't lie" is the thesis meant to express that financial engineering has its limits and may not be sufficient to generate dividends. In this context, it is often insisted on the fact that Enron also apparently very profitable did never pay a dividend.

Dividends do support the stock price

A sizable dividend supports the stock price in an important way. A regular dividend payment makes sure that investors will not ditch their share on the occasion of the first market crash. As long as they are able to view the dividend as safe (which may include the assumption of a slight increase similar to the one of the preceding years) investors find comfort in the idea that their investment generates incomee and that sooner or later the stock price will recover.

In case of a market decrease the dividend puts a floor under the stock price. If a stock priced $40 which pays $2 as a dividend drops to $20 the dividend yield is 10%. If the stock now slides to $10 the yield is 20% and the stock will not stay there for a long time as it will attract yield-hungry investors. In any time of crisis, high cap stocks with long records of paying dividends will be most looked after by investors.

Dividend payments impose financial discipline on management

The fact that financial markets expect a dividend payment corresponding to a certain percentage of the stock price keeps management of the company focused on the task to generate the cash required for such quarterly dividend cheques to be paid to all the shareholders. In this way, the company is precluded from making unsound investments which may be more suited to enhance the ego of the CEO for instance by acquiring overpriced companies, than to create shareholder value.

It may be interesting to note that Chinese State Owned Enterprises (SOEs) are also regularly criticized by Chinese authorities for not paying out sufficient dividends and using the retained earnings for unnecessary investments. The background of this criticism is that, according to Morgan Stanley Chinese corporations pay out 29% of their profits in dividends, compared with an average of 42% for emerging countries and 67% for developed countries.[20]

Dividend Investing

There is one school of investors, called Dividend Investors, which recommends to invest exclusively in dividend paying stocks. The scholars adhering to the said doctrine rightfully point out that dividends count for a very substantial part of the total shareholder yield which the investor may book at the end of the year. Indeed, the only payments shareholders receive from the company on an ongoing basis are dividend payments. It is true that stock repurchases are also payments made to shareholder but these payments are in fact (and in most of the cases) made to former shareholders of the company. However, remaining shareholders do also profit from such buybacks of own stocks by the company as their share of the company's profits increases over time due to the decrease of the number of shares outstanding. This effect may be surprisingly important, especially if companies generating high free cash flows are repurchasing large amounts of shares over many years.

Compounding dividends is essentially a long-term strategy which should only be considered by investors who follow a long-term approach.

As mentioned above, dividends are sticky which means that a dividend can hardly be reduced (at least not without major negative effects on the company's stock price). This means that a cautious company will typically refrain from paying out all or nearly all of its annual profits. If it did decide to do so any slight reduction of annual profits would mean that the expected dividend could no longer be paid. Hence, companies will decide to pay only a relatively low percentage of their annual profits as dividend. The percentage of dividend payments to annual profits is called the "dividend-payout ratio." This ratio should first not be too high and even more importantly it should not be rapidly increasing. The exact level of this ratio will to a large extent depend upon the business fundamentals of the entity: a consumer staples company will be able to have a higher payout ratio as its profit fluctuates less than in a consumer discretionary company. For instance, tobacco companies, as high cash flow generators with little capital expenditure, have payout ratios of 80 to 90%. A stable payout ratio would mean that dividends would increase in line with profits of the company. A low stable payout ratio would seem to indicate that there is room for future dividend increases whereas a high payout ratio signals that the company may presently already pay a dividend beyond its means. Payout ratios vary significantly from one business sector to the next which means that comparisons may be useful within the same business sector but a lot less from one sector to the other one.

Dividend investing does not consist in selecting the stock of the company which currently pays the highest possible dividend, expressed as a percentage of the current stock price. Dividend investors, who typically have a long-term approach, unlike the typical investor of nowadays, look for companies which are reliable dividend payers as evidenced by a decade(s) long history of dividends not interrupted by any blank years and even more, requiring never-decreasing dividend payments. A further improvement, which for some investors is a must, consists in an annual dividend increase at a rate at least beating the inflation rate. The gold standard of these dividend paying company are the so-called Dividend Aristocrats.

Dividend Aristocrats

Dividend Aristocrats is a concept which refers to corporations, which are part of the S&P 500 Index and which have increased their dividends during each of the last 25 years (at least). It is of course true that the fact that a company has continuously paid increasing dividends since 1995 does not mean that it will pay dividends during the next 25 years, that is until 2045 and beyond. The warning "past performance does not guarantee future results", as useful as it may be, tends to overlook one thing: a company which has been able to pay a dividend each year, and to increase a serious dividend payment during a quarter of a century is obviously in a stable business guaranteeing increasing per-share results over a long period of time. This is exactly the type of business any long-term investor should look for.

The fact that these dividend aristocrats represent stable businesses is not just a working assumption but is clearly confirmed by the companies who have made it to the actual list of Dividend Aristocrats. The number of companies qualifying for dividend- aristocrat status is fluctuating every year but it is remarkably stable at around fifty companies (51 in 2016)[21]. Many of these companies are in the consumer staples area like Coca Cola, Colgate Palmolive, McDonald's, Procter & Gamble, Kimberly Clark, Clorox, in the health service area like Johnson & Johnson, Walgreen Boots Alliance, AbbVie, the distribution area with Walmart and Target, natural resources like Chevron, utilities with Consolidated Edison, etc.

Many of these companies not only are in existence for more than 100 years but even do produce the same products as those they have produced for decades already, which again is testimony to the stability of their businesses. Compare that to what happens in the high tech world: no company is allowed to produce even for 5 years an identical product.

According to a number of studies made dividends are or at least have been over the 20th century the most important part of investor returns. Such is the case in the first place for the most comprehensive study made so far by Elroy Dimson, Paul Marsh, and Mike Staunton, authors of "Triumph of the Optimists: 101 Years of Global Investment Returns, published in 2002" which covers not only the US markets but includes 15 other mostly European countries for which sufficient data was available.

The conclusions are the same for Jeremy Siegel in both his books, Stocks for the Long Run The Definitive Guide to Financial Market Returns and Long-Term Investment Strategies, first published in 1994 and "The Future for Investors: Why the Tried and the True Triumphs Over the Bold and the New", published in 2005, dividends matter a lot.

All these studies assume that dividends paid are fully reinvested in the stocks of the company paying those dividends. Although, in practice very few investor do probably behave that way this is the only reasonable way to take dividends into account. It would be inconceivable to simply ignore dividends paid by companies: such way to proceed would render meaningless any comparisons between dividend payers and non-dividend payers (or even between low dividend payers (say, Apple) and high dividend payers (say, Altria).

Reinvesting dividends is *the* critical factor giving the edge to most winning stocks in the long run. In contrast to skeptics who claim that high-dividend paying firms lack "growth opportunities" the exact opposite is true. Portfolios invested in the highest-yielding stocks returned 3 percent per year more than the S&P 500 Index, while those in the lowest yielding stocks lacked the market by almost 2 percent per year."

Gordon Growth Model (GGM) Equation

The GGM is a simplified model for calculating the intrinsic value of a stock which only refers to the current dividend paid by the company and the dividend growth rate, neglecting all other factors like the competitive position of the company, the total profit of the company, the distribution ratio, etc. In fact, the GGM approach treats stocks as if they were bonds: bonds may be correctly valuated by reference to the cash flows paid by the issuing company, i.e. their interest coupons. Whereas the periodical coupons are the only remuneration bondholders may expect for their investment, such is not the case for stockholders which are entitled to a proportionate share of the annual result of the company which may be paid out only partly (and sometimes not at all, in case of non-dividend-paying companies). In this case stockholder have a reasonable expectation to be able to sell their stocks at a higher price on the moment of their sale of shares.

This means that this method is not of a general use and obviously it may only be applied to large companies with a reliable (and increasing) dividend flow.

The formula is:

V = d / (k-g)

where:

V = Stock value

d = Expected dividend per share one year from now

k = Rate of return expected by the equity investor

g = Growth rate in dividends (in perpetuity).

Assume a stock valued at $20 per share which pays a $2 dividend per share and predicts its dividend will steadily grow by 4% per year. The investor's rate of return is 10%.

Solving the equation, we find: V = $2 / (.10 - .04) = $33.33.

DRIP

By participating in a DRIP (Dividend Reinvestment Program), the investor accepts to not receive a cash dividend. The after-tax amount of the cash dividend is directly reinvested in the underlying equity and will participate immediately in compounding. Some DRIPs do not charge any commissions for reinvesting dividends, others do. Some authors consider value investors should not participate in a DRIP if shares are overvalued. This is absolutely correct in theory, as by definition, the share price does not allow for a margin of safety in the said case. However, the advantage of DRIPs is to put the investor on autopilot: shares are automatically purchased each and every quarter without any need for the investor to take any decision. Once the investor has to take quarterly decisions, the risk is that for each purchase of overvalued stocks he avoids, he will miss two purchases when stocks are really beaten down and are seriously undervalued. It is at these moments that the stocks get really bad press from the media and that the herd avoids them like the plague that the risk to shun the stock altogether is highest and with it the considerable gains investors miss if reinvestments would have been made at such depressed prices (which means that more shares may be purchased for the same amount of dividends reinvested).

In any case, participants in these DRIPs benefit from this dollar-cost-averaging effect in the form of lower average purchase prices (as less shares are purchased when prices are high and more shares when prices are low).

Companies with excess liquidities may do two things to have their shareholders participate in their prosperity: either pay dividends or buy back shares. In sharp contrast to the situation prevailing 20 or 30 years ago, the payments made by way of stock buybacks do considerably exceed the payment of dividends. The principal reason for this development is manager compensation as we shall see here below.

Stock Buybacks

As indicated here above, dividend policy is relatively sticky in the sense that it requires consistency, otherwise it will cause a lot of irritation with investors and a suppression or even only a reduction of dividends will harm the share price (and this especially if the company has a long record of paying dividends, and even more so if dividends have been constantly increasing).

Stock buybacks are an alternative possibility which can be used more flexibly and in fact it *should* be used more flexibly. Companies should proceed to buybacks of shares only if share prices are relatively depressed so that the share buybacks are made at prices lower than intrinsic value. However, studies made on buybacks of shares show that corporate treasurers, when buying back stocks, seem to make the same errors as individual investors investing in stocks: they buy many shares when prices are high and a lot less when prices are low! This conclusion is confirmed by many studies made for instance also by Thomas G Macpherson, author of "Seeking Wisdom: Thoughts on Value Investing"

Stock buybacks are a capital allocation decision of tremendous importance: it will either result in increasing shareholder value or destroying it. If the shares are overpriced, the buyback results in destroying shareholder value. It is easy to see that the effects of such buybacks are similar to those of financial leverage. If the return on investment is higher than the interest on debt incurred, the result is to increase the return on equity, and the opposite will happen if the cost of the debt is higher than the yield on investment.

Let's assume the following very simplified balance sheet. Assets of $1,000 (all in cash and cash equivalents) totally financed by equity of $1,000. The 1,000 shares outstanding have a market value of 80 cents (whereas, obviously, intrinsic value of these shares is $1). If 50% of these shares can be bought back at 80% of their intrinsic value we will finally have 500 shares outstanding with an intrinsic value of $600. If immediately after the buyback of these shares the company will be liquidated, any remaining shareholder will receive $1.2 for each share they hold whereas in the absence of the buyback they would only have received $1 per share.

Now let's change the assumptions and let's assume that the company will buy back half its shares above intrinsic value, namely at $1.2 per share. After paying out $600 for 500 shares the remaining cash ($400) will on liquidation be paid out to the remaining shareholder leaving each one with 80 cents per share. The bottom line is that the remaining shareholders will be left with $0.8 of value per share whereas before they had $1, the difference going of course to the pockets of the leaving shareholders.

What is the impact of share buybacks? If we answer this question from the company's point of view the shares bought back will result in a decrease of the company's equity. The shares bought back will be cancelled, the number of shares outstanding will decrease, which (from the shareholders' point of view will entail an increase in the profit (or the loss) attributable to one share).

Let's assume a company has 1,000 shares outstanding which represent the company's equity of $1,000,000. By buying back 5% of the shares, equity of the company will decrease to $950,000. The number of shares is now reduced to 950. If the profit of the company before and after the buyback was $100,000, then the portion attributable to one share will be increased from $100 to $105.263 (100,000/950).

This effect may be remarkably powerful for the remaining shareholders (i.e. those who have not been bought out) as they see their earnings per share increase every year and this without any tax impact or transaction costs. An alternative way to obtain that same result would be that the company pays out a dividend, and this dividend will then be used by the shareholders to increase their shareholding by reinvesting the dividend proceeds in additional shares of the company. This alternative has one significant disadvantage compared to the buyback scenario: the dividend will give rise to a tax levy in the hands of the shareholder, a tax which is avoided in the buyback scenario.

At this point it may be noted that the United Kingdom has several years ago abolished any withholding tax on dividends paid by UK companies. For any investor who does not have to pay taxes in their home country on dividends perceived it may be useful to consider some UK high-dividend payers like Shell, BP or BTI.

Buying back shares is the same thing as the remaining shareholders buying a proportion of the company (via the company's management) and the remaining shareholder has every reason to avoid paying too high a price "borrowing from the future" and discounting future profits of the company. The problem is that management may have different objectives in mind, meaning that it may want to keep up the share price allowing it to sell their own shares at an interesting price even if this may be to the detriment of the long-term shareholders. This is one aspect of the so-called "principal agent dilemma" which means that whereas in theory the agent should act as a fiduciary agent for the principal having in mind nothing but the interests of this

116

principal, in practice the situation is different as the agent may have their own agenda and just be interested in increasing the price of the shares in the short term even if this goes against the long-term interests of the shareholders.

Increasingly buybacks occur to support the stock price, even if the prices paid exceed intrinsic value of the stocks. Whereas such actions may benefit those shareholders who will sell in the near future they do harm the long-term shareholders: their interests are sacrificed.

Thirty years ago the announcement of a share buyback had an immediate positive effect on the share price as it seemed to demonstrate that management believed the shares to be undervalued. This does no longer seem to be the case anymore: Wall Street has learned that share buybacks do not have great significance anymore as the purchases are made indiscriminately i.e. regardless of the stock price compared to intrinsic value.

If shares should not be bought back at a price higher than intrinsic value (otherwise there is shareholder value destruction) and ideally should be bought back at a price significantly lower than intrinsic value one can only say that this rules is frequently disregarded. For instance, for GE (General Electric) the number of shares outstanding has hardly changed over the years 2003 to 2014. In 2003 the number of shares outstanding amounted to 10.063 bn compared to 10.057 bn in 2014. In 2009 the share price had decreased to a low level of $5.7 before slowly recovering over 2010 (range from $13.8-$19.7), in 2011 (range from $14-$21.7) in 2012 (range from $18-$23.2) and 2013 (range from $20.7-$21.8) 2014 (range from $23.7-$27.9). Then in 2015 and 2016 massive share buybacks have occurred reducing the number of shares to 6.78 bn and 6.17 bn. The problem was that these purchases were made at a time where stock prices were a lot higher than in previous years; 2016 (range from $27.1 – $33) and 2017 (range from $17.3 – $31.8) and 2018 (range from $6.7-$18.4). If we compare these repurchase prices to those of the following years we will have to conclude that the difference is also considerable. In other words, share buybacks were made precisely at the wrong moments, when the shares were most overpriced: it was shareholder value destruction on a massive scale contributing significantly to the weakening of GE's balance sheet where shareholders equity decreased by roughly $30 bn in 2015 and $23 bn in 2016.

At first sight one would assume that companies would carefully select the moment when they buy back their shares and in any case not proceed to buybacks when shares are at historically high levels. Unfortunately this is clearly not the case. In a nutshell, companies seem to have the same problems to time their purchases as regular investors as they are highly active when shares are expensive and inactive at market bottoms. There is however a difference between share buybacks made at high prices and a regular share purchase made at such high level: the regular investor who has bought at a high price may get bailed out by a raging bull market. For the company buying back its stock the damage is final: the shares repurchased result in an excessive decrease of the company's equity.

The Principal Agent Dilemma

In today's business world it is common for a person (group of persons) or organization, to not act directly but via another person who represents the first one. Such relationship is then called a principal-agent relationship: the agent acts on behalf and for account of the principal and they should act only to the best interest of those principals. The problem is that the principal is often a very large group of people that is not very well organized and may even not have clearly expressed (or it may not even know) what it actually wants. Take the citizens in a democratic state: as the principal they elect their representatives but those representatives may not really know what their principal actually want when a new issue comes up. The agents, on the other hand, are generally a very limited group of persons (maybe just one) and instead of pursuing the best interest of the principal they may tend to follow their own interests: the agents have their own agenda. Such situations of conflicting interests are by no means limited to the business world. Politicians do not necessarily follow the best interests of their constituents but do use their political mandate to increase their power, to place family members or pals in lucrative jobs, to enrich themselves, etc. People employed by altruistic organizations, like charitable foundations or charitable trusts, may be more interested in following their own career objectives than to realize the specific altruistic goal for which the charitable organization has been set up.

Another issue is that it is not that certain what actually is the purpose of a commercial company in the 21st century. In the US, the dominant position has been that the objective is a purely financial one and meant to maximize the shareholders' fortune: maximize shareholder value was the mantra as propagated by Milton Friedman, the Nobel Prize winning Chicago University economist, in his book "Capitalism and Freedom" published in 1962. The author argued that a company does not have any social responsibility whatsoever to the public or to society but only to its shareholders: "There is one and only one social responsibility of business – to use its resources and engage in activities to increase its profits." Friedman argued it was fine for shareholders to pursue social objectives on their own and with their own money. However, to do so through their company bears substantial risks and complicates the task of measuring the performance of companies.

This shareholder-centric view of the commercial company, while it has certainly been very dominant in the US has not been entirely shared in continental Europe and Japan where the approach has been more stakeholder oriented, term which refers not only to shareholders but includes employees, clients, suppliers, the communities where the company is located, the State, the public at large.

A relatively recent trend in investing consists in the fact that environmental, social and governance (ESG in short) criteria are increasingly used by companies and investors as standards for appreciating a company's performance. This tendency is especially strong with the young generation: as the Financial Times reported on March 9, 2020 figures published by Cerulli Associates, a research firm, show that more than two-thirds of investors under 30 prefer their investments to have a positive social and environmental impact.

Many investment funds, ETFs for instance, have been set up which select their investment based on ESG criteria. It is rightly insisted on the fact that a purely financial approach for appreciating a company's performance and an ESG inspired approach might not be fully incompatible in as far as ESG criteria may be considered as being part of risk management by investors.

Even if as citizens we may all applaud if companies behave well, as shareholders of such companies we should not lose out of sight that investing in employees, supporting suppliers, supporting communities, etc. in reality means that shareholders come last in the list of the company's stakeholders: for stock investors this is a mixed blessing.

In the business world, management of corporations is often more interested in increasing their own remuneration and to set in place extremely lucrative stock option plans than to maximize shareholder value or more generally to look after the interests of the other stakeholders in the company. This danger has already been underlined by Adam Smith who in 1776 wrote in the Wealth of Nations: "The directors of such [joint stock] companies, . . . being the managers of other people's money than of their own, it cannot well be expected, that they should watch over it with the same anxious vigilance with which the partners in a private copartnery frequently watch over their own.

Negligence and profusion, therefore, must always prevail, more or less, in the management of the affairs of such a company."

Such criticism has some merits for the reason that it is an undisputable fact that the remuneration of management has increased disproportionately over recent decades and more importantly it has evolved in a direction where it has become really disconnected from management performance. During the financial crisis of 2008-2009 (also called the Great Recession) public opinion got a shocking insight into the unacceptable practices which have taken over in the financial sector: management with a lousy performance which forced a government bailout received bonuses in the tens of million dollars amounts.

Shareholders should closely watch management remunerations which have become an important part of corporate expenses. It is obvious that a company will only be able to attract competent management if it pays competitive remunerations. Furthermore, if management does an outstanding job, it should not be denied a corresponding remuneration. This means that the bonus policy should be designed to align the interests of management to the one of the shareholders and it should not be so that management will always win, sometimes more sometimes a little less. Some practices followed in this field are abusive and sometimes even illegal: like revaluing one's stock options.

A very convenient way to solve the principal agent dilemma is to invest in companies in which managers hold a significant share of the capital of the company. In this case, the interest of the investor (the principal) and those of management (the agent) are really aligned. In such cases it can be safely assumed that the members of management do not lose the shareholders interests out of sight (which is not granted if the managers do not have significant skin in the game). Unfortunately this is seldom the case for companies with a certain age, for instance those being part of the Dow Jones Index, say Boeing, Coca Cola, Procter and Gamble, etc. For those companies Value Line the standard statement concerning the repartition of the company's stocks goes something like this: " Officers/directors own less than 1% of the common stocks; BlackRock, 6.9%; Vanguard 5.8%... ." In other words, investment funds (who themselves are part of the principal/agent issue which is why investment funds investing in publicly traded companies is sometimes referred to as the "double principal agent issue") are the only meaningful shareholders of these companies. However, some technology stocks which are of more recent origin do still have significant involvement of the founders in the functioning of the companies they have founded relatively recently (either as managers/directors or as significant shareholders): Alphabet (S. Brin/L. Page), Amazon (J. Bezos), Facebook (M. Zuckerberg), Oracle (L. Ellison), Salesforce (M. Benioff), etc. In investing in those stocks, although not guaranteeing success the chances are that you invest in companies displaying a shareholder-friendly attitude: if it is not a guarantee of success it is at least a guarantee for attention and focus; nobody having the bulk of their fortune invested in the stocks of one company will show a lack of interest in that company. Several studies actually confirm that companies managed by persons who are significant shareholders (say a holding of 10% as a minimum) do perform a lot better than those where management does not own meaningful shareholdings.

According to a study made in 2012 by Joel Shulman and Erik Noyes the historical stock-price performance of companies managed by the world's billionaires (and substantially owned by them) outperformed the index by as much as 700 basis points (or 7 percent annually).

Stock Options

Stock options have become a favorite way to remunerate top management and increasingly employees of companies. The granting of stock options to management and employees allows them to buy the company's stocks at a fixed price during a long period of time, 10 years for instance. The price at which the stock options may be exercised, generally corresponds to the stock market price at the moment the options are granted. The employee will not become a shareholder at the moment the options are granted but only if and when they exercise them. Such options may not be exercised immediately but only after a certain "vesting period" of 3 or 5 years for instance.

In many countries, including the US, employee stock options benefit from preferential tax treatment when compared to other forms of compensation. Whereas cash remuneration and remuneration in kind, valuated at fair market value, are generally speaking included in the income from employment the year the compensation is received this is not the case for stock options for which the inclusion in income is deferred until the exercise of the options.

In 1993 the US Internal Revenue Code was completed by Section 162 (m) disallowing the deduction of managers compensation exceeding $1 million. Incentive-based remunerations were specifically excluded from this limitation. In addition, the IRS (Internal Revenue Service) decided that stock options are to be viewed as incentive-based compensation. The bottom line of these decisions was that management compensation since that time very predominantly consisted of stock options and/or other stock award schemes which qualified as "performance-based compensation."

As investors may read in the Proxy statements or Annual Reports of any of the publicly traded US companies, the justification of stock options is the following one: "Stock options are designed to align the interest of the Company's executives and employees with those of shareholders by encouraging executives to enhance the value of the Company and, hence, the price of the Class B Stock. This is true "pay for performance", executives are rewarded only if the market price of our stock rises and they get nothing if the price does not rise or goes down.[22]

This statement, which is deceiving, requires some comments. Although Annual Reports and Proxy Statements of public companies diligently claim that granting stock options would guarantee that stockholders' and management's interests would be aligned, this is actually not the case: interests would be aligned only if management would also suffer losses in case the value of the stocks falls under the exercice price. In such case stockholders do suffer losses whereas option holders are protected against the downside. Another point showing that the interests of shareholders and those of management are not aligned is that the value of the options appreciate the more if no dividends are paid. Whereas dividend payments go to the shareholders' pockets, the value of management's stock options will get hurt. Such consequence may be avoided by simply cancelling the dividends, repurchase shares and in this way by decreasing the number of shares outstanding their value increases to the benefit of the optionholder. This point largely explains why nowadays, in the US, the capital amounts used for stock repurchases do exceed the amounts used to pay dividends.

Formerly, the principal advantage of these stock options was their accounting treatment: whereas cash bonuses paid to management have to be recorded as an expense (expense which was the higher because it was not tax allowable beyond $1m) which will reduce corporate profit, the beauty of stock options was that they did not have to be booked as such, so that they did not hurt corporate earnings. The reason justifying this solution was that no cash changes hands when options are granted. Nevertheless, these options were treated as an expense for tax purposes. A proposal of the FASB issued in 1993 was finally shot down by Congress under the pressure of intense corporate lobbying. In 2004 the FASB issued the rule FAS 123 which granted corporations the choice between disclosure and recognition. If the corporation choosed not to recognize the expense corresponding to the stock options granted on the income statement then the cost of the options had to be expressed in a footnote to the accounts as Pro Forma Basic EPS and Pro Forma Basic Diluted EPS. (In this case any reader of the company's financial statements was able to proceed to the required adjustments by simple reducing the company's result by the amount of the cost of the option as indicated in the footnote to the accounts.) At the time stock options were the only kind of executive pay which was a tax deductible expense for a company without it being required to be included in its books as an expense.

The OECD (Organisation for Economic Co-operation and Development which also takes an important role in company taxation (for instance in the field of bilateral tax treaties concluded between countries, generally on a bilateral basis) have published a study on taxation of stock options. The said study recommends a neutral approach with respect to the payment mix management receives: stock options would be fully taxable just as any cash payments, whereas all such payments would be entirely allowable with the company.

In fact there is little evidence that stock options actually boost a CEO's performance. There are no studies that would show that CEOs having received stock options would show better performance than their peers having not received such incentives. If such studies proving such better performance existed we would know it as they would be referred to by many greedy CEOs and armies of compensation consultants.

Under the old rules the cost of this equity compensation did not have to be expensed in the financial statements of the company based on the argument that such option grants did not constitute a real expense of the company. This argument was however very debatable as such options undeniably are a cost to the company's shareholders, although those shareholders did not incur a cash expense they "paid" in the form of a dilution triggered by the issue of additional shares by the company.

Under the new rules as outlined by FAS 123R (applicable since first fiscal year beginning after June 15, 2005) costs of stock option grants, which may be exchanged against shares of the company's stocks have to be expensed on financial statements over the vesting period. For instance, assume that 500,000 options are issued on January 1, 2020 allowing the purchase of shares of the company and that these options do have a fair value (calculated on the basis of the Black-Scholes pricing model) of $15 whereas the option exercise price and the current share price are 40. The total costs of the options are 500,000*15 = $7,500,000 amount which will be booked as a cost (let's say a deemed expense) over the 5 year vesting period of the shares, leading to an annual cost of $1,500,000. The counterpart to this booking entry is an increase of the account called APIC (Additional Paid In Capital), an equity account of the company issuing the stock options. The bottomline is that, unlike what was the case under the previously applicable rules, the financial performance of the company granting the option is impacted negatively. However, even if Wall Street does regret this aspect, by claiming that the so-called alignment of interests between management and shareholders would no longer be guaranteed, investors in common stock of the company should rejoice: the transparency of corporate accounts and of GAAP statements is enhanced.

Before entry into force of the Tax Cuts and Jobs Act of 2017 (TCJA) the deduction limit did not apply to so-called "performance-based compensation" as defined by Section 162 (m) of the IRC. Further to the TCJA employees covered by this Section are the CEO, the CFO and the company's next three most highly compensated executive officers for the taxable year. The TCJA includes a grandfathering rule pursuant to which compensation payable on the basis of a written binding contract which was effective on November 2, 2017 remains tax deductible for US federal income tax purposes.

It is at least ironic to note that as soon as the formerly existing accounting rules which allowed companies to give options to employees without recording any costs at the time of granting, were corrected and stock options were treated as operating expenses the effect of these very welcome adjustments was nullified by adding back these expenses to earnings in order to obtain "adjusted earnings", as these adjusted earnings go on to treat these options as non-events.[23]

Buybacks and Management Compensation

In the first place it needs to be stressed that management compensation (by which is meant in the first place CEO compensation) has increased considerably over time: if in 1965 the ratio of CEO remuneration to employee average pay for S&P 500 companies was 1 to 20 the same ratio is 1 to 278 in 2019. This median figure allows for some outliers like the CEO of Del Monte who for 2018 in his Schedule 14a filings declared earnings of $8.5m or 1,465 times of the $5,833 of its 39,000 staff. Even that is not yet the top position which goes to Kevin Clark, the CEO of Aptiv, formerly Delphi, who for 2018 declared compensation of $13.8m or 2,500 times the median earnings of its staff. Are these outrageous remunerations justified by a corresponding brilliant performance? Hardly: in 2018 Del Monte's return on equity was roughly 6%.[24]

A very important reason pushing companies to buy back their own shares has to do with management compensation. A significant part of that compensation is represented by shares in the company (mostly in the form of stock options). As a consequence, management has a clear incentive to do everything possible to increase the share price in the short term, not so much to the benefit of shareholders, as they would claim, but to their own benefits.

Another effect of share buybacks is that cancelling shares will reduce the shareholders' equity on the balance sheet and, all things equal, will weaken the financial position of the company. The debt to equity ratio will deteriorate by reducing the amount of equity. If buybacks are financed by debt, the debt level will increase.

On the other hand, the decrease of shareholders' equity does have an effect on ROE ("return on equity"), which (all things equal) will increase: by reducing the denominator of the fraction, the mechanical effect is to increase the ROE. (It is true, of course, that this effect will occur only if "earnings" will not be reduced more than the companies' equity: if such were the case, the ROE could even deteriorate. Such scenario is however extremely unlikely in times of very low interest rates.

The reaction of Wall Street to these buybacks is generally positive: the Street likes the increase in profit per share levels and the fact that the increased demand for stocks will support the share prices. Sometimes, the reaction is not so positive and the media will blame some companies but not all of them (IBM is a case in point here) for endeavoring in "financial engineering" in the form of buying back shares instead of investing in products and marketing in order to enhance its competitive position.

That the impact of share buybacks on a company's earnings position on a per share basis may be huge is demonstrated by AutoNation which, from 2002 to 2019, have bought back 70 percent of the shares outstanding, helping hugely to increase the earnings per share of the company (it increased from $1.19 to $4.98 although revenue increased only slightly over the same period, from $19,479 to 21,336 or 9,53%).

The financial impact of buybacks on earnings may be especially large if the company pays a high dividend whereas interest rates are low. If a company pays a 4% dividend, reduces its share by 2%, repurchase financed by debt incurred at a 2 per cent interest rate, then the impact on earnings is highly positive: there is a swap of a 4% (non-tax deductible) dividend against a (tax deductible) interest payment of 2%.

Buybacks in No-Growth Situations

Let's suppose a company with equity of $1,000 and which earns 10% on its equity. The P/E ratio is 10. The company might pay out all these earnings granting its stockholders a 10% dividend yield. However the annual earnings of $100 are paid out only up to 1/10th as dividends, a 1% dividend yield paid out over the year. In addition, the company uses the remainder of their profits over the year, namely $90, buying back stocks, buybacks which will have as a consequence to increase future per share dividend payments. As a consequence, equity of the company will not increase. Assuming the earnings rate and dividend-payout ratio remain unchanged, there will be an increase of dividends the next year from $0.1 to $0.10989, due to the decrease in the number of shares outstanding.

Assuming the number of shares is 100, each share has a value of $1 times 10 (= P/E ratio) leading to a market capitalization of $1,000). The number of shares bought back is 9 shares which will reduce the number of shares outstanding: 100 ./. 9= 91. This decrease in the share count will lead to earnings growth per share: $10/91 = $0.10989 compared to $0.1 in Y0. This represents an increase in EPS of 9.89 %.

In Y2 the retained earnings will again be used to buy back shares. The annual income is 10% of 1,000 i.e. 100 of which 1/10 will be paid out as dividends: 10 (dividend payment of 0.1086825) and the remainder of 90 is used for share buybacks at the value of 10.989: $90/10.989=8.19, results in a buyback of 8.19 shares. The share count goes down to 82.81 and each share is entitled to a dividend payment 0.120758. For the following years:

Y3: 75.3571 shares; $ Div.: 0.132701p.sh.; Incr.: 9.89%

Y4: 68.217861 shares; $ Div.: 0.146589; Incr.: 9.89%

Y5: 62.078254 shares; Div.0.161087; Incr.: 9.89%

Y6: 56.491211 shares; Div. 0.177019; Incr.: 9.89%

Y7: 51.407002 shares; Div. 0.194526. Incr.: 9.89%

Y8: 46.780372 shares; Div. 0.213765. Incr.: 9.89%

Y9: 42.570147 shares; Div. 0.234906. Incr.: 9.89%

Y10: 38.738834 shares; Div. 0.258139. Incr.: 9.89%

The number of shares outstanding decreases by 9% annually, whereas the EPS increase by 9.89%.

The merit of the example is that it shows that a no-growth company (the company realizes exactly the same amount of earnings from Y0 to Y10) may be an excellent investment for shareholders. The company shows a significant annual dividend increase (over a 10 year period the dividend increases by more than 150%). In addition the market value of one share has also increased from 1 to 2.5

If a low-growth company does significant share buybacks Wall Street's reaction might be quite negative by accusing the company of "financial engineering" which means that the company, unable to create real growth, would play foul by trying to "get there" in an indecent way.

In the first place it is somewhat strange that Wall Street, which generally speaking is not renowned for its high moral standards, does issue such criticism. For instance where were the critics of mortgage-backed securities (MBS) which caused the Great Depression or those criticizing the cyber currency hype?

Secondly, some companies are active in markets were growth is simply not obtainable: take regulated utilities where growth is guided by market factors with hardly any possibilities for utilities to influence demand for their product. If such no-growth company distributes all its profits as dividends then this behavior is hardly ever criticized (even if this dividend policy is far from optimal for existing shareholders as they suffer taxes on these dividend payments). Why then should it be criticized if these companies do return their profits to shareholders under the form of buybacks? These buybacks are a more tax efficient way to return profits to stockholders.

I am not denying that criticism of stock buybacks may actually be justified for the reason that they very often poorly done: lots of buybacks at overheated prices whereas none are done at depressed prices. Just look at General Motors before the Great Recession, General Electric in 2015-2016 or the large US banks over the period preceding the Great Recession. Such buybacks jeopardized the survival of these companies but this is not a reason to criticize buybacks as such. The big advantage of buybacks when compared to dividend payments is that buybacks do not impose on all shareholders a specific policy on their cash payments triggering the realization of a taxable gain: only those who sell are taxed.

Stockholders have a claim on the profits of the company. This claim may be partially settled by periodic dividend payments which transfers the major part of annual profits to the stockholders' pockets. The company paternalistically decides when this cash transfer occurs and how important it is. By comparison, in case of share buybacks the individual shareholders decides whether they want to dispose of their shares or not. In other words they may further delay the cash payment and with it the taxation which goes with it.

P/E ratios

The most popular instrument to assess the level of stock prices (or of market indices) is the classical P/E ratio. The P/E ratio is simply the division of the share price by the amount of the annual earnings per share. If the share price is $17 and the earnings per share amount to $1, the P/E ratio is 17. Simplistically said, this ratio expresses the number of years the investor needs to wait before getting back the money they invested (in the absence of any dividends paid by the company).

If the earnings figure refers to the last 12 months of reported earnings, the ratio is called the trailing P/E; the leading P/E (or future P/E) refers to an estimation of next years earnings. Value Line for instance when calculating the P/E ratio on top of the company page of the Investment Survey uses a mixture of reported earnings (the last six months of reported earnings and the next six months of estimated earnings). In any case the P/E ratio is recalculated each three month.

The price of a stock (P) is equivalent to earnings times the P/E ratio (P/E) or put differently:

$$P = E \times \frac{P}{E}$$

By deleting E in the numerator and in the denominator, what is left is that P = P, which is fairly meaningless and shows that the P/E ratio is nothing else but a tautology. Nevertheless the use of the P/E ratio is extremely pervasive and this popularity is understandable as it responds to Wall Street's (and Academia's) desire to have a simple quantified yardstick through which any company may be measured and accordingly allows for comparing companies of different sectors, size, countries and so on. This same desire also explains the popularity of the risk measure instrument, namely beta or the so-called fear index, the VIX).

Although P/E ratios are extremely popular they have to be taken with a lot of caution. In the first place it should be noted that in the P/E ratio there are two moving parts and not just one, the price. If the P/E ratio is historically at a high level, such high level may well be due to excessively high stock prices, to "P", but it may also be so for reason of a temporarily depressed "E", earnings. If at a given moment the P/E ratio of the DJIA reflects a level of 28 this certainly means it is high by historical standards. However, if the earnings are expected to double in the next 12 to 18 months then, all other things equal, this rise would lead to a P/E ratio of 14 only, perfectly in line with historical standards. For cyclical companies (say aluminum, steel or car industries) such wild fluctuations of the P/E ratio over the business cycle are quite usual. Whereas at the end of the cycle when profits are still very high, but signs of reversal are clearly there already, P/E ratios are extremely low, maybe down to 4 or 5, then this low level is certainly not a buying signal, to the contrary: Such P/E ratios show that investors do already foresee that profits will break away so that even with falling stock prices, the P/E ratio of next year will hugely increase, for instance to 18 to 20.

The P/E ratio has its share of shortcomings, most importantly in case of loss-making companies: a meaningful P/E ratio cannot be calculated in such case.

The P/E ratio varies extremely from one company to another, from one sector to another, from one era to another, one country to another, etc. However, its principal merit is simplicity: it allows to compare different companies one to another at least if they are profit-making. For loss making companies, a change of comparison metrics is needed: for instance a revenue multiple might be used. Possibly, a P/E's most useful part is that it allows to eliminate a certain fraction of stocks, those with the highest ratios and possibly also those with very low ratios. Some investors limit themselves to stocks with a trailing P/E ratio between 8 to 20. Of course, this rule has its share of disadvantages as it will exclude many fast growing companies which are still in their investing phase.

Generally speaking, P/E ratios are based on past figures and as such they are based on a rear-view-mirror approach whereas the value of a company is based on its future earnings to be generated on the income of the next 10 to 20 years if not beyond. The Shiller/Case ratio (CAPE, cyclically adjusted P/E) is based on the average inflation-adjusted earnings of the last 10 years.

P/E ratios (regardless to which species they belong), vary strongly from sector to sector and also within any given sector of the economy. These differences are fully justified and are easily explained: business economics vary strongly from one sector to the next one. The software business has completely different economics from a company of the steel sector or of the car manufacturing industry. Even within a certain sector there are big differences: the competitive position of the dominant firm is generally much different than the one of a marginal producer, i.e. one whose production costs are only slightly below the market price of its products (or maybe even above this market price).

All these differences (which in fact are a lot more numerous than indicated here) reflect themselves in the P/E ratio.

(It should also not be forgotten that it is far from easy to classify companies into different industries and the classification into one group or another is often somewhat arbitrary. For instance, Berkshire Hathaway is normally allocated to the Insurance Group (in the category property and casualty; such is for instance the case with Value Line). This classification may be justified in as far as the insurance/reinsurance business is probably the single most important one of the company. However, Berkshire Hathaway increasingly is a genuine conglomerate owning dozens of other businesses (like a railroad company, utility companies, numerous manufacturing companies, etc.), which means that it is not certain whether comparing it to pure insurance companies makes much sense.

Traditionnally, an investment in common stocks was based on upon three pillars: a decent and stable dividend, a stable earnings record and a reasonable coverage by tangible assets. During the bull market which let to the 1929 Depression the public completely changed its approach to common stocks and it was now assumed that the value of a stock depends only on the future flow of its earnings. The consequence was that dividends and even more so assets lost any importance and that past earnings were of importance only in as far as they indicated that changes to the earnings were likely to take place in the future

If at a certain moment in time P/E ratios have their justification to compare stocks of different sectors (and even more so stocks of the same sector) the situation is very different if P/E ratios are used to compare present prices with historic prices , or in other words in order to decide whether stocks are either historically cheap or expensive.

Such historic comparisons are very frequently made on Bloomberg or CNBC, which is legitimate only if one does not neglect the 800-pound gorilla in the room, namely interest rate levels. Unfortunately, very frequently no mention at all of interest rates is made!

If an analyst or market commentator concludes that at the beginning of 2020 stock prices are high because the average P/E ratio is, say, 16,8 whereas historically average P/E ratios were only 15 then this statement tells us a lot more about its author (who does not deserve much attention) than about the level of current stock prices. Low (and decreasing) interest rates mean that discount rates used to discount future cash flows in order to determine the value of stock prices decrease as well. It is well known that such valuations of stocks, based on discounting very long term cash flow projections, are extremely sensitive to discount rates and their changes cannot be outrightly ignored.

In order to somewhat cushion such wild fluctuations of the P/E ratio a modified P/E ratio has been introduced which instead of being based on the profit (or earnings) of a single year is referring to the average profits of a number of years. The is the so-called Cyclically Adjusted Campbell-Shiller P/E ratio, or CAPE which refers to the average inflation adjusted profits of a ten-year period (see hereafter).

If P/E ratios are by far the most-used measure of the value of stocks, other ratios do also exist as P/E ratios are not always available. If a company does not generate any profit or if the profit recorded is extremely low, no P/E is calculated. In such case a Price-to-sales ratio may be used to allow for meaningful comparison. Another classical ratio is the Price-to-book ratio: just as the P/E ratio compares stock prices to its profits, the Price-to-book ratio compares the company's stock prices to its book value. Book value is best reflected by the company's equity, which is the amount which remains over for the owners if all debtors are paid. Book value will correspond to equity only if assets may be disposed of at a price correspong to their book value and debts as well as other liabilities are fairly valued. Whereas traditional industrial companies, and nowadays also banks and other financial companies, trade at values relatively close to book value this is no longer the case for technology companies, pharmaceutical companies, consumer staples companies, etc. which tend to show high multiples compared to book value.

Growth Stocks and P/E Ratios

A question which haunts many investors is to know in how far they may conclude that a certain common stock is overvalued for the reason that its P/E ratio is "too high." Let us assume that a company has a P/E ratio of 30 to 35 whereas the average market ratio is about 15.

This stock may still be a good buy provided that the stock has above average growth expectations. The so-called PEG ratio represents an attempt to include a company's growth ratio into the assessment equation allowing to decide whether a certain valuation is or is not justified: this ratio consists in dividing the P/E ratio by the company's growth rate. Ideally the resulting figure is lower than 1.

For example, a company has a P/E ratio of 23. As long as its growth rate is higher than 23, for instance 25, the PEG ratio would end up to be lower than 1.

These calculations are useful but at the same time eminently dangerous. They are useful by stressing the fact that the earnings growth rate is a fundamental element in this context and that, as a result, a high P/E ratio may be fully justified provided the company is able to show a sufficiently high growth rate.

Unfortunately, these calculations are also dangerous, for the reason that the growth rate is looking into the future and there is no way to determine this rate with any significant reliability. The particular danger is that these forecasts of future growth rates quite generally err on the high side, by overestimating the growth rates, regardless of whether this is due to a general bias towards optimism or to more down-to-earth aspects pertaining to the attitude of those who want to promote the trading of the stock (self-interest). Another reason for a potential overestimation of the growth rate is that history shows that extremely high growth rates of say 20-30% are generally speaking not sustainable and they will sooner or later decrease to more pedestrian levels. Such high growth rates are frequemtly seen in the area of high technology, internet, biotechnology, in other words in domains which are viewed to be the hottest of the market and where the danger of valuation excesses is omnipresent.

Many investors are rejecting high-P/E-ratio stocks for being overpriced. However, this conclusion may not be correct. A stock with a P/E ratio double the market ratio is not overpriced if the stock is able to double its income in some 4 to 5 years of time. The conclusion of numerous investors is that such stock would anticipate the income of the next 4 to 5 years. However, this reasoning assumes that 4 to 5 years later this stock will be selling at the same price-earnings ratio as the average stock to with which they compare it. In fact this stock may go on to sell for twice (or maybe only one and a half time) the price-earnings ratio of the average stocks just as it is doing now and has done for many years in the past.

It is also worthwhile to stress that the PEG ratio is not the only important element to take into account. In fact the absolute level of the growth rate also matters. If a company has a P/E ratio of 12 and a growth rate of 12 then the PEG ratio is 1, just as for company B with a P/R of 24 and a growth rate of 24 as well. However these two companies should not be considered as being of identical value for the investor for the reason that the company with the highest growth rate is of hugely higher value, as over time it will produce higher gains for the investor as can be seen from the following table. A doubling of the growth rate translates to a value 21 times higher after 30 years. The real question here is to know whether and at which moment the higher growth rate will dwindle down to a lower level. It may be noteworthy that if the higher rate may be maintained only for 10 years then the earnings are already close to 3 times those of the lower growth rate company. This means that even if the growth rate did plunge to 12% as of year 11, company B would be an outstandingly good deal at double the price paid for company A.

Year	g = 12%	g = 24%
1	100	100
5	176.234	293.16
10	310.58	859.44

15	547.356	2,519.56
20	964.63	7,386.41
25	1,700.00	21,654.1
30	2,995.99	63,482

Stratospheric P/E ratios

With reference to historic market data, P/E ratios of 10-15 appear normal. Very low ratios, below 10, are often viewed as bullish signs whereas high market P/Es above 18, are considered as bearish signs as they tend to coincide with speculative excesses and forecast at least low future stock price performance. An exception to this "rule" is the case when P/E ratios are very high not due to share price increases but if profits are currently break away because of a severe economic recession. Such was the case in 1983 when the P/E ratio exceeded 130.

Very low P/E stocks are sometimes shown to perform best. This conclusion has to be taken with some caution. It may be biased due to the fact that often stocks which fell into bankruptcy were excluded from the studies which is of course a distorting factor. Any investor who gets attracted by a very low P/E should get suspicious and ask themselves what other investors do see what they may not see. It might be that the financial situation is so deteriorated that the survival of the company is in jeopardy or simply that the profit will soon decrease which will automatically adjust the P/E ratio downwards.

When P/E ratios have reached extremely high levels, investors should ask themselves the question what must happen for these ratios to come down to more "normal" levels. High P/E ratios are a reflection of the fact that the company under review has had high growth rates in the past and a lot more importantly they reflect the appraisal of the market that these high growth rates may go on at least for some time in the future. At this point, investors enter into really dangerous grounds and they have to be aware of the fact that a certain number of factors clearly play against them.

High growth rates are normally not sustainable for a long time. Sooner or later growth rates will revert to the mean. This is especially true if the target company has reached a certain size. At that point the limits of growth may become obvious: it may be that when extrapolating the present growth rate for another 5 or 10 years that the size of the company will exceed the size of the whole sector of which it is a part or even the size of the economy as a whole…

Wall Street is based on excessive optimism: there is a general tendency to err on the high side; such over-optimism is in the Street's self-interest, as they want investors to enter into securities transactions, which means in fact to buy stocks. Any shares can be offered to all investors whereas only those who own a share may sell it (if we disregard the possibility of short sales, which is not always possible and furthermore has several important disadvantages). This excessive optimism is often accompanied by another cognitive bias, overconfidence. Analysts are overconfident to correctly guess growth rates into the future for a long period of time. Investors are overconfident that they are able to forecast share prices, economic events and macroeconomic trends , like future growth rates, interest and inflation rates, etc.

On this subject, as on others, investors should bet with the base rate and not lightly go against it. The base rate is that growth rates which growth companies are able to realize will decrease over time. Markets will adjust to these decreasing rates as well. Nobody does exactly know when this downward process will start and at which speed it will develop. Even if one did know when actual growth rates will come down, it would still not be possible to know when the markets will adjust their evaluations. In other words, this type of companies which undeniably may make any investor rich, are a terrific investment but under the condition that you are a shareholder at a moment when the growth opportunities have not yet been fully recognized by the market but not at a later stage when in all likelihood the future growth rate is exaggerated and when the P/E ratios are coming down rapidly with the stocks going nowhere for a very long period of time.

On this question of growth rates it has to be added that the long-term return on a stock depends not on the actual growth of its earnings but on how those earnings compare to investors' expectations.

According to historic data US stocks of publicly traded companies did produce average real returns of 7% over a very long time periods. This return contains two components, namely dividends and stock price fluctuations (appreciations or depreciations). If the dividend yield is 2% (which is about the average of all the stocks part of the S&P 500 Index) then a 7% total return requires that stocks annually increase by 5%.

When calculating this yield, P/E ratios are not necessarily constant and in fact they fluctuate heavily: the incidence of these fluctuations is sometimes called the "speculative return" as it is not directly attributable to objective factors like earnings growth but influenced by the subjective appreciation made by investors who if in an optimistic mood will valorize earnings at a higher multiple as in normal times. It is those fluctuations of the P/E ratios which are at the root of market bubbles (as seen at the times of the internet bubble for instance). If over the period 1949 to 1969 the DJIA increased by a factor 5, earnings including dividends had only doubled. Hence, most of the increase was attributable to changes in mood of investors.

If the P/E ratio stays constant then we may express the dividend yield (expressed in per cent: annual dividend divided by the stock price) increased by the rate of growth of EPS (earnings per share). Again, if the dividend yield is 2% and EPS grow by 7% then we will reach the 9%

141

historical real return rate once we deduct the inflation rate of 2%.

Here comes CAPE

This ratio is frequently applied to market indices in order to judge whether stock markets are overvalued or undervalued with the conclusion that high CAPE ratios lead to below-average returns over the following 10-year period.

This approach, although confirming what was anyway widely believed already, does attract several critical comments. In the first place, the CAPE is based on "real" profits of a ten-year period. Although nobody would argue with the basic idea that such average approach allows for some smoothing of the annual earnings the question remains whether this period is not excessively long. Ten years is an eternity in business life and if the "E" in the P/E ratio is calculated in 2020 then profits over the period 2010-2019 enter into this calculation. Especially for strongly growing companies (take Facebook) you may wonder what the profit of 2010 has to do with the valuation of the company in 2020. The result is that the CAPE calculation will be based on an income which is too low as the more relevant recent years have been watered down by largely irrelevant older years. CAPE is an excessively pessimistic calculation (at least for strong-growth companies).

Another point of criticism is that the inflation-adjustment is not made on the basis of the CPI but on the basis of a relatively unknown index called wholesale price index. A third point of criticism is that by forecasting the earnings for the next ten-year period, is a period which is excessively long as investors are at best interested to learn what are the earnings of the next year or two to three years.

P/E ratios and interest rates

It is extremely remarkable and of course worrisome that when average market P/E ratios are analyzed (and especially if they are compared with the corresponding historic rates) there is generally no reference made to the prevailing interest rates.

For instance, a certain analyst interviewed on CNBC may say at the end of 2019 that an average P/E ratio of 19 is higher than the rate prevailing in 2007 without any reference to the interest rates prevailing during those specific periods. However, the connection existing between share prices and the level of interest rates is obvious. All assets classes (stock, bonds, real estate, commodities, etc.) are in permanent competition for funds available for investment. This is especially the case for fixed-income assets.

This is so because of the concept of opportunity cost as developed by economists. Each time an entrepreneur makes a particular choice on investing assets, this choice involves a cost which consist in not being able to pursue alternative uses of these funds.

The opportunity cost of an asset is the income that could be earned if the funds used to purchase the said asset had been used for another purpose. This concept is not limited to assets but it also applies to time which is used for one task and which could be used for another task.

If US Treasury bonds, an investment deemed to carry zero risk (in fact this statement only refers to the default risk) given the quality of the borrower who has never defaulted, bear an interest rate of 8 per cent, equity investments will suffer: no investor having all their senses will invest in equities if the P/E ratio of the market is 20. Such equity investments are risky and if they do generate less income than no-risk fixed-income investments it is foreseeable that equity markets will have a hard time. If, on the other hand, interest rates are low (as during the whole period stretching from 2009 to 2020), the P/E ratios may justifiably be higher: if Treasurys do yield only 2 per cent (which corresponds to a P/E ratio of 50 (!) with the additional downside that its coupon will never increase by a penny, that's for sure!), an equity investment in shares with a P/E ratio of 18 does not appear as clearly overpriced (the reason being that such investment does generate a yield of some 5.55 per cent still giving an equity premium of, say, 3.55 percentage points).

It is certainly noteworthy in this context that in 1979 the P/E ratio was the lowest ever, at a level of 6.8. Although inflation (CPI at 11.3%) and interest rates were still very high the results of the Volcker policy would soon take care of these factors and as of 1982 the P/E ratio would have more than doubled to 14.3.

In other words, and this statement is not really new, the P/E ratios of the markets are inversely related to market interest rates. In fact, what counts is not the presently applicable interest rate but the rate applying in the future. In a low-interest period like the one we are presently living in, there is always the fear that interest rates may increase in the near future. Because investment is a forward-looking activity, the investor does not escape the difficult task to make an educated guess about the (average) interest rates applicable over the coming decade.

Risk

Risk in investing is generally (if not universally) defined in a different way than is the case in other areas: whereas for a normal commercial business risk is associated with losing money, in the investment area risk is defined as a decrease in price below the acquisition price of the securities held if the investor sold these securities. A bond is risky if the issuer (a financially sound company when issuing the bonds) gets into financial trouble and defaults on interest and/or redemption payments. However, if bond prices decrease for the reason that interest rates increase (at very low interest rates it suffices for interest rates to only bulge by a tiny amount to greatly affect long term bond prices) then the investors' cash flow is not impacted at all if they hold those bonds to maturity. (In fact, in such case investors would benefit from the situation as they could profit from the now higher interest rates at which their annual bonds coupons could be reinvested). This means that the investor actually does not suffer any real risk in the traditional commercial business sense. The type of "risk" (if in line with Wall Street we continue to call it that way) of this investment only gets real if the investor is forced to exit their position: only if they have to sell do they incur a real and lasting financial loss. However, all such temporary price fluctuations should not matter to the genuine long-term investor for the reason that they have managed their financial situation (including their investment portfolio) in a way that they are never in a position where they are forced to sell their shares. Hence, such investors who are aware of Wall Street history are not panicking if stock prices decrease: either they do not react at all to such panic decreases, just sitting them out, or they will take such decreases as a welcome opportunity to invest at a higher margin of safety, in this way actually decreasing their risk: the risk to suffer a loss in case of a later sale.

A somewhat closer analysis shows that stock price variations and business risks are of different types (which furthermore are not all easy to identify). In theory it can be said these stock price fluctuations are either directly reflecting business risk (1) (as a consequence of deteriorating fundamentals like a decrease in earnings) or they are not relevant for the business at all (2) or finally they are of a mixed nature (3).

The elements of the first category (1) are news which straightly affect the company are mostly easy to identify: the information is often directly concerning the company (quarterly earnings statement, profit warnings, announcements of new products), analysts' comments, market studies on the business sector, etc.

The elements of the second category (2) are nearly all the macro-economic assessments of a general nature, like forecasts on GDP, inflation, the FED's interest rate adjustments, political events, like presidential elections, Brexit, the travails of the Euro, Japanese interest rates, etc.

These factors do, in general, not really matter for the company but of course in some situations they could. For instance if a company is heavily indebted, a steep increase in local interest rates could directly impact the business fundamentals of the company: The same is true for the banking sector.

Finally, the third category (3) is the most difficult one: here we have the very frequent situation of elements which impact the general economy and more or less each and every company. Investors should not be too nervous about these factors, especially not if they made sure to select only companies with a reasonably high financial standing. If that condition is met, they should simply discard most of the factors of a general economic nature. Clearly, any price increase of resources which are used by certain businesses to produce their widgets or services is bad news for such businesses which will see their costs increase. However, this is not a reason for that business to panic. In the first place, these price increases do affect competition as well; furthermore large businesses are huge operations which each and every day of their life are confronted with hundreds of changes which either increase or decrease their earnings. They get new mandates (or awards), they win new clients, they lose long-standing clients, they sue and get sued and they win or lose the corresponding trials. All this is part of their daily life and is part of the headache of management on high level and lower level. Assuming that management is reasonably competent and motivated, these managements will find solutions which will at least mitigate these problems. For the remainder, we may count on the rule that the impact of these multitude of factors will more or less compensate.

There is no reason that shareholders of such companies do try to treat those problems as their own ones. Investors should concentrate on what is important and knowable: even if some of these things might be important (which is far from sure) they certainly fall into the category of the unknowable things. 99.9% of these issues are not sufficiently important to get much attention from investors who unlike management of the company, do not have sufficient information on the company's business to make a valid assessment of the situation. Management, when compared to the public, has highly asymmetrical information advantages. In fact, for investors the fact to have some knowledge is worse than to have no knowledge at all. Take the situation of some sectors, like engineering companies, were new awards are generally widely publicized and clearly, large awards are cheered by investors. Unfortunately what is not known by those investors who are happy to drive the stock prices higher, is whether these awards are profitable or not. If they are not profitable (which will only be known with precision many years later, at the earliest when the work is realized and received by the client) then investors should not cheer for such awards but they should simply ignore them. Of course, there is no way for investors to know which kind of awards they are confronted with. They have to rely on their assessment with respect to the quality of the management of the company, as an honest and competent management will avoid deals which are sure to make losses just to be able to claim that the order book is full and increasing when compared to previous periods. If management does not comply with those standard and especially if it is dishonest or simply greedy there is trouble ahead for the companies and their stockholders.

Investing in stocks involves a different kind of riskiness than games of chance, for instance; in casinos the probabilistic distribution of outcomes are very well known for hundreds of years already. Stock investing involves risks of another quality sometimes also referred to as "uncertainty" where the outcome distribution is not known from the start and is by definition unknowable. Investors can only rely on their personal assessment of the various scenarios which they subjectively consider as possibly playing out and to allocate different probabilities to them.

Sometimes uncertainty may be in the interest of those investor who are able to separate uncertainty from real risks. Uncertainty as far as it only means that nobody knows how certain things play out precisely is not, or should not be, of concern for investors. Risks are involved only if a certain scenario involves either that the financial survival of a company is seriously in jeopardy and/or if the earnings of the company will be significantly negatively impacted.

Take as an example the case of a conglomerate which has taken up excessive debts in order to acquire new businesses as well as buying back stocks at quite high prices. Due to fallout of the Covid-19 crisis stock prices get severely punished. Some of the business lines of our conglomerate although not core of the company could easily be sold and the proceeds be used to deleverage the company. Uncertainty on the question of how the situation will precisely evolve will have scared off many investors who had beaten down the stock prices in an excessive way but which promptly corrected as soon as one of the possible scenarios foreseen by some smart investors does unfold. The advice for investors to distinguish uncertainty from risk and to discard the first unless it translates into the second.

Currently one area which is seriously affected by high uncertainty are several FAANG stocks which are subject to investigations by the US DOJ (Department of Justice) and the FTC (Federal Trade Commission) as well as certain non-US institutions, like the EU Commission. The various FAANG stocks are unequally affected by these investigations and it would appear that Facebook and Alphabet would be the most targeted, followed by Amazon.

To the extent that History may serve as a guide here it would seem that in general such investigations would not normally lead to incisive actions certainly not in the area of high technology. Investigations targeting IBM and more recently Microsoft, although lasting for many years, did not lead to a breakup of those companies. Such breakups did actually occur in US business history namely in case of

Standard Oil and AT&T. For Standard Oil the break-up was fully justified as the case at hand was clearly in the cross-hairs of the anti-trust legislation which was precisely enacted in order to sanction monopolistic behavior meant to crush competition and increase prices paid by consumers. The case of AT&T was similar as the U.S. government decided in 1981 that AT&T being a monopoly it had to be broken up into eight companies. Each AT&T shareholder received shares of the seven "Baby Bells" (regional telephone companies) and of the "new" AT&T.

Even if such breakup (which probably represents the worst case scenario) did occur for one or the other of the above mentioned FAANG companies this would certainly not mean awfully bad news for stockholders (even if it would certainly not make the number one scenario on the wish list of the incumbent managements). Furthermore, most competition lawyers do express serious doubts whether the presently applicable anti-competition legislation which goes back to the days of President Teddy Roosevelt (beginning of the 20th century) and targeted behavior of corporations intended to eliminate competition which behavior was directly and evidently harmful for consumers which paid monopolistic prices.

Such legislation is arguably difficult to apply in the case of services which are mostly free (at least for the consumer). In other words, it looks as if there is a lot of uncertainty involved here but the risks involved seem to be a lot less obvious; furthermore and in all likelihood these risks are already priced in by the financial markets.

Another point which needs to be stressed here is the following one: the US-China trade war is certainly something which will go on over the next years and decades (regardless of the fact whether Trump will be reelected or not and regardless of the fact that an agreement will be found eliminating the currently applicable tariffs or not). It is a fact that in the medium-term future the biggest competitors of Alphabet, Facebook and Amazon will be the large Chinese internet firms like Alibaba, Tencent, Baidu, etc. It is highly unlikely that these Chinese companies will be broken up by the ruling Chinese Communist Party which in their task of controlling the internet certainly prefer to have a small number of big actors to having dozens of smaller ones. The US internet behemoths will doubtlessly not fail to underline that on many third markets (possible even on the US market) they are competing with these Chinese firms which would have a competitive advantage if the US companies were broken up (whereas their Asian competitors do not face such headwinds). Arguably these arguments will not only find deaf ears with US Congress and US Government. However escaping existing trust legislation may not mean that the Faang stocks are getting out unscathed. The more direct danger they are confronted with is the same thing banks suffered after the Great Recession, namely an increase in cost due to new regulations which do not only result in explosion of the number of employees and "in compliance staff and infrastructure costs to deal with the new rules."[25]

Methodology of Risk in Finance

When it comes to risk, the situation is completely different compared to return. "Risk" cannot be expressed by a single figure. Risk can be assessed ex-post, after the fact: only then may we conclude that a certain investment was actually risky, namely when the risk realized. However, and to make things more difficult, even ex-post you cannot conclude that a certain investment was not risky for the only reason that the risk did not realize. It is not that because your house did not burn over the last 20 years that their was no fire risk over said period. We may only conclude that of the two scenarios which initially were possible – the house burns or it does not burn – the one which realized was the second one and the house did not burn. For instance, those "investors" who bought internet stocks in January 2000 (just because the name of the stock included ".com") and sold them with a nice profit several weeks later (just before the bubble burst in March 2000) had taken very high risks (whether they knew it or not), but by luck they escaped the financial bloodshed which they would have suffered had they held the shares just a little bit longer. Alternatively, the fact that certain trades did end in a loss does not tell us that these trades were particularly risky when they were initiated.

Academia has tried to express the riskiness of investments by introducing the concept of "beta." In fact, beta expresses nothing else than the volatility of stocks as measured by past data, which means it adopts a rear-mirror view. High-beta stocks (higher than 1) are those that do rise by a higher percentage than the market in a rising market and decline more than the market averages in a declining market. Hence, according to that school of thought, such high-beta stocks are riskier than low-beta stocks given that they fluctuate more than low-beta stocks.

In reality, the concept of beta is of little practical utility: beta does not measure risk, it only measures volatility. In fact, investors should welcome volatility, i.e. high-beta stocks, for the reason that this volatility will allow them to acquire shares at low prices (i.e. with a high margin of safety), and in this way will enable them to attain something which in theory seems difficult or even impossible to achieve, namely, increased return and decreased risk at the same time.

Furthermore, volatility tells us something about the behavior of <u>stocks</u> and not really something about the risks of the <u>underlying businesses</u>. A long-term investor, who by studying the Mr. Market metaphor (of The Intelligent Investor) should know to distinguish business fundamentals from stock market gyrations and they should be more concerned about the second than about the first: as long as the business does not incur serious dangers, the investor can do with a volatile stock, a high-beta stock. Low business risks will be given if the company has stable markets, a strong competitive position, growing income streams and a solid balance sheet, meaning in the first place, a low amount of debt (little financial and operating leverage).

Although losses are measurable, risk is not. Losses, once realized, are part of the return. Even in case of bankruptcy (where the loss is generally total and undisputable) this unfortunate outcome does not tell us much about risk as existing at the moment the investment was made. Imagine the following scenario: you have invested in shares of a US company which is a supplier to a company located in Japan and which went out of business due to the earthquake and the ensuing tsunami of March 11th, 2011. Due to this disaster, the outstanding claims held by the US Company in its Japanese clients were not paid with the consequence that it went out of business itself as this important client could not be replaced in the short term. The question is now whether this investment was risky, although the capital loss on investment was total. With the benefit of hindsight (in "the bright light of hindsight...") it would be easy to conclude that this was the case. However, in all fairness it has to be said that the investor, at the time the investment decision was taken, did probably not act in an unreasonable way by taking excessive risks.

Whereas in this case the outcome was bad, the investment decision was not highly risky, the opposite situation may also occur: a risky investment at the time it was made turns out as a big success. As an example take an investment in AOL made in mid-1997 for $3.5 (adjusted for stock-splits) and which became a 20-bagger at the beginning of 1999 when you sold for $80. Also in this case, the outcome does not tell as much (in fact nothing) about the riskiness of this investment.

Whereas risk is assessed at the moment of the investment, return is assessed after the fact, meaning at the moment the shares are sold.

The attempt to solve this problem made by followers of the efficient market theory (EMT) is the concept of risk adjusted return (ER= expected returm) which is defined by the following formula:

ER = rfr + β(mr – rfr)

Where:

rfr. risk-free return

mr: market return

Applied to stock investments, the element β(mr – rfr) represents the equity premium and our formula means that the expected return equals the risk-free rate of return increased by the equity premium.

A substantial part of the probability theory used in the field of stock investing goes back to games of luck, meaning activities with random outcomes, like roulette, black jack, horse betting etc. Those activities are of a very short duration and once the game is over, the accounts of all the participants are settled. Everybody is able to calculate the theoretical probabilities of their gains or losses. On stock exchanges such is not the case. The game goes on "forever." At no moment in time investors will close all their positions. Option traders live in a different environment: here the end of the game is called not in terms of minutes or hours, like in the casino, but in terms of months and years. The difference is that the option holder knows exactly that their options are worthless once a certain date is reached. The investor in stocks benefits of a very substantial advantage here: they have the opportunity to ignore any fantasy stock quotations which they are allowed to consider as not justified in fact.

It is true that sometimes it is the behavior of investors which puts them into a position which does not allow them to ignore the vagaries of stock market quotes. Take the investors who are highly leveraged and who get a margin call from their brokers. Such margin calls do only occur in case of serious market turbulences which led to extremely depressed stock prices with the consequence that the stocks are sold at a most unfavorable moment. (This point is belabored in more detail here below under Components of Risk).

Risk is probably the most difficult concept to grasp in investing. As the rule goes, risk and return are related: the higher the risk, the higher the return. This statement seems to imply that in order to get high returns, an investor needs to take high risks and if they are ready to run higher risks the unavoidable result is higher returns delivered on a silver platter.

Nowadays investment scholars attribute to this statement a higher degree of generality than was historically the case. Initially the rule referred to the comparative riskiness of different asset classes and it meant that stocks, whereas riskier than bonds (as creditors are preferred to shareholders of a company), produce higher returns than bonds, which in turn generate higher returns than short term commercial papers.

In this category one may quote Dimson Marsh Staunton, Triumph of the Optimists: 101 Years of Global Investment Returns, who after noting that over the long-haul, stocks, the riskiest asset class, have beaten bonds in every single country. Bonds have beaten bills almost everywhere. "Our findings thus provide support for one of the lasting laws of finance – the law of risk and return."

Later on, this rule has been interpreted to mean that any individual stock, bond, etc. generates a return in line with its degree of riskiness. That ain't so! The only thing the said rule says is that higher risks on average produce higher returns which is the same thing as saying that in reality some will cash in higher returns but others will get lower returns which might include the case of a total loss.

This "high risks, high returns" maxim is extremely misleading and quite frankly dangerous, as has been underlined many times by a number of authors; it gives the impression that higher returns are unavoidable once you are willing to assume higher risks. By neglecting the uncertainty on the return side of the equation, it is suggested in fact that at the end high-risk stocks are in fact not riskier than low-risks stocks but they only differ from them by having higher returns. However, it is completely erroneous to believe that all what is needed is to stomach higher volatility and to be compensated by higher returns.

The truth is that for any stocks, whether they are high-risk or low-risk ones, their value is determined by future events. The exact development of these future events is unknown at the present moment and for rational investors it is only possible to allocate a probability distribution to them. In fact this probability distribution is a very rough one and it may only envisage 3 to 5 outcomes which are deemed the most probable ones. To these outcomes the investor will allocate probabilities. For instance, outcome A: 5%, outcome B: 15%; Outcome C: 40%; Outcome D: 10%. This might be the probability distribution of a rather secure stock producing a return of 6% per annum.

Although risk and return are related (as we have just seen), there is a big difference between the two concepts: return can be expressed in a single number: it is either the return given by the market (i.e. the difference between the share price at the beginning and at the end of the year increased by the dividends paid, if any) or the investor's individual return (i.e. the difference between purchase and sale price also increased by dividends paid during his holding period). In either case, a single number will express the return, either the prospective return or the realized, the ex-post return.

Risk is a different ball game: defined as the probability of loss, risk is not measurable at least not by a single number even not ex-post. What is measurable is loss: if a company goes bankrupt all the investors lose their entire investment and they suffer a 100% loss.

This means that at best the investor may assume that they might *on average* get higher returns if they assume higher risks. But, in a given case it may well be that a riskier investment produces lower returns: in fact, far from being abnormal, this outcome would just be the confirmation that the investment actually was riskier than average…

To say the same thing in another way: if riskier shares did always produce higher returns for each and every investor they would not be riskier and by this very fact there would be no reason for markets to provide them with higher returns as these higher returns do precisely constitute the compensation for investors to purchase these higher-risk stocks.

Furthermore, the whole assumption may be challenged as not corresponding to reality. Instead of trying to realize higher returns by assuming higher risks (as a bond investor might do by switching from US Treasurys to junk bonds), the objective should be to decrease risks (by buying first class company stocks) with a substantial margin of safety which not only decreases risk but at the same time increases returns (given the lower costs).

The traditional belief that risk and return are positively correlated has had disastrous consequences for many investors as many took this rule too literally wrongly believing that it suffices to increase the riskiness of your investments to increase your returns in a correlative fashion. This would mean that by doubling the degree of riskiness of your investments you will double your rate of return (for instance from 4 to 8%). This reasoning ignores the fact that such increased returns do only occur <u>on average</u>. The problem is that hardly anybody gets the "average" return but whereas the majority of investors will record returns which are close to average return (think of the classical bell curve) many investors will get returns which are a lot higher or lower than the average. The risk is precisely to be among the unlucky few in the long tail of the distribution curve which are on the left side of the curve, meaning those who lost a substantial part of their investments.

Components of Risk

Risk, as far as investments in stocks are concerned has three component parts: financial position of the investor, quality of the issuer of the stocks and the stock price paid on acquisition of the stock.

1.Financial position of the investor

In the first place and perhaps surprisingly, 'risk' may arise from the financial status of the investor (and not of the issuer; Issuer risk will be dealt with sub 2 hereafter): this is for instance the case if the shares are bought on margin (a small decrease in the price of the stock could force the investor to sell at least part of their portfolio) or if the investor suddenly and unexpectedly needs the invested capital to pay unforeseen living expenses (which means that the investor did not have sufficient reserves for contingencies). Investors should not only simply assess probabilities of increases and decreases in value. They should also assess the financial consequences for themselves if these probabilities realize. They should avoid any scenario which could wipe them out, however low they may evaluate the likelihood that scenario could ever realize.

It is noteworthy that this first element of risk is the only one to be completely and exclusively under control of the investor, which explains why it should be handled first. This specific type of risk is entirely homemade and there is really nobody else to blame but the investor if it actually materializes.

2.Quality of the company

Minimizing risks involves purchasing secure companies, i.e. profitable companies with a solid financial position and enjoying competitive advantages. (Selecting interesting targets will be treated in Chapter 6.)

3.Stock Price

For the knowledgeable investor, selecting quality shares is not that difficult and as a consequence, the real challenge is to select quality shares at a decent price. Just as on the race-track it is easy to see that the lame horse with a fat jockey is unlikely to win the race, once the betting odds are taken into consideration the choices get way more complicated. In other words, for those quality stocks the essential element of risk lies in the price to be paid. The higher the price of the stock, the higher the risk; the lower the price, the lower the risk and, interestingly, the higher the potential return. If the price is low enough it may even be that a lower quality issuer is a lower risk than a higher quality issue at the current higher price.

If you buy the stock of Intel at $65 compared to the situation you buy it at $50 the probability of making a loss (i.e. your risk) is obviously much higher whereas your foreseeable return is clearly substantially lower (all things equal).

If this point is belabored here, it is so in order to draw the reader's attention to the central role played by the price paid for the stocks. Put another way, the question of risk is highly price dependent. It is hardly an exaggeration to state that any investment is extremely risky at a certain price and that at sufficiently low a price nearly any investment is safe, non-risky. This truth is also expressed by the old Wall Street adage is "there are no bad assets only bad prices."

In the extreme case of bankruptcy the loss is (generally) 100%, the same for all investors regardless of the price they actually paid. In all other cases, the amount of the loss is highly price dependent, i.e. it is closely linked to the price paid by the investor. The same holds true for risk. It is obvious that contrary to conventional wisdom (that risk and return are positively connected), the lower the price the higher the return but also the lower the risk (the possibility of a loss) will be.

Any investor may easily check that this "rule" of "higher risks begets higher returns" does not hold true in real life: if it did, then high technology stocks, as a group, would

158

produce higher returns than other industries. However, this traditionally has not been the case.

The incidence of security prices on investment risk cannot be overstated and it goes without saying that as in most other cases the crowd, fully supported by the "Street", behaves awfully wrong. In bull markets, when prices increase a lot quicker than earnings do, investors forget about risk and they do not ask for any compensation for assuming higher risks. The compensation for these higher risks could only consist in lower prices. Exactly the opposite occurs: prices increase rapidly, and any risk premium embedded in prices prevailing before the price increases will rapidly melt away. Risks increase exponentially (accompanied by diminishing returns).

Although most investors do consider that risk (unlike return) cannot be expressed by one single number, academia has viewed things differently and has exactly done this: expressing risk by one figure, and to give it a scientific guise, attributing it a Greek letter: beta.

Beta an Expression of Risk?

Albert Einstein once standing before his students wrote on the blackboard: "Not everything that counts can be counted and not everything that can be counted counts."

This statement comes to mind when writing about beta. Beta (β), the second letter of the Greek alphabet measures the volatility of a security (or of a securities portfolio) compared to the market, it displays the tendency of a given security's price to react to market swings. A beta of 1 means that the security is in tune with the market and that a price variation of x of the market will exactly (in fact on average and according to historical data) be matched by an identical move of the security in the same direction. A beta higher than 1 means that market moves will be amplified by the security's reaction, the opposite being true if beta is lower than 1.

It will not come as a surprise that conservative investments, like utilities or consumer staples, tend to have low betas whereas high-technology stocks tend to have betas higher than 1. A beta of 0 means that the stock or portfolio is totally independent from market moves. A beta of -1 would mean that the stock is expected to zig when the market zags meaning that a market increase of 5% will induce a 5% decrease of the stock (or portfolio of stocks). Finally, let's note that the average beta when all the stocks traded on a certain market (or other securities) are considered is necessarily equal to 1.

From its very definition, it is clear that beta does in fact not measure risk of the business but volatility of the stock (and not of the business). For value investors, volatility is Mr. Market in action and assuming that they are able to calculate the intrinsic value of a security (which they should be able to do) then high volatility, far from being a negative point, is in fact a welcome opportunity allowing them to decrease risk and increase return.

Beta has many shortcomings: in the first place (and as was explained above already) it does not really measure risk (but volatility which is in fact a different concept). The calculation of beta is based exclusively on past price movements and as such it gives a pure rear-mirror view which does not necessarily forecast the future. Disregarding the classical standard warning that "past performance does not guarantee future returns" the proponents of beta in fact say: future volatility of stocks is a true copy of the past.

Finally, it does not distinguish between price increases and price decreases of the security. Most people when they talk about risk they mean in fact risk of a decrease in value whereas they will not mind if the stock price surges. This point was already recognized by Harry Markowitz who changed his initial measurement of risk to the so-called "semi-variance" which assesses the risk that an investment might do less good than expected and which takes care of downside risk only. Take a certain utility company which in the past has had a very stable stock price and accordingly a low beta. Recently, the price of the security has decreased by 30% (in a stable market) without any concrete news justifying this price move. Beta of the security will have increased substantially but the question is did its risk increase as well (as the CAPM (Capital Asset Pricing Model) suggests)? For value investors the answer is clear: a decrease in the price of the security, far from increasing its risk, will have decreased it substantially (all other things equal).

Market practicians have argued repeatedly that it is totally ludicrous to say that a stock which has recently fallen from $60 to $30 which accordingly has a higher beta now, has got riskier than it has been at the formerly applicable higher price: it is obvious that this stock is not only less risky but furthermore it will show higher returns over future periods.

Let me conclude this chapter with a quote (which I reproduce in extenso and literally) from a blogger's statement which was made under an article published on Seeking Alpha: the article was extremely bullish which already results from its title "Tesla: World domination Lies In The Palm Of Its Hand" contained a number of rather groundless statements to talk up the stock. The quote goes as follows: "I am very risk averse. Therefore I invest in Tesla every month. This way if Tesla jumps in price I'm not caught waiting for a good price."

The said blog was written on May 8, 2020 at a moment when Tesla stock quoted around $820, giving TSLA a capitalization of $150 bn, more than fourth times General Motors.

The first two sentences are obviously a contradiction in terms: a risk-averse investor does not invest in TSLA at all at current prices. The last sentence envisages risk exclusively from the angle of missing an upside... which should be the least of the sorrows of a risk averse investor.

Chapter 3: Investor Preparation and Toolkit

The most important point for investors is to be emotionally prepared for coping with market vagaries. Temperament is way more important than having a stratospheric IQ.

Furthermore, investing in general and stock investing in particular, is a solitary activity. Teams, or committees are more harmful than useful. Committees are always about compromises and they will do less good decisions than an individual who is focused on his portfolio in which his own money is at stake. As the joke goes: a camel is a horse designed by a committee. In fairness, if an investor is inclined to take excessive risks, or makes impulsive decisions, working in a team might be useful in order to mitigate too aggressive behavior.

Let's start this chapter with some basic financial mathematics which investors should never lose out of sight and which in fact should help to guide their behavior.

Basic Mathematics in Investing

Although over the last 70 years Academia has introduced a lot of calculus in their papers on business analysis and investment management, most of these mathematical formulas are more harmful than useful and Graham's statement that in investing nothing more than basic arithmetic is really needed is largely still valid. However, some concepts are extremely important and investors should be highly aware of them. Let's start with compounding.

Compounding

Compounding occurs when an asset generates earnings which are reinvested in order to produce more earnings in the future, etc. The consequence is an ever-increasing annual income stream (assuming the income yield remains constant). This growth mechanism which produces only insignificant effects in the beginning, may reach impressive proportions after a certain number of years: this feature calls for a long-term perspective to be adopted by the investor.

The simplest form of compounding is shown by a regular savings account: assume such account is endowed with $1,000 in January 2015 and produces a constant 3% interest so that at the end of the first year, the balance of the account is 1,030. At yearend 2016 the balance of the account increases to 1,060.9, 1,092.7 (in 2017), 1.125.5 (in 2018), etc. If there were no "income on income" (no compounding) the balance of the account at the end of 2018 would not be 1,125.5 but only 1,120 (1,000+4x30). Hence the effect of compounding is rather limited only as it amounts to just $5.5 (in terms of increased interest return). This does not sound like much. However, if the same savings account is held in place for 40 years the snowball effect is very visible: the account would have increased to $3,262.03 and the effect of "interest-on-interest" would be $1,062.03.

The effect of compounding may also be shown on hand of the so-called "rule of 72."

The Rule of 72

The rule of 72 is a shortcut to calculate the time (in years) it takes to double a certain amount of capital at a given interest rate or more generally a rate of return. To this end, it suffices to divide 72 by the compound annual interest rate (or growth rate in general). For instance, if the interest rate is 8% the number of years to double the capital is 9 years, as 72 divided by 8 gives 9. If the interest rate increases to 12%, doubling of the capital occurs after 6 years already (72/12=6).

Without compounding, the number of years required to double would be given by a different formula, namely 100 divided by the annual rate of return. For instance, if the interest rate were 4%, doubling would occur after 25 year (100/4 = 25). In other words the difference between 72 and 100 is the effect of compounding, which in terms of years translates into the difference between 18 years (72/4 = 18) and 25 years, i.e. 7 years.

The results obtained by the application of the rule of 72 are reasonable accurate but not entirely so. It may be said that with very high rates of return the number of years required for doubling of capital is understated whereas for low rates of return the number of years needed for doubling is overstated.

Loser's Games and The Performance Illusion

Let's first insist on semantics: people often refer to a loser's game when they mean a losing game, which is a game that is rigged (say gambling in a casino) and cannot be won by the person playing it at least not in the long run.

Hereafter, a loser's game refers to a game where the outcome is the result of the actions of the loser and this by analogy to the tennis game. Tennis, in fact, is composed of two different plays: the professional players where the winner is the one who plays the highest ratio of winning points, which the opponent is unable to return, whereas the ordinary tennis player's game is characterized by the fact that the winner will be the one who commits the lowest number of mistakes, keeping the ball safely in play and waiting for the opponent to mess up his shots and giving the points to the risk averse player. Investing is sometimes described as a loser's game in this sense, meaning that it is more important to avoid losses than to realize high gains. This view is actually supported by basic arithmetic showing that high losses followed by gains of identical rates will not allow to come back to square one, i.e. the initial position (see here above).

If compounding is the long-term investor's best friend, the same cannot be said of performance fluctuations. To explain the issue discussed here, let's start with an example. Suppose in year one an investor realizes a 20% increase in value of their portfolio which means a $100,000 portfolio would increase to $120,000 at the end of the year. Imagine now that the second year the annual result is a 20% loss. This means that although the rate of change is the same as in the first year, the loss of the second year (which comes at the same rate as the first year's gain), will not simply cancel out the profit of the first year but it will go well beyond. At the end of the second year, the portfolio will have fallen to the level of $96,000. In other words, positive and negative performance rates cannot simply be added together. This allows us to state the following rule: *A negative performance rate will have a higher negative impact on the investment results than an identical positive rate.*

The higher the rates, the more visible and dramatic the discrepancy between those rates will get. For instance, in order to wipe out a 50% loss, a 100% profit is needed as shown by the following table.

Loss of:	Offset by gain of:
10%	11.11%
20%	25%
33.33%	50%

50%	100%
66.66%	200%
75%	300%
80%	400%
90%	900%

The above table shows that a certain series of annual return rates may not be represented by the arithmetic average of the said annual return rates. The correct aggregate rate giving the aggregate compound rate is the so-called geometric average rate as given by the following formula:

$\sqrt{a1 x a2 x a3 \ldots an}$ = the nth root of the multiplication of n growth rates.

Example:

Assume that we have the following growth rates:

Y1: 10%

Y2: 25%

Y3: 4%

the arithmetic average of which is 13%.

In order to determine the geometric average we calculate the cubic root (because there are 3 numbers) of 1,000 (i.e. 10x25x4) = 10% which, if applied to a capital of X at the beginning of year 1, will give us the same capital at the end of year 3 as the 3 above mentioned rates (10, 25 and 4% respectively) applied consecutively at each year end.

The reader will note that this geometric mean of 10% is quite substantially lower than the arithmetic average of 13% (which is based on the sum of the 3 growth rates). This is always the case if growth rates are variable and the more fluctuating the annual growth rates are the larger the difference between arithmetic and geometric averages will be.

The above method of calculation will not work if in one or other year growth is expressed by a negative rate, say, -4% or zero. The reason is that by multiplying several growth rates by a nonpositive number the product will be either a negative number or zero. But the solution is easy to find. It will be sufficient to add one to the growt rates, a1,a2,   an, which will be expressed as multipliers and afterwards deduct one from the product. In the above example if in the third year we have a decrease of 4%, our calculation wil be: $[1.10*1.25*0.96]^{1/3}-1 =[1.32]^{1/3} = 1.096962 -1 = 9.6921\%$.

The above table is a vivid reminder to investors how important it is to avoid substantial losses of capital. It may be close to impossible to recover from a 50-75% annual loss. Add to that the emotional status of a neophyte investor who has gone through such a devastating experience and the chances are high that the investor will no longer want to hear from stock market investing.

Another lesson for the individual investor with a long-term view is to avoid being too much focused on short-term performance. It is true that nowadays everything is counted on an annual basis or by reference to the annual rhythm. Also, companies report their results annually and even on a quarterly basis if their stocks are publicly traded. This is not a good enough reason for the individual investor to be mesmerized by annual or quarterly results. This said, it is true that even an individual investor should keep track of investment results.

With respect to performance, it may be useful to always calculate the average performance over a number of years, at least three years, preferably 5, in this way making sure that positive and negative results are balanced out. Such average results are more significant than annual or quarterly ones (as they fluctuate less than annual or quarterly ones). Investors should not be obsessed by the objective of beating the benchmark index (often the S&P

500 or for those more focused on small cap companies, the Russell 2000, etc.).

Beating the benchmark is a tall order and to beat it every year is close to impossible. More relevant than beating the benchmark is to focus on absolute performance (as opposed to relative performance compared to a broad-based market index). Such portfolios do have their own objectives, for instance in the form of giving a constant annual return, or giving reasonable assurance against downside risks (especially in economically difficult times). Such portfolios, assuming them to be rather concentrated ones, will more or less certainly underperform the benchmark index in case of very strong markets, but that fact is to be accepted as long as the performance is clearly better than the benchmark in case of serious difficulties like the ones experienced in 2000, 2008 or 2020.

Probabilities

The average investor, just as the public at large, does not have a good grasp of probability calculations. In fact, a correct risk assessment of future events cannot be found in past price movements but can only be based on a reasonable assessment of the future chances of business developments multiplied by the probability of each of the scenarios which might develop in the future. Any type of random event has a "probability distribution" which graphically shows every possible outcome together with the probability it has to occur. If all possible outcomes are known the sum of the probabilities is necessarily 1, a number which cannot be exceeded. A common mistake made by investors is to just focus on the most likely scenario and to disregard all the other ones, just for the reason that they are "unlikely" to realize. Such unlikely events (also called tail events by reference to the configuration of the bell curve) are regularly underestimated at best and in fact just ignored unless if they did happen recently in which case their probability is normally grossly overestimated.

Such approach may be acceptable if we have to do with a normal distribution of events where the low-probability cases are tail events with relatively unimportant outcomes. If however our distribution is not a normal (bell-shaped) distribution, abnormal events cannot be disregarded: despite their low probability, these events may jeopardize our investment survival and they cannot be neglected simply on the basis of their low probability. This is like playing Russian roulette and discarding the event that a bullet may be in the revolver barrel on the grounds that this event is unlikely. Everybody agrees that this would be an unreasonable way to approach the odds of this scenario.

Probability theory as it is taught today has historically developed out of the theory of games played in casinos: casting dice, roulette, different card games, etc. There are a number of important differences which exist between games of chance and stock exchanges, or financial markets in general. In games of chance the number of outcomes is limited: it is known with precision how many outcomes there are and what is the probability of each of them (coin tossing: two outcomes with 0.5 likelihood each (assuming an unbiased coin); casting an unloaded dice: 6 outcomes, with a likelihood of 1/6 each, etc.), for stocks the range of outcomes is unlimited as any stock may increase or decrease by just any amount, as assumed by the "random walk" theory. Furthermore, games in the casino are played for a short time at the end of which the winners and losers are known with mathematical precision. At the stock exchanges the game goes on and on until the company goes bankrupt. It would really end only if all publicly traded companies went bankrupt altogether.

Bayes' Theorem

Reverend Thomas Bayes, a British mathematician formulated this concept in a paper published in 1764, (after his death in 1761): "An Essay Toward Solving a Problem in the Doctrine of Chances." The formula is about conditional probability which requires updating probabilities (which means deviating from the base rates by customizing the calculations).

Let's turn back to the calculations familiar to the professionals of the health sector and construct an example.

A certain type of disease, is harming 0.5% of the population. Tests are available but we have to take into account the following:

99% of tests detect the specific type of disease accurately (genuine positives) for people having the disease,

97% of tests are accurate with respect to people who do not have the disease: this means that 3% of the people who do not have the disease are falsely tested positive (people tested positive but without having the disease)[26].

The question to be answered by Bayes' theorem is the following one: what is the probability of having the disease if the test is positive?

Bayes' formula is:

Prob (D I P) = Prob (D) x Prob (P I D)/ Prob (P)

Prob (D I P) = Probability of D (disease) given (represented by a vertical bar) a positive test (represented by P) equals the probability of having the Disease (Prob (D) * Prob (P I D), the latter being the probability of having a Positive test given the Disease.

Let's assign figures to the letters:

Prob (D) = Probability of having the disease : 0.005 (0.5%; this is the so-called "prior probability", the base rate of prevalence).

Prob (P) = Probability of a positive test: to assess this probability we have to be aware that a positive test may be either a true positive (which means either that a person having the disease is correctly tested positive) OR a false positive (a person not having the disease is tested positively but incorrectly so). We add up these two probabilities: 0.005*0.99 + 0.995*0.03 = 0,00495 + 0.02985 = 0.03480.

So, the result is:

Prob (D I P) = Prob (D) x Prob (P I D)/ Prob (P)

= 0.005*0.99/0.03480 = 0.142857 (or 14.2%).

This example shows that Prob (Disease | test) is not identical for everyone; it is highly dependent on the person concerned. If a person is at high risk for a disease to begin with (say she his been at a hot-spot for Covid-19, say in New Orleans at Mardi Gras of 2020), that information has to be factored in. On the other hand, Prob (test | disease) is the same for everybody regardless of the person concerned.

Normal Distribution

The normal probability curve (also called the "bell curve") represents continuous probability distributions which are very common in the natural sciences as well as in the social sciences. The most important characteristics of the normal distribution are the following ones:

1) Although the number of normal probability curves are infinite they are defined by only 2 parameters, the mean (μ) and the standard variation (σ).

2) The normal curve extends indefinitely to the left and to the right approaching more and more the x axis as it deviates from the high point of the curve.

3) The said high point is at the point where x equals μ (the mean). The various values cluster around the mean of the curve.

4) The standard deviation determines the spread of the curve about its mean. A high standard deviation implies a flatter curve than one with a smaller sigma.

5) It is extremely useful to know that under a normal distribution 68% of the occurrences are comprised within one standard deviation, 95% within two standard deviations and 99.7% within 3 standard deviations.

6) The curve being the graphical representation of a probability distribution the total area under the curve equals 1 and as the curve is symmetric about the mean the area to the left and to the right of the mean equals 0.5 each time.

Very often probability distributions do not exactly follow the normal distribution but they follow it in general terms. For instance, the actual distribution may not be exactly symmetrical. Such non-symmetrical distributions refer to the concept of "skewness", its degree of asymmetry, which measures the degree to which the actual distribution deviates from a totally symmetrical one (which has a skewness of 0). Skewness may be positive or negative. Positive skewness implies that the tail to the right of the distribution is longer or fatter (or both) whereas negative skewness implies the tail to the left is longer and/or fatter than the mode (the value which appears most often). Positive skewness (even if expected returns are negative) are clearly viewed as desirable by most people: think of gambling with very low probability of gaining an outsized prize (lottery).

Negative skewness occurs for instance in cases of low-probability events like floods, hurricanes, earthquakes, fires, etc. Most people will be ready to buy insurance in order to protect themselves against such disasters: as these events are unlikely to occur, the insurance premiums are moderate and allow to protect against high amounts of losses. In terms of statistics the degree to which these exceptional values occur more or less frequently than in a normal distribution is measured by the so-called kurtosis: a high kurtosis corresponds to frequent exceptionally high values also referred to as "fat tails" whereas low kurtosis is assimilated to "thin tails" or to low probability of exceptionally high or low values.

It would be quite convenient if share price movements did obey a normal distribution as described by the classical bell curve. This is however not the case in addition to the fact that price changes are far from being independent one from the other.

The first mathematical analysis of stock market returns was produced by Louis Bachelier, in his 1900 PhD dissertation, called "Théorie de la spéculation." One of the conclusions of his work was that stock returns are statistically independent so that today's returns do not allow to forecast tomorrow's returns. This assumption is still one of the cornerstones of the EMT. However, theory and practice do agree to a large extent that such independence in reality does not exist.

Statistical findings need to be interpreted and unfortunately this is often poorly done. An extremely common and worrying case may be found in the medical world. One might assume that this field, science-driven as it is, would escape this blame. Unfortunately this is not the case. For people not familiar with the health sector it may sound surprising that tests are only accurate to a certain degree but that is reality: there are no tests which are 100% reliable. Furthermore, the interpretation of the results of such tests is rather tricky as we will see hereafter. Tests are open to mistakes on two fronts: either they show false negatives which means that a person actually having a given disease will show a negative test (with the regrettable consequence that no treatment against the disease will be initiated). At the same time, tests may be excessively sensitive and detect the disease where it does not exist in reality: a perfectly healthy person is detected as having the disease, the test having shown a false positive. This time the danger may be that a treatment may be started against a non-existing disease. If the disease is a dangerous one, say cancer, such treatments may have severe collateral damages. These cases lead some health professionals to the statement that unreliable tests are worse than no tests at all.

What is the likelihood a person tested positive actually does have the disease? To answer this question it is needed to consider not probability percentages but absolute figures. Let's say we have a sample of 10,000 people. At a prevalence rate (which corresponds to the so-called base rate) of, say, 0.1% we may easily conclude that 10 people actually do suffer from this disease. Given that the accuracy of the test is 99%, we may assume that the number of persons tested positive will actually be very close to that figure of 10. However, as the available test shows false positives in, by assumption, 5% of the cases, 500 persons will test positive although they do not have the disease. The end result is that we have 10 (real positives) + 500 (false positives) or 510 in total, meaning that the few persons actually having the disease are drowned in the sea of false positives and that the chance that a person having tested positive to actually have had the disease is ... 1.96% only (10/510). This is a quite familiar situation: for rare diseases with tests the large majority of positive tests are false positives.

Although this is a purely theoretical example such situations do occur in reality. The problem is that medical doctors tend to be poorly trained in statistics, point which is confirmed by studies showing that they get it wrong in roughly 80% of the time meaning that a patient tested positive and asking what are his chances to actually have the disease will receive an answer which, by referring to the test accuracy rates, will be somewhat like 95% or 99%, or in other words close to certain. The tragic consequence of this gross interpretation mistake is that a person falsely diagnosed positive will seek treatment for a disease they do not have, treatment which may well have quite serious collateral effects. If however they had known that the correct probability is of only about 2% they would certainly not have taken treatment.

174

In order to avoid such harmful effects, US Preventive Services Task Force, in 2009, recommended that forty-year-old women should, as a general rule, not get annual mammograms as, at that age, a positive test is way more likely to be a false alarm than to detect cancer, and many women were unnecessarily terrified (and got unnecessary treatments as a result): only 3 out of 363 forty-year-old women (0.82%!) who tested positive for breast cancer actually had the disease.

However, if we do know more about the personal situation of an individual case, a test even for a forty-year-old woman might be advisable, say, if her mother died of breast cancer. This process of collecting additional information allows physicians to update the probability of having breast cancer. This is the core tenet of Bayes' Theorem.

One might consider that if a test shows as well false positive as false negatives at the same percentages that the effects of such imperfections would finally even out themselves. This is however not the case. Suppose a test which is 99% reliable meaning it truly shows 99% of the positive cases and 99% shows of the negative cases while testing on infections with a rare disease: only 1 in 10,000 persons have the disease. Assume we have a sample of 1,000,000 individuals which will all be tested. Given the data we have we may conclude that 100 persons (1 in 10,000) actually suffer from this disease. As the test is accurate at the 99% rate it will incorrectly show negative in 1 case in 100. So the test will, on average, underestimate the number of the persons infected by one unit: 99 instead of 100 persons. When moving over to the false positives we will easily note that the effects are significantly larger: 1% false positives means that we will actually have 999,900 persons which are not infected but as false positives represent 1% of that figure, this means that we have 9,999 persons who are wrongly considered as infected, whereas false negatives mean that 1 person suffers of the disease but is falsely tested as negative. This means that as the 1% of false tests is calculated on different bases if it concerns false positives or false negative the effects are not compensating at all.

Investor Psychology and Attitude

"Time is your friend, Impulse your enemy."

John Bogle

Frequently the reason why investors are not successful lies in themselves, in their psychological biases, in their general attitude or in the fact that they are poorly prepared for their task. In a first step I shall deal with psychological aspects.

Growth Mindset versus Fixed Mindset

"The illiterate of the twenty-first century will not be those who cannot read and write, but those who cannot learn, unlearn, and relearn." — Alvin Toffler, author of Future Shock

The notions of "fixed mindset" and "growth mindset" have first been used by Carol Dweck a Stanford University psychologist. Whereas for those who believe in a fixed mindset talent is a given granting those who have it an innate superiority, for those who adhere to a growth mindset it is always possible to improve performance through patient work[27]. Nothing reflects better the growth mindset than Mahatma Gandhi's statement: "Live as if you were to die tomorrow. Learn as if you were to live forever."

A crucial part of the growth mindset is the willingness to learn from one's mistakes. Even if for some people this is a really painful exercise, there is no question that this is an extremely important part of an investor's development.

The smart man learns from his mistakes whereas the wise man learns from the mistakes of others. From this point of view it is certainly better (for being less costly) to be wise than smart. However, the own mistakes, probably because they are so costly, hurt more and for that reason they may teach us a more lasting lesson.

In their excellent book Superforecasting The Art & Science of Prediction, Philip Tetlock and Dan Gardner explain that one of the basics for becoming a good forecaster is to develop a growth mindset meaning that abilities are predominantly the results of effort and that anybody can grow provided they are willing to keep on working and learning. Most people do not have that attitude and believe that one's abilities are more or less a given and can hardly be developed. Needless to say that only those who constantly read and progress have a chance to improve their investing performance.

The capacity to learn from one's own mistakes is definitely one point which distinguishes the successful businessman or investor from the other ones. In the first place, this supposes a clear willingness to learn from such mistakes. Most investors do not show that willingness at all. In case bad decisions have been taken they are inclined to play the blame game, looking for someone responsible for the bad outcome, their advisor, their golf buddy who give this surefire tip, the Fed chairman, the politicians, etc. With such mindset the best advice which could be given to that person would be to abandon investing altogether because the likelihood that this can ever be successful is extremely low.

In a very remarkable book titled "Black Box Thinking: The Surprising Truth About Success" written by Matthew Syed the author notes that in healthcare and the legal profession the willingness to learn from mistakes is somewhat under-developed and the attitude is one of denial, non-transparency and covering-up.

The title of the book (which is somewhat ambiguous[28] as it may suggest to advocate an attitude of non-transparency like a device which workings are mysterious) comes from the airline industry the security record of which is absolutely outstanding and gives an example for any area, whether in business or beyond. If an aircraft accident or other critical incident occurs there is a strict procedure to follow based on transparency and full disclosure of the results of the mandatory consecutive investigation. Learning from failure is hardwired into the system. This starts with the well-known obligation for airplanes to carry two black boxes, recording devices, one of which records all instructions sent to all on-board electronic systems whereas the other one is a cockpit voice recorder which allows investigators to understand what the pilots thought in the moments before the accident happened. If an accident has occurred, investigators who are independent as well of the airlines, as of the regulators and of the pilots unions will seek evidence which will be disclosed the more freely as it cannot be used as evidence in a court procedure. Accidents are not an occasion to stigmatize anyone but simply as an occasion to learn and to do better in the future.

Every accident gives rise to a report which is available not just to the board of directors and the upper management of the firm flying the crashed plane and the aircraft manufacturer but is made available to the whole world: any pilot or journalist in the world has access to the findings of the report.

One may wonder why it is precisely the airline industry which has set in place a safety culture like no other industry. One element is clearly that pilots are easy to incentive for diminishing the number of airline accidents. In case of a medical mistake, the victim will not be the doctor or the medical personnel (but the patient) whereas pilots are directly motivated to eliminate accidents.

Avoid First-Level Thinking

Investors (or maybe speculators) with little or no experience frequently commit the very common mistake to think in the first degree. A company showing good results, or presenting a promising new product (say Apple presenting the iPod, the iPhone or the iPad) will increase its profit substantially; the conclusion is, "I buy the stock." This tactic will not give good results. The reason is obvious: the moment our investor will read this message, the good news is already fully baked into the stock price, and for reasons explained elsewhere, the odds are that the price move has already taken place. These anticipations which are built into stock prices also explain why sometimes companies although showing record quarterly (or yearly) profits and still the stock prices get hurt. This means that the market had anticipated good results, but that they were probably somewhat disappointed by their magnitude (or maybe the outlook for the future).

For this reason investors should take the habit of second-level thinking which consists in analyzing the implications of first-order thinking: as everybody thinks that this is a good company this fact is already incorporated in the price which in fact is too high, so the thing to do may be to sell. First-level thinking, if pervasive enough, creates the conditions for second-level thinking to be successful.

Take the insurance industry. A devastating hurricane which hits the coasts in highly-populated areas will lead to much damage which if insured will hurt the results of insurance/reinsurance companies. First-level thinking leads to the conclusion that such companies should be sold. However, at a second glance, such major disasters do often have more far-reaching consequences which go beyond the results of the quarter of the year when the hurricane occurred. Take 9/11: this devastating disaster happened at a time when competition among insurance companies was intense and insurance premiums were driven down to unsustainable levels. With the New York Twin Towers going down, the consequence was that competition decreased and the cost of insurance cover did increase by 66% from 2000 to 2002 (according to the broker Willis Tower Watson). In other words, if major disasters like hurricanes or the 2019 forest fires in California lead to short-term pain for insurers and reinsurers the medium term effect may be overall very positive as price hikes are easy to justify and are accepted by clients who will find less insurers offering low bids.

As a general rule, any investor should be aware that they will normally be unable to make any significant money on following good or bad news: neither buying on good news, nor selling on bad news will give outstanding results. It is true, however, that some recent studies do conclude to the contrary in the sense that it appears that news are not immediately fully priced in but only over a period of several days after publication of good or bad news. Richard Thaler, the author on behavioral economics and Nobel Prize winner, together with Russell Fuller, has set up an investment fund based on investors' cognitive biases and whose purpose is to buy (or sell) shares not before but after the earnings announcements under the assumption that if the company beats the earnings forecast then the increase in the share price will not happen immediately after the earnings announcement but will spread out at least over several days.

Acting on bad news may, in carefully selected cases, be more promising: given the tendency of Wall Street to exaggerate, bad news may sometimes give a good entry point in case the shares have been beaten down by the markets.

Activity and Patience

"The big money is not in the buying and selling but in the waiting."

Jesse Livermore

"Patience is a virtue, have it if you can. Seldom found in women, never found in men."

Thomas W. Phelps.

Investors should focus on results not on how active or how inactive they are (or their asset manager is). In a famous study Terrance Odean, based on data supplied by an internet brokerage firm, analyzed more than 100,000 stock trades made by individual investors over a period of 15 years, found out that the stocks they bought underperformed the market by 2.7 percentage points whereas those they sold outperformed the market by 0.5 per cent. The conclusion was that investors paid up dearly for their activity, and that even disregarding tax aspects and trading costs they would have been better off by 3.2 percentage points on average if they had just been sitting on their hands doing nothing at all. Other studies come to the same result: a buy and hold strategy would generally benefit investors.

Overtrading is also caused by one of human's most pervasive cognitive biases, namely overconfidence. Peter and Paul, both suffering from overconfidence, will gladly (and confidently) enter into a transaction on a certain stock, as Peter thinks he is smarter than Paul, and Paul believes he is smarter than Peter.

It seems that patience would even have decreased over time at least if we estimate patience by the average stock-holding period: From roughly 6.5 years in the 1950 it has decreased to 1 year and 10 months in the 1990s, to 11 months in 2010. It is true, however, that these average holding periods may be heavily influenced by algorithmic trading.

The public image of the modern Wall Street stock trader is rather more in line with a testosterone-laden male, an action-junky who does one profitable deal after another and turn around their entire portfolio at least once a month if not more often. A good example of this kind of attitude is given by the daily shows on Bloomberg TV or on CNBC where a group of traders (whose portfolios are followed in order to show their monthly and yearly results) explain the different deals they have done over the recent several days.

This representation is actually in line with our dominant cultural conceptions in most areas and certainly in business. Our education system wants to produce young adults who enthusiastically and confidently put their hands on any task, handle it with a pragmatic approach and will bring it to a rapid and successful end. Children are raised in an environment where they are compelled to have a large number of extra-curricular activities in sports, arts, etc. otherwise they will be viewed as non-normal. All this leads to activity-biased adults.

Although this image may comply with public perception, it is not an approach followed (or recommended) by successful investors and certainly not by those from the value investor camp. As George Soros once said: "If investing is entertaining, if you are having fun, you're probably not making any money. Good investing is boring."

Long-term investors will insist on a different approach, namely one based on extreme patience requiring standstill for years before entering into a position and then regardless of the day-to-day fluctuations and the emotional moods of Mr. Market again patiently sit on their hands for years and hopefully even for decades just watching the market values (and intrinsic values) increase.

In fact, this attitude requires more effort than one could think at first glance, only that that kind of activity does not result in market actions. It requires the investors to follow the target company for years and years, to analyse the company not only before purchasing the stock but on an ongoing basis thereafter, its annual and quarterly reports, (its 10-Ks and 10-Qs), its management, its products, its competitive environment, its moats, its strengths and weaknesses, and so on.

This type of investor will have a clear idea of the intrinsic value of the company and hence of its stocks. At the occasion of any quarterly results presentation, this intrinsic value calculation may be adjusted in one way or the other being understood that the result of such a short time period should in no way be overestimated. It is by comparing this intrinsic value with its market value that the investor will decide whether the margin of safety is sufficient to allow them to jump into the water and finally enter into a position in these shares. It is even more important to anticipate changes in the competitive position of a company, changes which may affect its competitive moat and this even before these changes reflect themselves in the company's books. For instance, the effects of e-commerce on traditional retailers, the incidence of sharing companies like Airbnb on the hotel industry, of Uber and Lyft on personal transport business, the incidence of electric and self-driving cars and trucks on traditional automotive car companies and on insurance companies, truck companies, railway companies, etc.

Over the last two decades, trading costs have come down in an impressive way: since the liberalization of brokers fees' (by a Ruling of the SEC dated January 23, 1975 which entered into effect on May 1, 1975) and since the development of the internet the costs at the most important internet brokerage firms have been below $10 per trade. In October 2019 the internet brokerage firm Charles Schwab announced the elimination of all trading commissions (which were charged at $4.95 per trade before their elimination) on all stocks, ETF and base options on all trades placed on US and Canadian exchanges immediately followed by the most important competing firms like Ameritrade, E*Trade, Interactive Brokers, etc. Furthermore, the spread between bid and ask has also been reduced significantly at least for mid- or high-capitalization stocks. This spread will not go to zero as market makers need to be paid for their services. In addition, on US securities markets, SEC regulations impose a minimum spread of one cent per share. Accordingly, transaction costs on securities may nowadays be considered as incidental. Add to this the rapidity at which an investor may sell even significant positions without influencing the price in any substantial way and you have one of the most important advantages of investing in securities. Compare this situation for instance with real estate transactions (where costs are high, and delays extremely long in practice) and you will agree with me on this account.

Unfortunately investors, by and large, do not make proper use of these inestimable advantages of stock markets: its liquidity and its extremely low transaction costs. Instead of just taking the liquidity as a given which allows investors in case they have unforeseen needs of money, they take this liquidity and the low transaction costs as an irresistible invitation to do mindless trading. Furthermore and this is even worse they take the totally erratic prices which are quoted daily as market wisdom.

The issue of transaction costs does not make the top position of the important items of Wall Street professionals but it should be one of the top priorities of investors. Wall Street lives from making money *from* investors (not *for* investors) and it will always downplay the importance of any costs either by simply not mentioning them or qualifying them as incidental. Transaction costs and taxes may be controlled by investors and efficiently reduced by avoiding mindless overtrading.

Know Yourself and Know Your Adversary

As Sun Tzu (The Art of War, p. 14) wrote some 2500 years ago any war commander should know himself and know his adversary. He said: "If you know the enemy and know yourself, you need not fear the result of a hundred battles. If you know yourself but not the enemy, for every victory you will suffer a defeat. If you know neither the enemy nor yourself you will succumb in every battle."

In investing, it may be more important to know yourself than to know the market. The first reason is that markets do change all the time. Investors having their emotions in check will be able to profit from the opportunities offered by Mr. Market.

Investors should make sure that they will not panic once markets go in reverse mode. The easiest way to do so is to analyze how they reacted at the occasion of the last market correction, on occasion of the internet meltdown of 2000 or during the Great Recession of 2008-2009.

Frequency of Transactions and Results

"A lot of shavings do not make a good carpenter."

Unknown

Stock markets are extremely dangerous terrain, in fact they are a minefield where activism is the sure recipe for disaster (just as in a minefield). It is true that Wall Street does view things differently: it is its self-interest to do so. Clearly, Wall Street wants to make money not *for* the investor but *from* the investor, and magnificently succeeds in this endeavor. The intelligent long-term investor resolutely takes the opposite view and reduces to a bare minimum the number of trading decisions.

If at the 1998 Berkshire Hathaway's annual meeting, Warren, Buffett said, "We don't get paid for activity, just for being right", Wall Street is paid for activity not for results which means that the Street professionals have a natural bias to do many trades as opposed to few but successful ones. The fees are collected upfront regardless of the outcome and long before that outcome is actually known. This fact creates a bias in favor of frequent trading where the success of this activity is, at best, of secondary importance only.

Once an investor has reached the target asset allocation (the ideal mix of stocks, fixed income assets, cash, commodities), the question comes up whether this portfolio has to be rebalanced as soon as the portfolio has deviated from the target portfolio. It does appear according to recent research made by Michael Edesess and Andrew Wise there is no clear evidence that rebalancing will beat a buy-and-hold strategy. For some critics, rebalancing relies on the questionable assumption that all securities are cyclical and that they revert to their mean.

However, rebalancing may be beneficial for returning a portfolio to the investor's investment time horizon and risk tolerance. Risk avoidance is the principal goal of rebalancing. My personal view is that on asset allocation questions one should not have dogmatic views, meaning that the proportion of one stock (or of a group of stocks) in a portfolio may vary significantly. A sale or partial sale of a position may occur, or perhaps even should occur if the share price has significantly outgrown its intrinsic value or if a stock shows durable fundamental weaknesses (for example the newspapers industry with the ascent of the internet). The keyword here is significantly: Given all the insecurity which is inherent in any valuation of stocks the rule should be to stay with stocks which have done well.

The prudent long-term investor will trade very little, which as such is a significant advantage in terms of transaction costs. Such transactions costs include brokerage fees (which tend to decrease significantly), the bid-ask spread (for more details please refer to Chapter 4.) and tax costs (taxes on capital gains). This policy will make sure that the portfolio turnover will on average not exceed 0.1 to 0.2 per year (meaning that on average the portfolio will not be turned around more than once over a 5- to 10-year period).

The careful reader will have noted that all this is the exact opposite of what most investors are constantly doing nowadays: even institutional investors will turn around their portfolio roughly once a year (on average), and they will try to time the market (by selling a substantial portion of the portfolio and holding cash positions awaiting a "market correction" of 5 to 10 percent at least). It is undeniable that such market corrections are frequent and that they may be quite substantial. The problem is how to make money out of this situation: if there is one thing on which everybody agrees, it is the difficulty to determine the moment when to get out at "high" prices and the exact moment when to get in again at lower prices. If you succeed once in this endeavor you should not tempt your luck and try to do it a second time because the chances to get away successfully with this game are slim.

To show how successful Wall Street has been in selling the idea to investors that activity is beneficial for investors portfolio a look at average holding periods is very instructive. Whereas in the 1950s the average holding period was roughly 6.5 years this figure had dropped to less than 1 year and 10 months in 1990. By 2000 it was 11 months and by 2010 it was 6.8 months[29]. Those who time the market in this way are not looking at the underlying business but they do consider stock prices as something disconnected from the business which these shares represent.

Contrarian Investor

One prominent school of thought in the investment area is contrarian investing which means that those adhering to this approach buy and sell shares in opposition to the prevailing mood of the market. Contrarian investing at the end of the day is not really an investment doctrine but more like an attitude which avoids herd (or crowd) behavior and in this way avoids some egregious mispricings of stocks.

Contrarian investing does not consist in observing what the majority of traders do and then do the opposite: For instance, if markets are bullish and most participants buy, the contrarian investor would simply sell. Such simplistic approach, which implicitly would seem to assume that markets are always wrong, will not give good results for the reason that markets are not always wrong. In fact markets are mostly right. What a contrarian investment approach means is that investors should follow a highly skeptical approach not run after market trends or chasing stocks. The results of this attitude will for instance be to not buy in a

187

raging bull market (here the market are definitely wrong and getting more wrong by the day) and even more not selling when panic is taking over and everybody runs to the exits.

This behavior applies also to the approach towards certain sectors of the market: If financial stocks are in high demand and if prices are already on the high side a contrarian approach would tend to alleviate on these shares instead of contributing to drive these prices higher.

There is a lot of warmth in the herd. However, as often in investing, what seems to be intuitively correct is the wrong thing to do. If there is general consensus on one thing then it is that following the herd (even if the herd is right) is certainly the wrong thing to do and this point can easily be explained. If everybody is bullish on stocks, the price of these stocks (as those of any asset) have been driven so high that basically there is only one direction left for them: down. Even if the stock price does not go down immediately it remains inevitable that the future yield which may be generated by this asset in the following years will, all things equal, be lower compared to the one obtainable at lower prices. Hence, once again, higher present prices mean not only higher risks but *lower* future returns.

Even if stocks do not correct immediately it may happen that that stock price might very well go nowhere for a decade or so. In such case investors should simply avoid to follow the herd which means they should simply stay on the sidelines. Going one step further, investors may consider not just to abstain from taking a long position but even sell short the stocks: As explained elsewhere (Chapter 6.) this is not my preferred choice but is definitely an option for investors provided they are convinced not only that the shares are overvalued but furthermore that they will correct in relatively short order. As it is objectively difficult to have any assurances in this respect my advice is to simply abstain from shorting at least generally speaking.

Any investor should avoid the current darlings of Wall Street. This is not to say that the darlings may not be good stocks. More often than not they actually are good stocks, even excellent stocks, but that again does not mean they are certain (or even likely) to be good investments. They are good investments only if they are bought at reasonable prices. However, this last condition is clearly not met if the stock is cherished by everybody, which is only another word to say that it is overpriced.

There is no other way to look at the future than by studying the past. The one who does not study history is forced to live it again. All this rearview mirror approach is fine but it will not tell us what the future result of any given company will look like. Nobody will drive a car by looking exclusively in the rear view mirror.

Whether one refers to contrarian investing or to the EMT, stock market reality is somewhat more complex. It may safely be stated that by always following the dominant fad the investor will NOT get rich. The reasons for this conclusion are obvious: The investor who buys the latest fad will pay premium prices which means that the upside of these stocks is limited (whereas the downside risk is considerable which leads to an extremely unfavorable risk/reward relationship). Even worse, and especially if the momentum to the upside has been very strong, following the trend might lead the investor to sell low, after having bought high, as has happened for many investors when the internet bubble had burst.

The question in how far markets are efficient is very much debated. Academia claims that they are, meaning that any information which is publicly available will immediately be reflected in share prices. The consequence is that it is pointless to try to "beat the market." Although few people will still claim that markets are *always* efficient, most people tend to consider that although markets are often irrational this does not mean that one could invest on the premise that markets are always wrong. Markets are mostly right; such was the case when the internet bubble has finally burst starting in March 2000 and also in 2008 when after the market indices have been cut in half (and even more for the NASDAQ), investors finally started buying shares again and this at fire sale prices.

As Benjamin Graham put it: "You're neither right nor wrong because the crowd disagrees with you. You are right because your data and reasoning are right."

The challenge for investors is to think independently, meaning that they need to have the courage to take a position against the consensus view and at the same time to know when the consensus view is the right one and should be followed. Needless to say that from time to time even the best investor will make errors at this game.

Further to one study dating back to 1985 by De Bondt and Thaler on the so-called winner-loser effect, investors are excessively optimistic on past winners and excessively pessimistic on past losers. As a result, those past extreme losers (defined as stocks classified in the lowest tenth percentile during the previous 3 years) are under-valued whereas past winners (stocks in the highest tenth percentile over the last 3 years) are over-valued. As shown by their study, the situations of mispricing are not permanent and tend to be reversed: over a 5-year period past losers will clearly outperform past winners as shown by De Bondt and Thaler.

At its core value investing is contrarian investing for the reason that the key tenet of that investment strategy is to invest with a margin of safety. Such margin of safety cannot exist if the stocks bought are the current darlings of Wall Street. In order to find such stocks allowing for such margin of safety the investor has to look somewhere else.

Michael B. O'Higgins related that on reading the Saturdays newspapers back in October 1983 he noticed that 7 publications showed headlines announcing the bankruptcy of the airline industry. On the following Monday he purchased 4 airline stocks whose value increased 57%, on average, over the following 15-month period.

A contrarian approach is also advisable with respect to emerging markets. As the Financial Times reported on June 26th, 2019 John Dehn, head of research at Ashmore the British investment manager a contrarian approach based on media headlines of 33.000 publications over 20 years; the researcher found out that buying at times when negative media coverage on emerging markets was highest would have generated excess annual returns of 10% beyond the normal profits of 4.1% produced by an approach which consists simply in investing the same amounts constantly and ignoring media. The conclusion of Dehn was that media exaggerate bad news whereas investors extrapolate problems in a few countries to the whole EM world with the consequence that periodic sell-outs create buying opportunities.

Investors' Market Preparedness

Any investor, before starting to trade, should have carefully thought of the investment philosophy at the roots of their market strategy. Said investment philosophy could for instance consist in trading shares as a day trader, based on charts, or buying the 3 lowest performing stocks of the Dow Jones Index during the previous year. Alternatively, it could be a value investment approach buying undervalued securities, with a margin of safety, to be held for the long run.

Whatever their philosophy, investors should be consistent in their approach and avoid to amalgamate different styles for the reason that those styles have an inherent logic which could be seriously challenged if non-compatible elements were combined.

Whatever the philosophy followed, investors will have to answer the following questions: what types of assets they will invest in (asset allocation and in which proportions), in which markets, how frequently they will trade, how to select their positions, when to sell, etc.

In this respect investors could decide to be only long in stocks, or only short (which I would not advise), or be opportunistic which would allow them to follow the market conditions and get into short trades once the market gets seriously overvalued. A lot of other investment philosophies are available. But in any case, if there is one thing investors should never do, it is to allow themselves to be drifted along by the media and follow the latest fad. They should also refrain from changing their strategy once they think they lag behind the market (this is what is called FOMO, Fear of Missing Out or that other strategies generate better results. Such changing of strategy is potentially disastrous.

Of course, most investors come to investing without giving much thought to these questions. They do not cogitate about investment philosophy, strategy, etc. but do just get started as soon as the brokerage account is open and duly funded.

As Warren, Buffett puts it, excitement and expenses are the enemies of the stock investor. The fact that expenses are harmful to performance does not need belaboring. Excitement is the enemy of any investor as soon as real money is on the line. In the Introduction (under Paradoxes of Stock Markets) this aspect has been analyzed in more detail. "If investing is entertaining, if you are having fun, you're probably not making any money. Good investing is boring," as George Soros had put it.

Emotions are in most cases the single strongest obstacle preventing investors from being successful. Investors typically do have exactly the wrong mindset with respect to fluctuations of stock prices. Instead of selling when prices correct they should resist that impulse and either sit out the price correction and even better, buy additional shares, but without doing so blindly. Conversely, in case of a strong increase in prices they should resist greed and avoid getting carried away by their excitement.

As soon as the average investor has identified a stock which they consider as having above average potential they think they have to get it, come hell or high water, which means they will purchase it at any cost. Very often, the real reason for identifying this specific stock is at the end of the day that it has increased substantially in a very short period of time. Buying this stock under these circumstances is the first step to financial disaster. It is an unavoidable fact that our investor will generally overpay and inevitably the share price will correct somewhere in the future. (Even if they get out with a gain, the return will be seriously lower than the one they could have obtained if they had waited for a moment when prices are weak, i.e. for a moment where the stock is out of favor. Given that our investor did not have very solid reasons for buying the share in the first place (they never analyzed the fundamentals of the company), it happens all the time that they will sell the share again for the wrong reason, namely for the reason that the share price did correct. This leads to a very common result but harmful result: buy high, sell low.

Plan Your Play and Play Your Plan

"If you fail to plan you are planning to fail."

Benjamin Franklin

Take the situation at the turn of the 20th century when traditional companies (e.g. consumer staples) where totally out of favor and were sold out and replaced by stocks of companies belonging to the so-called "New Economy", a tragic misnomer. The worst thing to do was what many (if not most!) investors have actually done, i.e. to sell out their "blue chip" investments (at already depressed prices) only in order to purchase companies of the New Economy at inflated prices. (This was another example for an unpleasant experience many investors go through namely to be wrong twice in case of a change of stocks: sell a winner and buy a loser).

It is undeniable that the most representative companies of the New Economy did actually have a huge impact on the lives of everybody (just take the internet or social media).

193

But what has been forgotten in the hype over the New Economy was that the past major technological advances tended to benefit the consumers more than they benefited investors. This was not something new but it was a repetition of what had happened previously for other technological breakthroughs namely the railroads, the car industry, the airlines... All of these innovations have been great for consumers, but hardly for the companies involved, neither for their stockholders.

Any investor needs two qualities: patience and the emotional capacity to suffer (book) losses. As Warren Buffett rightly stated, if you are not able to suffer that the value of your shares is divided in half then you do not belong in this game. This statement needs some comments: it does not mean that, in any case you should quietly watch your stock prices tumble and be divided by two or three. It is possible to be as sanguine about share price fluctuations only if at the start, on buying the stock, you have bought under sound principles, for instance under value investing principles. If so, you have closely analyzed the fundamentals of the company and bought with a margin of safety. Any investor should take comfort in the fact that if their principles are sound, the market will eventually turn to their favor. The alternative (all too often followed) consists in selling the shares at a very bad moment and to invest in something else.

Assuming that the fundamentals have not changed (or at least not substantially changed for the worse) since the purchase of the shares, you are ill-advised to sell in panic when the share price drops considerably. To the contrary and assuming you control your emotions at a time when all around you doom and gloom dominate, you may consider that this is a great opportunity to add to your position.

The above quoted Buffett statement also implies that value investors do not use stop loss orders, the objective of which is to limit losses. This strategy is often recommended by advisors or traders. Such stop loss orders trigger a sale at market prices if a certain price is reached. For instance, you are buying Intel shares at $54.5 and place a stop loss order at $50. If Intel shares drop to $50 (or below), a market order is triggered meaning that the shares are sold at market price. It may be that the sale takes place at $49.98 or at a slightly lower amount. In case of very bad news like a profit warning, it may well occur that the actual price at which the sale is made will be substantially lower than the limit price indicated by the seller, for instance only at $48.33 in the preceding example.

If for value investors (having studied the fundamentals and investing for the long term) the use of stop loss orders does not make sense, the situation may be completely different for a chart trader: having no clue whatsoever what the shares are actually worth, and having purchased without any margin of safety it is certainly good advice to at least avoid catastrophic permanent losses of capital, by a loss-limitation strategy, which can indeed be achieved by the use of stop loss orders.

Another point to stress here is that investors should stick to one method of investment only and furthermore they should not blend elements of different methods. For instance, if any given investor decides to act as a day trader giving their buy and sell orders based on chart signals, oscillators, etc. they should do so and not pyramid down (meaning in case of a drop in price buy additional shares). In this way, they avoid confirming the old saying: "double-up, triple-up, belly-up."

Again, developing a solid and trustworthy strategy will take time, several years as a minimum. Before doing any purchase of shares the investor should first very thoroughly reflect on what they intend to do in the market. What asset classes they will invest in (stocks, bonds, the respective proportions of the two), what are their goals, what is their time horizon and above all what investment approach proper she will use. Whatever the results of this thinking process may be, it is important that once conclusions have been reached, the methods adopted will not be changed, at least not without good reasons.

So, the first thing to do is to choose one investment strategy and to stick to it (even if temporarily it seems that it does not work or at least not work out for you). Any investor should be aware that there is no such thing as a method which will always work and be superior to all or any other methods all the time. Even investment systems which provenly have worked in the past for very long periods tend to lose their edge once they get widely known and followed by too many investors. The market continuously follows fads which means that during one period a certain type of investments is favored whereas on another occasion another one is in the pole position. In such moments, comfort may only be found in the fundamentals of the underlying business: if it continues to grow, the balance sheets gets more solid by the year, maybe the dividend payments increase consistently, the vagaries of the stock exchanges are always unpredictable and as sure as spring follows winter the Wall Street favorites change with time and often sooner than one thinks.

The different aspects of such strategy should be given a lot of thought, they should be analyzed from a theoretical point of view and of course also from their practical side, their implementation. It is of primary importance that the philosophy designed for themselves suits their temperament. If it doesn't, they will most certainly not be able to stick to it through thick and thin. They should at least mentally consider how their philosophy will perform and how they will react once the currently prevailing conditions will change and will give rise to either a bull market (even going to bubble territory) or more importantly, what they will do when the markets go through a very serious contraction as was the case in 2008-2009 when the financial crisis was raging.

Of course, when looking at old stock charts, it is easy to figure out how one should have reacted back in 1999-2000 and 2008-2009. There is no guarantee that in real life one's behavior will correspond to these intentions. Reality of a market crash is a lot worse than most investors are able to figure out from the outset. Most people will overestimate their standing power in the face of hardship: it is extremely tough to see one's life savings melt away like snow in spring over months and months, if not years. Are you really sure that if the market which has touched an all-time high 15 months ago and in the meantime has lost 40 per cent (and your portfolio even 50%), you will be able to stand still and you will not run out and sell a substantial part of your remaining portfolio? Most investors are unable to just sit it out.

No investment strategy is cast in stone forever, but it has to develop over time. Securities markets change, the investor also changes and their attitudes are always evolving but with all flexibility they should cultivate they should never chase the latest fad.

When the facts change, the investor cannot just ignore this and do as if all this were just a temporary aberration. Any investment decision is a wager on the future of a company, of a product, of a market, etc. That such forecasts are wrong from time to time goes without saying. It is pure stubbornness to do as if such forecasts were always right: in fact they are typically wrong at least on some points. Such changes in the forecast scenario cannot be ignored or discussed away and they will have to be taken into consideration by at least minor adjustments with regard to the investments made. This mean that the investment decisions have to be reconsidered. The calculations have to be redone and possibly some investment decisions will have to be reversed.

Fundamental changes to the investment philosophy should be only few and far between but adjustments to the policy are absolutely vital. Nobody in the investment world has a longer-term view and a stronger investment approach than Warren, Buffett. He adheres to this so-called value investment doctrine with very few and simple tenets: buying companies (or their stocks) in a simple and understandable business, with a significant moat around their castle, with able and honest management, at a sensible price, i.e. with a good margin of safety. This philosophy has been taken over from his mentor Benjamin Graham but not without having been significantly changed over the years. The most important change has been that whereas Graham was buying a very diversified portfolio of companies with net currents assets reduced by all of the company's debts higher than prices, Buffett, also under the influence of Charlie Monger, did put a higher weight on moats (competitive advantage of the business as often evidenced by a strong brand), was willing to pay higher prices than Graham would have considered as acceptable and favored more concentrated investments. In this development the investment in See's Candies (a fully owned subsidiary acquired in 1972 for $25 million) and the investment in 400,000,000 shares (9.2 per cent in 2016) of the shares of The Coca Cola Company were important steps in the fine-tuning of their investment philosophy. See's Candy had sales of $30 million and a profit of $4.2 million. According to Warren, Buffett, in 2007 sales had increased to $383 million with profits of $82 million. To say that See's Candy yields every year more than three times the money it cost, as some market commentators do, is falling prey to the money illusion. Based on the official inflation figures 1$ in 1972 is equivalent to $4.91 in 2007. Accordingly, the annual inflation-corrected (by the CPI) profit would be $16.7 million (in $ of 1972) which still represents an annual yield of 66.8%. In the same time Berkshire Hathaway, although having tried for decades now, has never been successful to scale the business of See's Candy over the whole of the US. It simply did not work (which once again shows the point on which Warren Buffett has repeatedly insisted heavily, namely that retail has its one rules which are not always easy to understand but still have to be reckoned with).

The importance of moats is that they act as a weapon against reversion to the mean. Let's assume that a certain company has an attractive gross margin. Unless that company has a "moat" in one form or another it is unlikely to profit from these higher margins for a long time. This phenomenon is due to market forces meaning additional competitors will invest in this business or existing competitors will offer improved goods simply by imitating the strategies of their more successful competitor. Erosion of the profit margin may be avoided if the company has a moat for instance if it is a low-cost producer which has a lasting competitive advantage which is more difficult to be taken away.

Typically, the neophyte investor is attracted to the stock market by accident. Before they know it, they have an account with an internet broker charging low amounts in fees (nowadays this generally means no brokerage fees at all). Once they have funded their account, they are eager to get into the market by buying stocks. Excitement overwhelms them, especially if the prices of their stock selections increase. Very quickly they will be "fully invested", the investment decisions being based on the news headlines or on the stock recommendations of one or the other market commentator or analyst.

This sequence of events is typical and at the same time unfortunate, as in all likelihood it translates into financial disaster. It is very likely that our investors have overpaid for their investments (the principal reason being that most investor are attracted to the market at the very wrong moment, i.e. when the markets are booming and stock prices are already heavily inflated) and when the inevitable market correction occurs, they will sell out their shares and finally start to reflect on the decision-taking process and frequently they will try another approach. Maybe their next step will be to study charts. If this does not give good results, they will try another foolproof way to riches, maybe buy options, invest in gold, trade commodities or foreign currencies.

Formalization of The Investment Policy

It is highly advisable for investors to take the time to draft an "Investment Policy Statement" (IPS) summarizing in a short paper of maybe 1 or 2 pages their investment strategy addressing the purpose of the portfolio, the investment horizon, the expectations, the criteria of selection, diversification policy, and state a number of "don'ts." The fact to write down something always has very special and in fact unexplainable merits: not only that it forces the writer to thoroughly think over the subject but it also greatly increases the intensity of their commitment to the substance of the statement.

Periodically reviewing this statement does allow the investor to verify whether or not they are still in harmony with the particulars set out therein. If so, this is fine. If not, and if there is "style drift" they should reflect on the question whether their behavior should be amended or whether the IPS should be changed.

The latter solution is certainly acceptable but it should not happen all the time, otherwise the IPS has probably not been sufficiently thought over at the start, or the investors are (too) versatile in their approach. In any case, the IPS should be well thought of and it should not result in important trading volume. Activism is harmful to any investor's portfolio, not only in terms of trading fees and taxes paid (those two points treated in Chapter 4. are, or should be, obvious) but also in terms of not being invested at the right moments and last but not least in terms of emotional energy which is lost by continuously buying and selling stocks.

Keeping Track of Investments

Any business (beyond the one of a microscopic size) is based on keeping proper accounts, not just for complying with tax and accounting laws and regulations but more importantly to allow the entrepreneur to keep track of their investments, their obligations (debt payments) and to assess their performance as objectively as possible. Similarly for an investor it is important to know how much they have gained (or lost) over a given period. Portfolio statements are useful to track the allocation of assets to different asset classes, to different sectors, countries, currencies, etc.

Such assessments on a periodical basis are useful to see whether one makes money or loses money in absolute terms and in relative terms, that is to say when comparing to market indices which may serve as a benchmark. This is far from saying investor should be obsessed by such comparisons: the obsession to "beat the market" is one of the favorite games of Wall Street. It should not be the same for the individual investor. Depending on their investment objectives, investors may perfectly accept to lag the market indices.

Nowadays, keeping track of one's investments is extremely simple, at least for investors having an online account and especially so if they have only one such account. In such case, logging in to this account will give all information needed to be fully informed on the situation of one's investments and this on a real-time basis. The situation is different for investors having accounts with different brokers and/or banks. In such case an app is needed to consolidate those different accounts into one.

Unfortunately in 2017 Google Finance has stopped its Portfolio Feature to be available for investors, Yahoo Finance, although less performing than the one Google Finance was offering in the past, is a reasonable cost-free alternative. Internet brokers render the same services by continuously supplying the total value of the portfolio to their clients.

Any investor when assessing their portfolio composed of a large number of shares is well advised to base their judgment on the figures as shown by data supplied by their brokers and not on their gut feelings. There is a high likelihood that their gut feelings make them think that their performance is significantly better than it actually is. This is the result of some cognitive biases which are part of our human heritage. For that reason we may trust that they will still be around in the near and not so near future.

Keeping track of investments should in no way trigger a burst of activity. If, for instance, you note that you're lagging behind all the indices over the last quarter, this should not now lead to panic transactions consisting in turning around half of your assets in favor of other hopefully better performing stocks. Such reactions are ill-advised and they would just result in giving away what is probably the biggest advantage of the individual self-directed investor, namely not having to pursue short-term performance goals (like monthly or quarterly results).

With respect to investor performance the whole is more important than its parts, meaning that what counts is not that 30% of your positions are in the red (showing losses compared to the acquisition price) but what counts is that overall the portfolio shows a gain in line with your investment strategy and somewhere in line with the market indices not day by day or quarter by quarter but over a long period, of several years at least.

Cherry-picking by bragging on your ten-baggers on a tiny position is nice for the small-talk at cocktail parties but irrelevant for the performance assessment of your portfolio or of your investment strategy.

Technology and Change

A long-term investor is confronted with major difficulties in the technology sector. The problem is that that this sector, with all the blessings it brings to society at large, is changing extremely fast. Long-term competitive advantages which have been built up over decades and on which people counted to continue for an extended period do not seem to exist. The dominant rule is rapid and disruptive change. Just consider what happened to Nokia and RIM (Research in Motion the manufacturer of Blackberry), two of the dominant players in the mobile handheld device area at the time Apple launched the iPhone (in 2007). Both companies were reduced to irrelevance in a very short time. The new dominant players became Apple and Samsung (with its Google supported Android operating system). Nobody knows how long this domination of the smartphone sector by these two companies will last. What has happened to Nokia and RIM may be the future for Apple or Samsung or both of them once another disruptive technology is launched by a competitor. Similar examples may be found practically in every sector of high technology.

Another example for this relentless change is given by the semiconductors industry. The semiconductors industry is ruled by Moore's Law (named after Gordon Moore, together with Robert Noyce co-founder of Intel Corp.) according to which the capacity of computer chips doubles every 18 to 24 months. This breakneck speed requires the competitors to invest heavily in R&D in order to allow to place ever increasing numbers of transistors on the same surface of silicon and to put in place the corresponding production facilities to produce the newest generation of chips.

According to the Financial Tmes of December 30, 2019 productivity of research is falling: the economy has to double its research efforts every 13 years just to maintain the same overall rate of economic growth. More specifically concerning Moore's Law, in order to keep the speed up, eighteen times as many researchers are needed as in the early 1970s.

It also means that at a given moment Intel is not only working on the next generation of chips to be shipped in a year but already the following one planned to be launched in about three years and also on the third generation to be launched in maybe 4 to 5 years from now only.

In 2019 the Swiss watch industry sold 21 million watches (a 13% decline) outsold by the Apple Watch which was only launched 5 years ago with close to 31 million watches an increase of 36%. Even if the Swiss industry as a whole generates more revenue ($21 bn compared to $11 bn) that could also invert in a few years' time given the opposing respective trajectories these products face.

Compare these relentless and brutally disruptive changes in technology to the extremely slow speed of change applicable in more traditional sectors of the economy, for instance in the beverage sector. The Coca Cola Company (KO), although it has added a long list of products over the twentieth century, most of its profit still comes from a product which has already existed in the same form on the date the company went public in 1919, a century ago. In order to stay competitive, no need to spend heavily on R&D or to retool the factories every 2 or 3 years: by the way such need does not exist at all for KO as the factories are owned by the bottlers generally distinct entities from The Coca Cola Company.

What is mentioned here for Coca Cola does apply for any beverage company: a machine once installed can be used until it is worn out which means after some 8 to 12 years. Even if the end product is slightly changed (which does not happen frequently), such change does not require any meaningful change on the production level. Furthermore there is not much room for major changes on that level: machines are anyway already fully automatized and human intervention is only needed for supervision and troubleshooting purposes.

Once bottling has taken place, the product has to be shipped to the client by putting the product on a truck and deliver it manually to the premises of the client. Also at that level there is little room for major changes: the internet will not disrupt the production and supply chain. The bottom line is that change, if it takes place at all, is slow and very gradual. There is no risk whatsoever that a new product will render obsolete from one day to the next the products supplied by The Coca Cola Company or the way these products are manufactured and delivered to the customer in the same way as the iPhone did render obsolete the mobile phones sold by Nokia and Blackberry.

Investors should be highly aware of these differences (and others) which exist between different business sectors. The fundamental economics of one business sector compared to those of other ones are hugely different. It is far from irrelevant whether an investment is made in the one or in the other one. These business economics are rather stable over time although it cannot be ruled out that one sector characterized so far by relative stability will in the future not be subject to an abruptly increase in the speed of change. As examples consider the sector of taxis (UBER and LYFT being the most important agents of change), Airbnb for the hotel sector or, in the oil and gas exploration sector, the fracking revolution (for technological changes in the areas of hydraulic fracturing and of horizontal drilling have allow the exploitation of oil and gas reserves which formerly could not be exploited, or at least could not be so on economic terms.) Likewise, newspapers represented an extremely interesting business sector for investors, attracting a considerable amount of advertising dollars combined with only low capital expenditure. These business economics have fundamentally deteriorated over the last 30 years during which period people turned to the internet for supplying news: correlatively advertisement dollars increasingly found their way to the internet search firms and social media.

If a company is active in a sector with bad economics (for instance for the reason that the rate of change is extremely high or that excessive capacities put pressure on prices), these conditions apply to all competitors of this sector. This means that all companies face the same headwinds. The investor may now select those companies that are doing best in coping with this situation. However, the question is raised whether the investor may not be well advised to avoid such sector(s) altogether. It is not doubtful that such bad economics will have an impact on the rate of return which the investor may reasonable expect from their investment and also perhaps more important even, it will directly have a significant impact on the degree of risk of the investment: A high rate of change is synonymous with increased risk of serious financial problems up to bankruptcy of the company.

The question whether the investor should not stay clear of the technology sector is valid for one other important reason: the technology sector (including new media) for a very large proportion of investors companies like Apple, Facebook, Google are glamorous, modern, sexy, cool whereas companies like Coca Cola, 3M, Johnson & Johnson are old-fashioned, boring. As such, these perceptions could be disregarded as being just an aspect of free speech. However, if many investors think this way it is likely that the shares of these fashionable companies are overbought and the prices high compared to their intrinsic value. This is exactly and provenly the case. Peter Lynch was one of those who favored such no-growth industries and especially so if the company had a silly name, with a repugnant activity and located in a place difficult to access, in one word those type of companies shunned by Wall Street analysts. Peter Lynch/John Rothchild, One Up on Wall Street, p. 131

Buffett consistently says that he avoids the technology sector for the reason he does not understand technology. In my view, what in fact he wants to say is that nobody understands the technology sector. There is no arguing about the fact that there are several thousand of persons in silicon valley and elsewhere having done their whole career in this sector and who, for that reason have a better knowledge about the newest trends and their implications than the most diligent investor outside of this sector may ever have, but that does not mean much: investing is about the future and forecasting which company will prevail. For the lay investor it is very naïve to think that they, unlike Buffett, understand technology. A lot of investors view this point differently as can be seen on various message boards on the internet.

It is however noteworthy that the technological sector (say, the internet) like other business sectors go through a cycle of quick growth followed by a period of maturity. At the beginning there are a large number of competitors and it is very difficult to know which ones will ultimately be the winners and the losers. At least in the developed countries (say, the US, Western Europe and Japan) this period of strong growth is largely over in the field of the internet and social media; in those sectors market visibility has increased a lot: it is a bet with low odds to say that the winners are Amazon (in e-commerce), Google (in search) and Facebook (social media). It is basically certain that these companies will continue to dominate the said areas mentioned between brackets. This does not exclude that other companies may prosper as well in the said fields but in all likelihood they will have a hard stand against the industry behemoths mentioned here. For start-up companies active in the areas covered by the megacap technology companies of the likes of Amazon, Apple, Alphabet, Facebook, Microsoft, etc. do have huge hurdles to overcome: in the first place, if they have anything interesting to offer they will be turnover target of the incumbent megacap companies mentioned above. The cost of such take-overs, say a $1 bn is really peanuts for the said companies. If they refuse to be taken over they are exposed to quite stiff competitive behavior pushing them either to accept the offer or to get them out of business. In a number of court cases all over the world this reckless behavior is disclosed. Another hurdle is that obtaining financing by such start-up companies competing with the technology behemoths is extremely difficult as the venture capitalists' policy is not to finance such companies given that they do not consider it likely that they will eventually be able to successfully compete with such powerful companies.

Base Rate

The so-called "base rate" (also known as "prior probability" under Bayesian Probabilities) tells us how often something normally occurs without taking into consideration any facts of the concrete case. So, for example, if in a certain town 5,100 people out of 10,000 are female, then the base rate for being female is 51 per cent. Any randomly assembled group of people meeting in this town may be expected to be composed of females in that proportion. This concept can refer to any characteristic of any specified group.

The concept of base rate tells us that intelligent people (or, let's say rational people) do not gamble, gambling being a loser's game: The base rate (or the odds) are in favor of the House which means the gamblers' expected value is not nil but negative.

Applied to the stock market, base rates tell us what to expect from a certain class of stocks (e.g., all stocks with high dividend yields) and what that variable generally predicts for the future.

Base rate neglect, which is considered as a cognitive bias means that base rates are correctly taken into consideration only in the absence of precise data. If such basic data is completed by colorful but largely irrelevant information then people think their exceptionally deep insights allow them to disregard the base rates and to come to their own conclusions which will ignore those base rates.

This attitude of investors is very useful for those analysts who want to talk up our down a given stock. They need a nice story to explain why a stock is a buy at a P/E ratio of 150. Base rates heavily go against such investment to be a good buy.

However, the so-called narrative fallacy is a reminder that what sticks is the narrative not the statistics: the story will generally trump the base rate. A rational investor will always take the base rate into account and as a principle will only invest if the base rate is in their favor. The base rate for IPO's is that in 80 percent of the cases stocks bought at the moment of the IPO will underperform. Similarly, stocks with high P/E ratios will also underperform most of the time. This said, investors are free to bet against the base rate but they should always be aware of that rate and bear in mind that they should not neglect it lightly and only go against the base rate if they do have really good reasons. In the long run, the base rate should prevail (just as the casino will win over any longer time period if you wonder why this is so: it is due to the base rate…).

Another example taken from the investment management world: generally speaking stock prices do increase on average by about 7% per year (in real terms). Hence, a trader who decides to short stocks is going against the base rate. This does not mean that they should always refrain from shorting stocks but in any case they should be able to explain why in a specific case the base rate will not prevail.

It is a fact that a number of studies have found that so-called base rate neglect is extremely common in practice. This is for instance the case for the book of Philip Tetlock, Superforcasters (cf. Chapter 3.).

The case rate, as opposed to the base rate, is the actual rate applying after taking into consideration the concrete facts and circumstances of the precise case. Investors should start with the base rate and make their initial forecasts on that basis. Of course, the facts and circumstances of the case at hand do have to be taken into consideration in a second step. This may then lead to an adjustment to be made to the base rate in the sense that it will either be increased or decreased.

Short-Term Price Fluctuations

It is undeniable that stock prices do not always reflect the intrinsic value of stocks. In other words, prolonged periods of over-valuation and under-valuations are extremely common: this statement applies as well for individual stocks as for broad market indices which reflect the prices of large numbers of stocks: in such cases market commentators will state that markets are grossly undervalued or overvalued.

Managers of companies are interested to see stock prices grow and this at least for two reasons: firstly, if the company wants to increase their share capital via the issue of new stocks then the dilution of existing shareholders will be minimized. Secondly, if a company wants to acquire other companies and if it intends to use own shares as currency for those acquisitions then the fact that the currency with which the purchase is paid being high, the consequence is that for existing shareholder dilution is reduced.

The long-term oriented investor does not really care about short-term market price fluctuations. As explained in Chapter 2., they have taken care that they will never be in a situation where they have to sell their assets in order to provide for their living expenses or those of their families. Once that last condition is met, long-term investors who know the intrinsic value of their stocks do not complain if the stock prices linger for extended periods. Regardless of what

Wall Street preaches, such depressed prices do have a number of advantages, namely:

1) They allow investors to get in at lower prices, which, all things equal, will lead to higher yields over the long term;

2) If the company concerned buys back stocks, the number of stocks which can be bought back with a given amount of capital increases which will increase the number of shares outstanding and automatically increase the value of one share of that company;

3) As management's compensation is generally fixed as a function of the company's stock price, high stock prices mean, all things equal, higher costs which decrease the share of profits available for investors.

Market Fluctuations

When assessing your own decisions, you can be either over-indulgent or over-demanding. Of course, when a market after having made a new historical high mark, tanks and loses 12 to 15 per cent, you might think that not selling a substantial part of your assets at the market high mark (or close to that mark) was a mistake. This is not the right kind of reasoning to follow. Nobody is able to time the market successfully over years and investors are definitely excused if they do not even try to do so.

Issuers of market newsletters are constantly bragging with all the events they (allegedly) have called. A smart investor should just ignore such newsletters as being totally unprofessional. Indeed, calling such corrections and being consistently right is simply not possible, and furthermore is in no way needed to be an outstanding investor. Some people, or better some crooks, go a long way to convince the gullible public of their investing skills. The scheme goes as follows: a stock recommendation prediction is sent to a large number of targets, say 500: half of the addressees receive the forecast a certain stock, say, Amazon will go up, the other half get the opposite forecast. If the stock did a big move those who received the correct forecast will again be split into two halves the one receiving a prediction on, say, Tesla stocks, going up the other one it will go down, etc. Those having received the wrong forecast will be dropped and will never hear again from the forecaster. After a number of repetitions of this game this scheme has singled out a group of individuals, those having received half a dozen of correct forecasts, who are convinced the issuer of those recommendations is a stock market genius and, on request, they are ready to trust him a lot of funds, funds they will never see again. For investor this example is a vivid reminder to not suspend their disbelief if they are confronted with persons claiming to be able to forecasts stock price fluctuations (whether they concern individual stocks or market indices).

Market corrections are part of the game and investors should just disregard them: as long as they have carefully selected their investments and as long as the underlying businesses produce good results, maybe pay a decent dividend, which is sustainable for being covered by a low payout ratio as well as by a stable business, there is no reason to panic. The company's business is just going on to prosper (albeit with some fluctuations) and will earn as much money as it did during the time when its stocks showed new highs every day. The long-term investor should either consider these corrections as non-events or, and especially if they have the necessary dry powder, use them as occasions to buy in at lower rates, by investing any available cash and maybe even by incurring some debt (provided the interest rate is low, the overall debt level is moderate and finally that there is a reasonable chance that the debt may be reimbursed over a short period, say one year, by means other than the selling of shares, for instance, future dividends or new funds coming from other sources).

Uncertainty

In the stock market anything may happen at any time. Put another way: nobody has any certainty on what the markets may do the next day or the next year. Anybody who claims to know what will happen are charlatans. However, this is far from being a negative, fatalistic or even defeatist statement. As markets are unforeseeable, they will always offer unforeseen opportunities (in addition to unforeseen risks!). More often than one thinks the shares of first-class companies will strongly correct either for no (apparent) reason at all or they correct in an excessive or disproportionate way when compared to the actual incidence the news recently disclosed may have on the intrinsic value of the business and its stocks. For instance, Wall Street has a considerable dislike for litigation and the decline of the securities' price may be out of all proportion to the merits of the case initiated against the company.

Uncertainty is often a reason why prices may represent interesting buying opportunities. Wall Street hates uncertainty: this means that if some news comes out which hangs over a company's stock (say an SEC investigation on its accounting practices or a court case initiated by a competitor) the market often corrects in an excessive way. This creates opportunities for those investor who do not run with the herd to the exits, who do their own assessment of the risks and will be able to buy at rock-bottom prices which will quickly correct once the markets find out that the correction was excessive. As an example one may take Buffett taking a participation in American Express at the time of the so-called salad oil (or soybean oil) scandal in 1963.

A dangerous case is the one where the shares correct violently without any news or only trivial news. In such case, investors should be extremely cautious and not enter into any position before they know what is going on. The "market" (or better: some investors) may know something which has not (yet) been published by the media. Maybe a hedge fund is massively shorting the stock, which they will only let the public know after having built up their full position of the shares (and at the latest when they publish their quarterly earnings statement or 13F statement). An example of such situation is the famous short raid of Pershing Square the hedge fund managed by Bill Ackman on the Herbalife shares. During 2013 the shares of Herbalife (HLF) tanked for months without any obvious reason. As was known later on, the reason for the decrease in the value of the shares has been that the hedge fund Pershing Square had taken a massive short position in HLF. Another similar case has been the UK hedge fund Prescient shorting the shares of Chicago Bridge & Iron (CBI) before announcing their thesis that CBI had committed accounting fraud.

Generally, however, the reason for which a stock corrects are quite obvious (or they seem to be so): some news has come out and as a reaction to this news the share price adjusts. The most obvious reason (which concerns any publicly traded company) is the quarterly earnings publication. Either the average earnings forecast given by the community of analysts following a given stock is met, it is missed or it is beaten. The earnings announcements are typically made out of the opening hours of the stock exchange, i.e. either before 9 30 a.m., or shortly after the closing time, meaning after 4 p.m. E.T. The reason is that in this way investors have at least some time to digest the numbers before acting by trading the shares: in fact this restriction does only apply to large, generally institutional investors, for whom the volume during the afterhours trading will not be sufficient to trade at reasonably satisfying conditions. This will also give them the opportunity to first dial in to the earnings call which typically takes place at 4 30 or 5 p.m. (ET) i.e. very shortly after the earnings announcement has been made by the company.

This delay between the announcement of the quarterly (or annual) results and the moment the shares can be traded does of course not guarantee in any way that the ensuing price changes of the share are commen**surate with the results annou**nced. Far from it! If any proof of the emotional character of the market is needed, it can be seen here. The reactions to earnings announcements is literally immediate or instantaneous and generally extremely violent: the stock soars or tanks in the afterhours trading by a significant margin even before anybody has been able to fully read the entire earnings announcement made by the company.

Another noteworthy point and which very often puzzles neophyte investors is the fact that often the reaction of the stock exchange seems counter-intuitive. It happens that the so-called consensus estimate is beaten and the share price drops or that the earnings forecasts are missed and still stock prices increase or do not move. The reason for such reactions, which at first glance seem nonsensical, is that a certain result is priced in. This means that the market does expect a certain amount of profit, and that the so-called consensus estimate ("the Street expects a profit of 11 cents per share and a quarterly revenue of $1.842 bn") which is used as a benchmark is not necessarily what the market has priced in.

One important lesson from this is that investors only make real money on the stock exchange if they <u>know something the market does not know</u>. This is obviously the reason why the activity of company insiders is followed closely by many market participants. The assumption is that, notwithstanding all efforts made over the last century with respect to information disclosure to all market participants at the same time, there are still unavoidable information asymmetries, meaning insiders do know things, and act on such things, which are not disclosed or which are not disclosed yet.

What is the real reason for mispricing of stocks following some events? The real reason lies in human nature which does not change (and will never change) and more particularly in its emotional character.

It is true of course that nowadays a substantial share of the trading on the large stock exchanges is in fact no longer done by humans but by algorithms using artificial intelligence. It will be interesting to see over the next years when algorithmic trading will certainly develop further, whether markets will become more or less volatile. At first glance, it would appear that as robots lack emotions less volatility could be the consequence. However up till now it would seem that such is not the case and that the relevant algorithms take any news at its face value and for instance on negative news simply sell off their long positions.

Investors suffer from numerous cognitive biases which have important impacts on their market behaviors. These biases are dealt with at another place.

It should also be noted that prices (and hence price moves) do not necessarily reflect the majority view of all the shareholders of the company at a given moment. Prices are made by the small minority of people who buy and sell the shares on a given day. The percentage of shares traded on any day varies from one day to the other (low volume during summer months for instance) and more importantly even from one company to the other. One may estimate that on average per day 0.1-1 per cent of the shares of a company are traded. As the number of shares traded during the day are published for each company it is easy for each investor to calculate the ratio for the companies they follow.

Like time and volatility, uncertainty is one of the investor's best friends. Uncertainty means shares can be bought at an undemanding price. The reason for such uncertainty can be manifold, for instance a rare earning's miss (the uncertainty resides in the fact that investors do not know whether this is a one-time accident or the first step of a downward spiral), the company is in the middle of a restructuring process, it is in the process of a merger, a major acquisition or a spin-off is in the making.

"What everybody knows isn't worth knowing." Joe Granville.

This statement has to be taken with a lot of salt. It is obviously true that nobody can make any money with information which is widely known as it will simply be priced in. However, if such information cannot make money it will still be possible to lose a lot of money by not knowing what everybody else is knowing. As an example take the Herbalife saga where hedge funds had sold short a large proportion of shares of the company. It would certainly have been interesting to know the rational on which this short sales have been based, namely that Herbalife might be viewed as a pyramid scheme and as such could be declared illegal by the US Federal Trade Commission (FTC) as was the thesis of Bill Ackman and his hedge fund Pershing Square. As we all know in the meantime this thesis was not confirmed by investigations made by the FTC (Federal Trade Commission) but still it has led to a long-lasting decrease in the stock price of the company concerned.

Outcomes of Decisions and Time Horizon

When investors assess the quality of their decisions they should always proceed to an honest and unbiased *post mortem* analysis and they should not forget that their assessment will highly depend on the moment at which the assessment is made. Assume that an investor has sold their Microsoft position on August 23, 2013 at a price of $35.20 (the high of the day). After the steep rise due to the announcement that Steve Ballmer resigns. At that moment the stock increased! by more than 7 percent from $31.61 to $34.20 (by the way making Steve Ballmer, owner of 333 million Microsoft shares richer by 778 million US$) only to fall back to the 31.5 level at the beginning of September 2013. Looking at the stock charts in September 2013 the investor may rightly consider that their decision to get out was a smart one. However, if they had another look at the Microsoft chart in March 2014 they would have to admit that her decision was not that smart after all, given that the shares have blasted by her sale's price: on March 20th 2014 the share price easily took the $40 hurdle a price level it hadn't seen for more than a decade. At that moment the assessment of the decision to sell would be different and it can only be rated as not a smart decision (at least when judged with respect to the share price). As we all know by July 2020 the stock price exceeds $200. What may initially appear a smart (dumb) decision may later on be viewed as the opposite only again to be reversed later on, etc.

By the way, it is not correct to assess those decisions only on the basis of the following evolution of the stock market prices: although largely used in the media, the only merit of that method is that it is easy to apply. It may well be that the stock is either beaten down or bloated up due to irrational market behavior influenced by fear or greed. Furthermore, a decision may give good results but still be a bad decision: this is for instance the fact if inconsiderate risks have been taken when the decision was executed.

Long-term investors know that the stock market is not a reliable guide on the value of shares, and that its only purpose is (or better should be) to be their servant, supplying liquidity by allowing them to buy and sell stocks.

Depending on their investment philosophy, the time horizon of investors will greatly vary: from minutes, to hours, to days, to one or two years, to one or several decades, and finally to the famous "forever" of Buffett (who gave that answer when asked what his favorite holding period was). Depending on one's time horizon an investment in the shares of a given company may either be a bullish bet on the perspectives of a company (for the long term investor) or meaningless (for the chart investor or other daytraders)

Quality of Decisions

Investors should concentrate more on the quality of their behavior than on their results. In other words, they should privilege process over outcome. The reason is that outcome is to a very large extent beyond their control whereas process is not. Investors having very limited experience should be aware that they are at the beginning of a more or less lifelong learning process. In his book Outliers, Malcom Gladwell concludes that in order to dominate a complicated skill a human being needs roughly 10,000 hours of practice. Disregarding any differences which may exist between the various activities researched by the said author it is obvious that the said amount of hours of practice cannot be accumulated in less than 5 to 10 years at least.

It is a fact that most people seriously underestimate the difficulties involved in investing. The reason is that this activity is simple which is far from meaning that it would be easy: it may be practiced by any adolescent who has been endowed with a brokerage account by their uncle as a Christmas gift. A crash course in the basic trading activity will allow that schoolboy to claim to be an investor after a minimum training period, falsely believing that the difficult part of it is to select and buy a number of different stocks. The said adolescent will have ample time to find out later on that the real difficulties start when the markets go in reverse mode and when their portfolio financed with "real money" shows losses over an extended period of time whereas nobody so far has warned him that this is a frequent reality.

In investing (as in many other areas) there is no automatic connection between quality of decision and outcome. This means that a bad decision may have a good outcome just as a good decision may have a bad outcome.

The following table shows all the existing possibilities.

Case	Quality of decision	Outcome
1.	Good	Good
2.	Bad	Bad
3.	Good	Bad
4.	Bad	Good

Whereas cases 1. and 2. do not create problems as the result is "fair", this is not so for cases 3. and 4. which are in fact very misleading (and which may be seen as "inconsistent situations") for the reason that inexperienced investors, if they frequently experience these situations, may tend to erroneously conclude that there is no connection between quality of decision and outcome and hence they may be led to follow a wrong track. If their decisions have been successful two or three times in a row (by pure luck and possibly helped by the fact that the stocks are in bull market mode), they may easily be led to believe that they have found a water-proof system to make money, lots of it. However, if there are few things of which we can be sure, we can count on the fact that bad decision-taking will sooner or later produce bad results. The results of decisions based on luck only will doubtlessly revert to the mean.

Unfortunately, this learning process, which most investors will go through in their investment life, is very expensive. Once again, it is more efficient, for being more cost saving, to learn from other people's mistakes than to learn from the own ones. As Eleanor Roosevelt put it: 'Learn from the mistakes of others. You can't live long enough to make them all yourself.'"

Hence, the advice to study as much investment literature as possible covering the experiences of other investors: the price of books is very incidental compared to the sums which may gained (and especially be lost) in the markets in a very short period of time.

It will not come as a surprise that investors should build on solid grounds and not fall for the "How-To-Get-Rich-Quickly" schemes: there are sufficient good authors available in order not be led on wrong tracks by those who are not worth your money and/or of what is even more precious, your time.

The lesson to be learned is: concentrate on process not on outcomes. Once again, process, like costs and taxes, is one of the few things investors can control. They cannot control the outcome (i.e. the stock price). By concentrating on process, investors improve their odds, and eventually they will become better investors although they will never completely rule out what was called here above the "inconsistent situations" especially of the type number 3: good process followed by bad outcome. Just as in tennis, the objective is to increase the ratio of successful operations even only marginally (which is known by the term "percentage tennis") which may lead to a significant improvement of the results.

Consolation may be found in the saying that investing is more art than science and/or that mistakes are part of the game.

Smart investors, when assessing the quality of an asset manager do not just look at the results (for instance if a manager has beaten the market, say the S&P 500 by 10%) then they will not take this as conclusive evidence in itself but they will "look under the hood" in order to identify how this results was obtained. For instance if an asset manager does hold 80% of their portfolio in 3 FAANG stocks then in most of the recent years they would have shown excellent results but these results could have been different and are attributable to luck for a large part. Such concentrated portfolio could easily show bad results in case FAANG stocks would fall out of favor, for instance for reason of anti-trust pressures.

The situation described here is similar to the one experienced by Bill Miller, asset manager of Legg Mason.

He achieved cult status by showing excellent and market-beating returns over 15-year period from 1990 to 2005. He lost heavily during the great recession of 2008 and had very volatile performance since then, showing a 120% gain in 2019. Although renowned as a value investors he did over all these years invest a significant part of the assets under his management in technology stocks.

Value of Forecasts

"Often in error, never in doubt", correctly describes the behavior of many forecasters in financial markets.

The August 1979 Business Week issue opened with the following cover story: "The Death of Equities." The article started with the following sentence: "The masses long ago switched from stocks to investments having higher yields and more protection from inflation… The death of equities looks like an almost permanent condition – reversible someday, but not soon." The said article preceded the market revival signaling with a comfortable previous notice the greatest bull market in history. At the moment the cover story was published, the moment of maximum pessimism was reached: all the sellers having left ship and the market couldn't do anything else but reverse.

Some twenty years later, in January 2000 Business Week's cover story dealt with "The New Economy" defending the absurd valuations of Technology Stocks which allegedly were part of a new normal.

These articles, and others which made it to the cover pages of business magazines over the last decades, which have proven to become real embarrassments for their publishers, are nowadays viewed as representing a first-class contrary indicator of the forthcoming trends or events.

Studies made with reference to GDP forecasts show how consensus forecasts never get the extremes and they always forecast a middle ground. The same results occur when the forecasts concern stock prices or per share earnings. The problem is that it is at the extreme that the big money is gained or lost.

Whether we like it or not, investing is about forecasting the future not about studying the past. The standard warning "past results do not guarantee future performance" is there to remind us of this reality. In this sense it is fair to say that good investors are made not born.

This means that efforts to improve our forecasting abilities are potentially extremely helpful and that slight improvements in this respect may have a high multiplier effect on the investment results. Tetlock has set up a program which is available to anybody (see www.goodjugment.com) and which allows participants to make forecasts which consist in precise questions with a fixed deadline, the objective being that a feedback is possible allowing the forecasters to assess how well they have been performing. It is clear that some forecasts are so vague and not limited in time so that it is very difficult to ever call the forecast wrong. Take for instance the forecast that hyper inflation will be the result of past and present stimulus packages. Such forecasts if made without a precise timeline will allow the forecaster (who apparently has been wrong) to claim forever that it has not yet happened. Compare this situation with weather forecasting, where forecasts concern generally very short periods of say 24 hours, and several days as a maximum and are always tied to a certain clearly defined area: if the forecast was wrong, the forecaster will know it within 24 hours at a time when everybody still clearly remembers the forecast. The result is that weather forecasters are not those who suffer from overconfidence. In the realm of investing the problem is not so much that forecasts are not limited by precise deadlines but that the forecasters tend to make countless forecast without keeping score of the accuracy of their past attempts.

If forecasters are not held liable for their numerous wrong past forecasts they are obviously strongly motivated to make many forecasts: By doing so, they are sure to be right many times which they will not refrain from recalling to their audience (even if their past record overall is actually disastrous).

The media, instead of keeping track of the past record of the forecasters, are always happy to give a stage to an "expert" who speaks with confidence and tells us why the income from Apple iPhone 5 will soon break away and why TESLA shares will soon reach $5,000. Imagine such bold statements to be accompanied by a scrolling line stating that the currently talking expert over the latest 5 years has been wrong 82% of the time.

The point which I want to drive home here is not that these forecasts will be wrong. If I said that, I would do precisely the same thing for which I am blaming those forecasters here, namely that many of these forecasted things are UNKNOWABLES and forecasters should not do as if they knew: instead of knowing something they are just guessing which is far from being the same.

Chapter 4: Financial Markets

Let me start with explaining the concept of "efficient market" which is the dogma of many investing scholars although heavily criticized by market professionals as well as by some academicians.

Efficient Market Theory

In the 1960's this theory (sometimes called the "Efficient Market Hypothesis", EMH) has first been proposed by Eugene Fama (of the Chicago University) and it is based essentially on the assumption that securities at any moment in time are correctly priced as the price-fixing mechanism takes into account all available information so that it is impossible to "beat the market" by selecting certain stocks. In an efficient market, stock prices fluctuate on the basis of new information, which as it is either favorable or unfavorable follows a so-called random walk itinerary which is totally unpredictable. As with reference to market expectations news are randomly positive or negative the implications for stock prices is that their changes are random as well: this is the random walk also called the "drunkard walk" which took his origins in the statistics classes. Applied to finance, the implications of the random walk theory are that as stocks follow such a random walk adding one random daily step to those of prior days it is impossible to forecast future market moves which do not follow any forecastable pattern and hence cannot be predicted for instance based on past moves. The random walk theory is one of the cornerstones of the efficient market theory.

Under these assumptions, market outperformance can only be due to luck (just as in any coin-tossing competition some participants will have a better performance than others, which outperformance may however be explained only by luck). This point is proven by the fact that if the same competition is repeated a number of times the winners are certainly going to change. If they do not change at all or if they only change slightly (as would be the case in tennis, chess, or bridge), this would be more than a hint that luck is involved only marginally.

It needs to be stressed that in the eyes of their more reasonable defenders the EMT does not mean that markets are always fully efficient. In the eyes of Eugene Fama, one of the most notorious proponents of this theory, market efficiency is a continuum meaning that securities markets are more or less efficient, this degree of efficiency being dependent on the one hand on the number, the quality and the capital intensity of the "arbitrageurs" i.e. those market actors who endeavor to all the time correct market inefficiencies by profiting from over- and undervaluations of the markets or of individual securities. One of the decisive factors of market efficiency is that transaction costs, including the cost of information concerning stocks, are low. On this point it may safely be stated that the efficiency of stock markets has enormously increased over the last 20-30 year period especially as the internet developed. Information has never been so available (and especially available in an equal and non-distortive way) at no cost or very low cost, as it is now. This transaction cost advantage is huge, especially when compared to other asset classes like real estate characterized by very high transaction costs and also by the fact that in some asset classes assets are not fungible at all. If you buy Apple common stocks you will easily find out that there is only one class of such Apple stocks and regardless of who is the seller or who is the intermediary intervening in the operation you can really be certain that any share representing a partial ownership of this more than $2 trillion company has exactly the same rights as any other of the 4.3 billion shares outstanding. No due diligence is needed to confirm that fact. Compare that situation to buying a house, in addition to the high transaction costs and cumbersome regulations, each and every real estate item is different and requires its own research to analyse whether the price quoted is acceptable or not. (Needless to say that the same is true for other asset classes like works of arts, antiques, expensive wines, etc.)

In fairness it must be stated that the efficient market hypothesis does not mean that markets can never be wrong. Efficient is not synonymous with all-knowing. At a certain moment, markets may have estimated the Fed will increase interest rate by 0.25%. On the announcement made by the Fed to keep interest rates stable stock prices will soar. This correction is not an argument that stock markets would be inefficient. The problem however is that is difficult to consistently profit from such market mistakes.

Furthermore, the fact that some investors are outperforming the market is not inconsistent with the market efficiency theory. The real difficulty is again to determine which investors will be able to outperform the markets *in the future*. As decade-long experience in the investment fund industry shows in a convincing way, relying on past performance does simply not work. To the contrary: as the star managers of yesteryear revert to the mean by falling in the rankings of fund managers, they have attracted record additional capital amounts from those investors who relied on those favorable past rankings. (Incidentally, the fact to have to invest significantly higher capital amounts represents an additional reason for the fund manager to do worse than they did in the past.)

Although the efficient market theory is still predominantly taught in business schools, it is heavily criticized by market practice and also by a growing number of academicians.

Indeed, market practice shows numerous examples of inefficiently priced securities which tend to indicate that stock markets are certainly not efficient all the time, and even worse that markets can be irrational for very long periods of time. Just three very well knows examples of obvious market inefficiencies.

1) In June 1989, "The Spain Fund Inc." (a closed-end Fund seeking long-term capital appreciation in Spanish equity securities), sold at 92 percent of NAV, an 8 percent discount whereas three months later the shares traded at more than 260 percent of NAV (!) and remained at more than twice NAV until February 1990. Any investor could have bought the shares held by The Spain Fund at market prices and have built exactly the same portfolio without having to pay any premium to market prices (let alone one amounting to 160% of those market prices).

2) A similar example of market inefficiency may be found in the internet bubble area in 1999-2000. 3Com, a company active in the area of networking of computers, had acquired all the shares of Palm, producer of a so-called handheld computer called Palm Pilot. Although the business of 3Com was profitable, its share price did not really advance so that in summer 1999 the company decided to spin-off Palm. This was done through a public offering by which 5% of the shares of Palm were sold on the market, the remaining 95% being retained by 3Com. The next step was that the 95%-shareholding would be distributed to 3Com shareholders at the ratio of 1.5 Palm shares for one 3Com share. As of the separate listing of Palm shares, each 3Com shareholder could consider (for each share held) to own two assets: 1.5 shares in Palm and one share in the remaining 3Com operations. The interesting part of this story lies in the relative level of share prices. The day the spin-off of Palm was announced, the 3Com shares were traded at $40 a share. On the IPO the price of Palm was set at $38 a share but this price quickly increased to $95 as soon as the stock

began to trade. What was the price of a 3Com share? As mentioned above, any holder of such shares, in addition to holding a part of the 3Com business did own 1.5 shares of Palm. In other words, a 3Com share was worth at least $143 to be increased by a share of the 3Com business. Mr. Market did not come to that conclusion and the 3Com share price declined to a level of $82 with the unavoidable conclusion that the value of the (profitable) 3Com business was negative in the magnitude of some $23 billion. Although this valuation discrepancy was extensively covered by the media, it took several months before it was more or less corrected by the markets.

3) Another example challenging the validity of the EMH is the crash of Monday October 19[th,] 1987 when stock prices dived all around the world, starting with the Asian markets, then followed by Europe and finally by the US markets. The US markets shed more than 20% of their value and this without any significant financial, economic or political news justifying this move. For Yale economist Robert Shiller, Black Monday was just a further proof that the EMT was "the most remarkable error in the history of economic theory. This is just another nail in the coffin."

One of the principal implications of the EMT is that "the price is always right", meaning that is is impossible to beat the market as all relevant information is immediately incorporated in price moves so that cheap stocks (or expensive stocks) do not exist. This statement is totally incompatible with value investing. Indeed if the price were always right than there could be no margin of safety and no value investing. As Buffett once quipped: "I'd be a bum on the street with a tin cup if markets were always efficient."

The EMT is also a dangerous theory: if markets are efficient and if accordingly the price is always right, then there is no reason to act against market incorrections like bubbles (or assumed bubbles). One interesting point here is that Grossmann and Stiglitz [30] argued that perfectly efficient markets from an informational point of view are impossible as the return on research on collecting such information would be zero and trading would make no sense with the consequence that markets would eventually collapse. This reasoning does not appear absolutely water-proof as there may be other possibilities: what if the return of research on collecting information were actually zero (or even negative) and through good salesmanship these researches were able to convince investors that they are actually adding value, say beating the benchmark index by more than the amount of their fees? It is only after the fact, when it is too late, that investors discover that the promises made were not kept.

At the basis of the EMT lies the assumption of the rational investor, consistently maximizing their profits and in pursuit of this objective always arbitraging away any discrepancies which might (temporarily) affect securities prices. Unfortunately this assumption of the rational market operator (the *Homo economicus*) is not credible or at least is an ideal (an approximation) which suffers numerous exceptions.

Behavioral economics did undertake the task to check these assumptions of rational, calculating subjects as provided for by classical economics. One of their numerous tests was the "Ultimatum test" which involves 2 participants. A receives a certain amount of money, say, $100 which he has to share with B in any way he likes, even keeping the full amount to himself. B may either accept the proposed division or reject it. In this second case none of both players receives anything. Experience shows that very low offers are in all likelihood rejected as unfair with the result that, generally speaking, A does not even propose such unbalanced offers and that often A proposes at least a third to B.

These results seem to conflict with classical economic theory which would require B to accept very low offers of say $1 as by accepting such a low offer he would still be better off than by rejecting it outright.

Countless studies show that market operators are often behaving very irrationally, in other words emotionally: instead of following their own research they follow the herd and base their market moves on research heavily influenced by cognitive biases.

One of the tenets of the EMT is that any information generally available is immediately fully taken into consideration and priced into share prices. This point is not confirmed by the so-called "Post-Recommendation Drift", which refers to the fact commonly observed that if an analyst changes their recommendation this change does not only have an immediate effect on the stock price (in the sense suggested by the change in recommendation) but will exercise an impact for a significant period thereafter, say, of several trading days at least.

Recently the EMH received a surprise blessing from an unlikely authority, the US judiciary. A Delaware Chancery court in a case initiated by a plaintiff called Verition Partners Master Fund Ltd. and Verition Multi-strategy Fund Ltd. v. Aruba Networks, Inc. argued that the price paid by Hewlett Packard for the stock of Aruba Networks was insufficient as the fair value was $32.57 per share. Vice Chancellor J. Travis Laster decided that on the occasion of the acquisition of Aruba Networks the fair value was just $17.13 instead of the $24.73 Hewlett Packard had paid. How did the court determine the fair value price? The judgement explained that it based itself on the EMH, holding that the price at which the stock trading before the acquisition of the company reflected its fair value adding that "the efficient market theory is generally a more reliable assessment of fair value than the view of a single analyst." The fair value was the 30-day moving average before the deal was announced. However, on March 27, 2020 the Delaware Supreme Court reversed the Chancery court's decision. While the unaffected share price may give an informative view of fair value it does not represent an irrefutable measure of it. In the process of acquisition, corporations conducting a due diligence in which non-public information is disclosed may well reach a different amount of fair value which may include a premium compared to the unaffected market price. Finally, the Supreme Court overthrew the first instanced judgement by upholding the traditional Delaware case law which for strategic buyers consists in deducting the synergies from the deal price when determining the price to be paid to dissenters which claimed that the price paid to shareholders of the target company was insufficient to be considered as a fair price. Hence, the blessing received by the EMT from the US judiciary was only short lived.

The question may be asked whether the collection of the very large number of traders which daily operate on financial markets are not to be seen as collectively representing the wisdom of crowds?

Wisdom of Crowds

This subject has been treated in James Surowiecki's well-known book, "The Wisdom of Crowds: Why the Many Are Smarter Than the Few and How Collective Wisdom Shapes Business, Economies, Societies and Nations," published in 2004. It is a fact that under the right circumstances crowds can be remarkably intelligent and are often smarter than its smartest members. This finding contradicts previously held beliefs that groups are only as smart as the most stupid of its members. As the above mentioned book explains, in order to benefit from this wisdom, a number of conditions need to be met, namely, diversity of opinion, independence, decentralization, aggregation, and trust. It is beyond doubt that these conditions are not fulfilled by today's stock market: especially diversity of opinion as well as independence are not really met as opinions are heavily influenced by the media, by analysts and other opinion makers. This again confirms a classical finding in finance, namely that markets are not a weighing matching but a voting machine.

Reversion to the Mean

Quoting Horace, Graham/Dodd on the opening page of their "Security Analysis" 1934 edition, "Many shall be restored that now are fallen and many shall fall that now are in honor" insisting in this way on the changing fortunes which affect companies, entire businesses, fund managers, etc.

This phenomenon of "reversion to the mean" known for a long time already (first discovered towards the end of the 19th century by the English scientist, anthropologist, mathematician and eugenicist Francis Galton, half-cousin of Charles Darwin) who among other things, analyzed the statistical data on the height of children of extremely tall parents and he found out that on average they have children who are taller than average but smaller than themselves. Similarly extremely small parents do have children who are taller than them but still smaller than average.

In nature, a common observation made already centuries ago is the phenomenon of reversion (or regression) to the mean, which means that the average acts as an anchor pulling down higher values and pulling up lower than average values. Regression to the mean basically means that "on average extremes do not survive."

This phenomenon is not restricted to genetics but it may be observed as soon as repeated measurements are taken, meaning it will also apply in financial markets. Concretely, it means for instance that very high ratings have just one way to go, namely down. Statistically speaking it is more correct to say that such high rates are more likely to decrease than to increase, just as it is more likely that in a very hot summer extremely high temperature days will be followed by a day of lower temperature.

The rule of reversion to the mean is full of applications in the investing area: a company with high growth rates (say

20-25%) will not sustain this break-neck speed for decades. Sooner or later growth will decelerate. If high growth rates just kept on increasing, the fast-growing company would sooner or later be bigger than its industry or even the national economy…

This rule is not entirely symmetrical as lower than average rates cannot be deemed to always revert to average rates: indeed a company may go bust and the rates go to zero instead of going up to the average.

Fund managers who beat the market for a number of years by high margins are extremely likely to fall back to average rates. Many investors follow closely fund managers' performances on an annual or even quarterly basis. Those who are doing well in these comparisons will see the funds entrusted to them grow rapidly. The problem with this strategy is that those fund managers who have deviated considerably from the mean for several years will, generally speaking, revert to the mean very quickly again (and the more so as their capital basis grows rapidly making it much more difficult to outperform the market indices and so becoming victims of their own success). This means that if an investor whose investment fund had for the last two years missed its benchmark index (say the S&P 500) switches to another fund who over the same period has beaten this same S&P 500 index it may happen that that new manager's performance now drops considerably (his past performance was to a good part attributable to luck) so that he now has also sub-average returns: here again switching carries the risk of being wrong twice.

The result is that investors who follow assets managers' performances are typically always too late if they are betting on those managers who recently have had outstanding performances. It would appear that a more promising strategy would be to invest with those managers which over the past decade(s) have had a decent record but with a below average recent performance, which on the basis of the mean reversion principle will, in all likelihood, improve again in the near future. (Alternatively, investors who do not want to change managers very frequently may of course just sit out periods of below average performance of their managers counting on the reversion to the mean principle especially if his investment performance over a medium and long-term period has been decent.)

Some authors (for instance Michael J. Maubouissin) explain that reversion to the mean is the more reliable as the role played by luck is more important. If the game played is exclusively a gamble (say roulette in a casino) the player who has had a winning streak is assured to fall down to average (or very close to it). If the game played is a game of skill, (or predominantly a game of skill, like chess or tennis) the stronger players will always have a record which will be way above average and they are in fact unlikely to revert to that average. Investment is not a pure game of skill and luck undeniably plays a substantial part. This explains why reversion to the mean is heavily involved in assessing the performance of asset managers (as undeniably luck is involved when outstanding performances are involved).

Reversion to the mean is sometimes interpreted in the way that if recent results have been substantially above average it would mean that future results would have to fall below average. For instance, if fund managers have outperformed the markets for a period of 3 to 5 years, regression to the mean would require that during the following year the rate would be below average. This view is in the first place not covered by the semantics of the discussed phenomenon: it is called regression to the mean and not regression *below* the mean (or *above* the mean). It is easy to see where this interpretation comes from, namely from the so-called gambler's fallacy. If in a casino roulette is played and if 5 times in a row the color red comes up people tend to believe that the sixth time black is due and that the likelihood of red is higher than 50%. People tend to consider that the number of reds and blacks will be roughly the same if the game is played even only a small number of times. So the reasoning is that if in the first part of a series the color black has been preponderant this would mean that in the second part red will catch up as at the end the two colors would come out even: that assumption is obviously a wrong one.

Readers should be aware of the fact that if investor sentiment will directly have an impact on markets the reverse is true as well: strong price moves will impact on investor's mood. Nowadays everything is measured, and investor sentiment (as measured for instance by the so-called Bullishness Index reflecting the sentiments of writers of market newsletters) is no exception. After markets have gone up, bullishness increases, in this way creating a self-reinforcing mechanism which is prone to the development of market bubbles.

As could be observed during the end of the 1990s and beginning of the 2000s, after a long period of price hikes, investor totally abandon the view that prices should be somewhere connected to intrinsic value of the business. Conversely, in case of a market correction and even more so in a bear market (20% decrease at least) bearishness increases which leads to further market losses and regularly to underpricing compared to intrinsic value and in this way creating opportunities for investors who are able to resist the herd instinct. However, the Bullishness Index does not tell us what the market will be doing next but nevertheless being aware of the relations between sentiment and market moves may be helpful to investors.

It might be so that reversion to the mean is stronger in areas involving human behavior. In the context of the dire predictions made by the Club of Rome in the 1970 Barbara Buchanan commented: "The doomsayers work by extrapolation; they take a trend and extend it, forgetting that the doom factor sooner or later generates a coping mechanism... you cannot extrapolate any series in which the human element intrudes; history, that is the human narrative, never follows and will always foil the scientific curve."

Market Bubbles and "This Time Is Different"

One of the distinctive characteristics of market bubbles is that many commentators claim that the prevailing high valuations are fully justified because of one or the other variation on the theme: 'this time is different'. However, when the bubble eventually bursts, the conclusion is that in fact the situation was not at all different than what was occurring in all previous market bubbles. This rule should not be extended beyond its real scope of validity; in fact it is based on human behavior and human nature. It is a fair assumption (confirmed by historic events) that these human characteristics do not change over centuries. But it is less certain whether this maxim may be extended to other areas of economics and finance or even to technology. Technological innovation is precisely about changing things and once an innovative technology is out, things are different than what they used to be.

The problem with bubbles is its timing: If at the first signs of high valuations (or better, "perceived" high valuations) investors get out of the market, then they miss a big part of the stock value increases. In the current bull market they would have been out of the markets probably already since 2015. At the end of 2015 the DJIA was at 17,600 and the S&P 500 at 2,060.

Is there any chance to assess whether current stock markets prices at a given moment in time are so high that they entered into bubble territory so that the only reasonable choice is to exit the market? This is rather tricky and hard and fast reliable rules are not easy to find.

Still, it is sometimes possible to spot the signals of unsustainable growth. As the dot-com bubble grew in the late 1990s, a common justification for rising prices was the claim that internet traffic was doubling every 100 days. This explained why infrastructure companies were being valued at hundreds of billions of dollars and investors were pouring money into internet providers like WorldCom. But it was soon found out that these forecasts were wild exaggerations[31].

Behavioral Finance

In 2002 Daniel Kahnemann, although a trained psychologist, received a Nobel Memorial Prize in Economic Sciences (shared with Vernon L. Smith) for his work in behavioral economics. According to his findings as described in his seminal book "Thinking Fast and Slow" (published in 2011), humans tend to use two distinct modes of thinking namely our automatic and intuitive mind, named System 1 (think fast) and our more controlled analytical mind named System 2 (think slow). Whereas System 1 allows us to take quick and effortless decisions gives good results in current everyday situations it quite frequently gets us into trouble in a world where a number of different variables are involved when quick and intuitive reactions may lead us to do severe mistakes. In such situations, System 2 thinking is needed. This same distinction was later on taken on by another Nobel Prize laureate, Richard Thaler, who only used different names namely Automatic System, for System 1 and Reflective System for System 2.[32]

Investing is about estimating future developments which is nothing else than forecasting uncertain events. In this task, humans make use of heuristics (rules of thumb or mental shortcuts or simple and efficient rules allowing for quick decisions) which are meant to reduce the complicated task of assessing probabilities and quantifying values. Whereas such simplification is generally helpful in our day-to-day life it also leads us to commit serious mistakes.

The thinking of us humans is plagued with an impressive number of cognitive biases which do handicap us considerably in the decision-making process and unavoidingly lead to decisions of poor quality. When we take a decision, we get excessively influenced by the immediate examples coming to our mind (availability heuristic). If shortly after a major disaster occurred somewhere on earth (say the March 11, 2011 tsunami in Japan doubled by the Fukushima nuclear disaster then people asked how much they are afraid of such a nuclear catastrophe will immediately think of this incident and will consider that such event is way more dangerous than other causes of death say car accidents or even more so domestic accidents: the reason is that such accidents although happening all the time are not as immediately present as the more publicized and accordingly more available spectacular low frequency accidents.

Anchoring is involved when a certain often irrelevant element influences our opinion on a certain subject, for instance the price of an asset, in an excessive way, meaning that later on adjustments made and based on new information is insufficiently taken into consideration: the anchor carries too much weight. The effect of such anchors may be observed on any market: the price quoted by the seller will act as an anchor in the following bargaining process.

We are way too quick to make up our mind on the basis of just a very small fraction of the information available. Once we have adopted a certain position, we do not test our views by comparing to all the available data: we will more or less exclusively look for information confirming our position which will make us feel good (confirmation bias), and frequently, overconfident.

It is not surprising that our forecasts are often far from the shot and nevertheless we think we did see it all coming: hindsight bias is extremely common in all walks of life. That hindsight bias is not unknown on Wall Street may be illustrated by Bernard Baruch the famous American financier of the beginning of the 20th century. In his memoirs

240

published in the 1950s Baruch explains to have warned of the forthcoming market crash of 1929, whereas this point is in no way confirmed by his publications made in 1929 which show that he was just as bullish as more or less anybody else.

Forecasts tell us more about the forecaster than about the future (which means they are far from objective assessments). Our economic models are based upon the assumption that humans are rational optimizers (the model of the *Homo economics*) which unfortunately is far away from the real people with their brain largely formed in the Paleolithic era, if not earlier already. These models at the end of the day do not warrant extremely accurate results.

People are risk averse but in a myopic way which does not prevent them from taking substantial risks at gambling. (On risk aversion, see below.)

In this section of cognitive biases let us also say a few words on fixed ideas which may dominate our thinking. Max Sterner a German author in a book written in 1845 explained that it is not people who have ideas but ideas which have them. In markets people with fixed ideas are legion: the perma-bears who forecast a market crash at least every month, the gold gurus who recommend to sell all securities and place everything in gold, etc. although since more than 500 years at least (if not since biblical times) gold has done little more than conserving its value.

Risk Aversion

Risk aversion is deeply anchored in the psychology of the *Homo sapiens*. In ancient times, during the era of the hunters and gatherers, the very few possessions people had were absolutely vital for their survival and they could not dispense of them. Risking to lose their hunting weapons or their winter clothes could directly mean death by starvation or freezing of the hunter/gatherer and/or of their entire family. Under these circumstances, it is understandable that people were willing to enter into a risky bet only if the odds were significantly in their favor. Numerous studies have shown that humans of the 20 and 21st centuries require a 2-3 odds in their favor in order to risk losing their property. This means people risk to lose $1,000 only if they have an equal chance to win $2-3,000 as a counterpart. This risk aversion does not prevent people to enter into bets which are clearly losers' games and where the chances are stacked against them. This comment applies of course to gambling: buying lottery tickets does not make any sense for a rational and educated person. Nevertheless, people do so on a big scale.

The explanation for this apparently foolish behavior is that people are not able to fully appreciate very low probabilities of success as is the case for lottery tickets. In addition, it is true that lottery tickets generally carry a very low price which the gambler can easily afford to lose. Recently, neuro-psychiatrists have supplied another explanation which could be an important element of explanation: buying a lottery ticket allows people to fantasize that they will hit the jackpot and become insanely rich. This creates the same feelings as the use of drugs and begets addictive behavior. Day traders do apparently experience exactly the same sensations.

In general, risk aversion is a good thing in any situations of life (say when driving a car) and when it comes to investing in particular. The primary obligation of investors is to preserve their capital and to avoid severe losses. It has to be insisted on the fact that in order to recover a 20% loss of capital a gain of 25% is needed. If the loss is 25% the required gain is 33.33%, and for a loss of 33.33% a gain of 50%, etc. (Please refer to the paragraph on Performance Illusion in Chapter 2.)

The problem is that the actual behavior of these supposedly risk averse investors is not consistent with this risk aversion rule: people tend to be attracted to the stock markets not when stocks are inexpensive (for instance when the markets have corrected severely), but after stock prices have already increased in an important way. Such price increases mean that the risk of these securities has already significantly increased and the Expected Value of the investment has become negative and that from a risk assessment point of view any investment should be avoided.

Furthermore, when assessing investment risks, investors do not always adopt the correct perspective which has led Richard Thaler to coin the expression of "myopic risk aversion." Confronted with the equity risk puzzle (stocks produce a significantly higher yield than bonds), investors concentrate on the short term and choose investments in the form of bonds because they are less volatile in the short term but eschew investments which over the medium and long term produce higher income.

Due to myopic risk aversion (or myopic loss aversion) it is arguable that many investors do hold excessively conservative portfolios (too little in stocks and too much in bonds) for the reason they focus excessively on the potential for short-term losses. As explained elsewhere, the investor's time frame is all-important here. However, this cannot mean that any risk should be avoided: the irony here is that by avoiding any risk one takes the biggest risk of all: the risk to not being invested in stocks and in this way avoiding the asset class which is by far the highest-yielding one. If not taking any risk at all means keeping one's money in a savings account, the investor will in all likelihood have taken the highest risk at all, namely to be sure (under normal circumstances) to lose out compared to equity investors who are able to double their capital roughly every 7 years (on average).

Investors who in March 2009 sold their share in panic in order to invest in safe assets like Treasurys or high-grade corporate bonds in fact paid a very high price for their risk aversion. The lesson here is that shareholders should learn to manage risks in a cautious way by making sure that the odds are clearly in their favor. If you foresee a 60 per cent change of a gain of 30 but a 40 per cent chance of loss of 10 then the Expected Value is determined as follows: 0.4x(-10) + 0.6x30 = 14. This is a positive outcome, i.e. the odds are in your favor. Whether you should enter into this deal or not is another question and it depends on a number of factors, namely your risk aversion and also on the alternative investments which are in competition with the said investment; in fact, by calculating the mathematical expectation for all investment alternatives we can easily compare the different available alternatives.

The difficult part here is of course to assess the probabilities and the potential gains and losses. Although difficult, this exercise should not be avoided. Take the situation where there is a 80% chance that an investment is going to appreciate by 50% over a period of 3 years but that there is a 20% chance that it will go bankrupt which could mean that the investor themselves as they own a very concentrated portfolios will themselves become insolvent. Despite the favorable odds, the investor should pass the opportunity.

Investors are often severely misguided when they withhold their investing decisions until uncertainty disappears. The problem is that once uncertainty has disappeared the investment opportunity has gone as well, or it is a lot less interesting as stock prices have adjusted as soon as uncertainty has gone away.

Investors should be aware that uncertainty is first unavoidable (see above) and it does exist even (and especially so) if the general agreement is that times could not be better and that the future is brilliant; furthermore, uncertainty is useful for the investor. The difficulty for the investor is to go against the general consensus of the markets and to come out with a personal and correct forecast. Granted, this is easier said than done. To have a contrarian bend is certainly helpful but will not be sufficient: it has to be backed up by serious work. Uncertainty is often the investor's best friend as uncertainty is frequently accompanied by low prices offering a high margin of safety.

Many investors strive to realize a specific rate of return on their investment portfolio, say 8 or 10% per year. Quite generally these goals are unrealistically high and as such they reflect the overconfidence bias which afflicts most humans, not just investors. Beyond that, it has to be noted that it is unwise to believe that a certain rate of return can be obtained each year: an average rate over a longer period of say 5 to 7 years is a more realistic goal. Also, markets are more or less favorably oriented which means that it is easy to realize a high single-digit result in a market similar to the great bull market starting in 1982, whereas it would have been a prowess to only come out even in the Great Depression starting in 1929.

Things are made even more difficult due to the fact that there is no correlation between efforts put in and results obtained. In other words, by spending double the hours on investing there is no guarantee that the results will double or even that they will increase at all. Any efforts put into forecasting results of one's portfolio are a waste of time. All that investors can do is concentrate on their investment policy and apply it in a disciplined way. In that way results should come by themselves.

Another danger of focusing on a certain level of investment return is that it leads investors to concentrate more on upside potential than on downside risk. In this way they may be pushed to risky behavior, like investing in stocks of companies which are in a weak financial position or chasing stocks which have known strong price increases recently. Investors should concentrate on risk instead of return: this means that the starting point would be the risk-free investment return offered by sovereign debt of triple A rated states. If that rate is 3%, a rate of return always accessible for everyone, investors should accept the higher risks of equity investments only if those risks will, in all likelihood, be more than compensated by commensurately higher returns.

Information in the Internet Age

The rise of the internet has significantly levelled the playing field with respect to information available to everybody and hence also to investors. A huge amount of information is easily accessible on the internet and much of it is for free. The problem nowadays is definitely not that information would be scarce or expensive but that the volume of available information is excessive. The challenge is to separate the chaff from the wheat or the noise from data that really matter. The media followed by eager analysts have a tendency to concentrate unduly on stories; such stories, although they make nice headlines, are often only anecdotes which do not matter that much. Again, it is not difficult to find examples. In 2015 Costco announced that it would stop to issue a common credit card with American Express and in this way that credit card company would lose a significant proportion of its turnover. This story was repeated again and again in the media whereas the fact passed over in silence was that the margins American Express made on these operations were razor-thin so that if American Express lost a lot of turnover it did not lose that much in terms of profit.

Analysts

Analysts frequently behave as if they were true followers of the efficient market theory (EMT): they implicitly assume that stock prices at any time correctly include all relevant information. Assume a company's quarterly earning's report was outstandingly bad (or any other negative and unforeseen event is reported in the media), analysts will not immediately reassess their rating and price target of the company but they will wait until the market reacts. Only when this market reaction is clearly established, will they adjust their ratings of the company and the new price target:

this new price target tends to follow closely the amount of the correction set by the market.

Analysts, very often, instead of guiding investors are in fact behaving as if the markets knew better. Suppose that a given stock goes into a strong movement (an increase or a decrease) without that move being the consequence of some new fact directly impacting the stock's value. If due to that move the stock loses some 15-25 p.c. of its value, the analysts will enter the scene and downgrade the stock (from overweight to hold for example) and lower the price target. It is all too clear that these analysts take care that there price targets do not too much deviate from the most recent daily stock quotes.

If, for instance, a company misses "the Street's" earnings forecasts, analysts (which are as short-sighted as the rest of the so-called "professionals"), will reassess their recommendations downwards, triggering selling pressure on the stock. It is quite interesting to note that the analysts will give new price targets not without giving some fundamental (and sometimes technical) reasons for their revised assessment but at the end of the day the real reason is ... the decrease of the share price and the new price range, very coincidentally, is a close match to the decrease in price which recently occurred but which they were unable to forecast in the first place. In other words, despite calling themselves professionals, these analysts, by and large, behave like the proverbial dumb money, which instead of looking at the playing field, the business, gawks at the scoreboard, the stock price fluctuations: they will feel totally at ease only if their forecasts are not much at odds with the current stock prices. The added value of such "forecasters" who are only looking in the rearview mirror is not very high, the more so because these analysts have a very acute herd instinct.

Behaving like this, analysts signal that they consider the market to be smarter than themselves and instead of

247

profiting from the market's liquidity they want to profit from its wisdom: a sure recipe for disaster.

As an example let's consider TESLA which as it is well known, at the beginning of 2020 started to increase considerably (by 128% over a three-month period) from already very extended levels, and without any substantial news, giving the company a market valuation of more than $150 bn more than the combined value of the 3 legacy US car companies GM, Ford and Fiat Chrysler. On February 18, 2020 Barron's reported that in the morning trading of that day Tesla stock was up 5% to $835.78 whereas three bearish Wall Street analysts had increased their price targets. Toni Sacconaghi (Bernstein) raised his price target from $325 to $730 (an increase of 120%) noting that his price target was 13% below the prices quoted the day before. Adam Jonas (Morgan Stanley) with a Sell rating increased his best-case scenario from $650 to $1,200.

A good piece of advice is that one should listen to analysts only when they give information and not when they issue opinions.

As soon as one analyst has started to reassess the company's perspectives, their peers which follow them in short order, will do the same thing which will put additional pressure on the stock. The behavior of these analysts is a violation of the advice to profit from Mr. Market's pocketbook not from its wisdom.

This observation seems to be confirmed by research studies. Tom Bulkowski (The Encyclopedia of Chart Patterns) "found that in a bull market only 25 percent of downgrades occurred within a third of the stock's yearly high, when they would do the most good. In a bear market the forecasts were even worse, with only 13 percent near the yearly high, meaning 87 percent had already gone down when the analysts shouted "sell."

Are stock recommendations by analysts of any good? It is obvious that these recommendations (which by the way are generally bullish) are beneficial for the firms which do issue them. But the more relevant question is whether they are beneficial to investors. In other words, does an investor who follows these recommendations do better than by buying an index fund representing the entire market? It seems that this is the case although market outperformance is only weak.

Let's also mention that the rating agencies Moody's and S&P had maintained the investment grade ratings on Enron's debt until just four days before it filed for bankruptcy.

Sometimes analysts who have the courage of their opinions live dangerously as was experienced by Marvin Roffman an analyst with Janney Montgomery Scott who in 1992 predicted the failure of Donald Trump's Taj Mahal casino complex in Atlantic City. Donald Trump asked to his employer either to fire the analyst or to have him aplologize, which Roffman refused to do. When the casino went bankrupt Roffman sued his former employer and Trump for reparations, a demand accepted by the court.

In hopefully rare instances, companies literally blackmail investment bankers to give a favorable rating. Representatives of Enron apparently bluntly approached investment bankers that they could expect business from the energy company but under the condition that they rate their stock as as a strong buy as reported.[33]

Financial Advisors

If you are in continuous contact with an advisor, banker, investment manager, the nice person who calls you at least once a week to tell you about the market in general and of course about the latest investment opportunities, do yourself a favor and get rid of them under all circumstances. Do not forget that advisors have their own agenda and their objective is not to make money *for* you but to make money *from* you.

This point was again underlined by a recent article in the Financial Times: "Remember the point of financial markets is not to make you money, but to device ever more elaborate ways to take your money." The author warned investors against investing in global datacenters like Equinix or Digital Realty.[34]

If you maintain the contact with your advisor who calls you up on a daily or weekly basis you will do your best to reject most of the investments proposed to you, but from time to time you will give in and purchase their newest investment idea. In this way, you will not only trade more than you should but even more than you actually want. The old rule of reciprocation (as shown by Robert B. Cialdini, Influence, The Psychology of Persuasion), according to which we try to repay favors, invitations, gifts which have been made to us and in this way paying back our debt is at play here and will guide you to follow the moves suggested by your advisor.

Investing is difficult enough; it should not be rendered more difficult than needed by interferences of third persons with their own objectives not aligned with yours.

However, many people do things differently and in fact use advisors very abundantly: once again psychological reasons may be at play here. If an advisor is involved, the investor may make use of a kind of psychological call option: if the outcome of a certain investment is favorable, the investor is able to call the credit for himself; in the opposite case the advisor may be blamed for the bad decision. This is an absolutely non-valid reason for hiring an advisor. Investors have to get rid of such childish behavior consisting in playing the blame game and they have to take full responsibility for all their decisions, good or bad ones, and not just for those which prove to be successful ones. It is only in this way that they will be able to learn from past mistakes and to progress as an investor (see under "Growth mindset").

Absolute Level of Stock Prices

Although this may appear very strange, it seems that some investors get influenced in their stock buying decisions by the absolute level of the stock price. These investors may tell you that they do not buy Google (or Amazon) because at a share price of $1,500 (or $3,000) it is "expensive." It goes without saying that such a statement is utter nonsense. The price of one share does not say anything on the expensiveness of a stock and it can be changed easily either by splitting existing stocks in 2, 5, 10 or any other number of shares (which will simple divide up the capitalization of the company in a higher number of stocks) or by doing a reverse split, meaning that the number of shares will decrease and each share will be traded at a higher price. In order to not make mistakes on this point the best advice is to focus on the business as a whole in a first step. Company X has a capital of $1 billion and each year it realizes a profit of $100 million. The capital may be divided into any number of shares: either for example into 1 billion shares (which would imply shares with a nominal or par value of 1$) or into 100 million shares (par value of $10), or into 10 million shares (par value of 100), etc. It has to be added that this nominal or par value will not strictly coincide with the prices at which these stocks are traded on stock exchanges which fluctuate around wildly, but this par value, which refers to the book value of the shares gives a first approximation of the intrinsic value of this stock.

It is a fact that traditionally most companies tried to have share prices which are part of a range extending between $10 and $100 (although nowadays this last amount is more and more often exceeded). This means that if price fluctuations make that the stock gets out of that range, the company might proceed to a stock split (and more rarely a reverse split in case the prices are very low) which involves for instance that the stock price is divided by two, three, ten or any other number. For every share having a market value of $500 the investor will, for instance, receive 3 additional shares (as on the occasion of the recent stock split done by Apple on August 31, 2020)[35]. On the day of the stock split, Apple shareholders found out they owned 4 shares at a price of $125, so that in fact nothing has happened, neither for them nor for the company which, in future will pay half of the dividend it previously paid on the stock before the split.

If most companies try to avoid that their shares do get too expensive, some companies have adopted a different policy and have never proceeded to stock splits. This is the case for Berkshire Hathaway Inc. whose A-shares increased in value from $49.50 (in 1965) to currently some $300,000. The attitude adopted by many companies over recent years is a similar one: companies like Amazon and Alphabet do no longer proceed to stock splits even as their stock prices did not stop from increasing beyond the four-digits level.

Again this does not mean that stocks of Amazon, Alphabet or Berkshire's A–shares are expensive (when compared to intrinsic value) nor that the Berkshire B–shares would be inexpensive: the question whether a stock is expensive may only be answered by reference to the classical metrics used to determine the value of shares, meaning profit per share, sales or book value per share, etc. It stands to reason that the A–shares of Berkshire will have a considerable higher profit, sales or book value per share than, say, the shares of General Motors which trade at about $40.

Momentum investing

Momentum investing is based on the idea that a certain market trend tends to persist for some time (rising stocks tend to continue rising and falling stocks continue falling…) so that it may be worthwhile for investors to follow that trend "until it ends": by selecting stocks which are in a strong uptrend move, or downtrend move, followers of this investing strategy hope to obtain higher returns than the overall market return. Sometimes momentum strategies are designated by the phrase: "buy high, sell higher." The entry and exit points are generally determined by following some technical indicators, for instance different moving averages (MA): if the 50-day MA crosses the 200-day MA from below a buy signal is generated, a crossing below the 200-day MA gives a sell signal. It will not be a surprise to the reader that there is no consensus on the merits of such momentum strategies.

Momentum investing consists in buying stocks that have outperformed over the past three to twelve months, and selling those that have had poor returns over the same period. Although this strategy results in higher trading expenses than a buy-and-hold strategy, some studies show that it may actually be profitable even after taking these trading costs into account.

The effectiveness of such momentum strategies is clearly difficult to reconcile with the EMT and more particularly with the tenet of the independence of stock prices.

Some investors label themselves as "momentum investors" which means that they are less concerned with the fair value of stocks and are attracted by stocks with rising prices counting on the assumption that this trend will go on, following the motto: "The trend is your friend… until it ends." Is this a promising approach? Hardly! The reason is that in fact most investors are such trend followers (or momentum investors) anyway, and if you do what most investors do … you will never have superior returns.

The point is that prices you have to pay for such so-called "momentum stocks" will be on the high side and thus not allow for a decent profit. Investors following momentum stocks will buy the Street's darlings, the fashionable stocks. Before long, they will hold a consensus portfolio and will find a lot of comfort in the media, and whether they know it or not, they follow the herd. This consensus approach cannot and will not be successful and the thoughtful investor should try to avoid it.

The successful investor will not chase shares with runaway prices but using a contrarian approach they will buy shares which the "Street" hates and which for a long time are beaten down by the media, with prices either going down or showing no trend at all for an extended period of time. This does not mean that such a momentum investor cannot make money from time to time. In investing luck is certainly a non-negligible factor. It does however mean that it is not in line with a value investing approach which calls for an assessment of the intrinsic value of the shares and for an adequate margin of safety.

Momentum investors also follow a very common mistake: they are attracted to the market when prices are rising and they (generally) move to the sidelines when markets fall. They buy shares like they buy perfume or jewels whereas they should buy them as if they were consumer staples, meaning the lower the prices the more they buy. Again, these investors move with the herd whereas only a contrarian bent (which in this context means only buying stocks that have fallen in disgrace) is successful in the long run.

Different studies made over the past half century show that the best-performing firms for investors have been those with strong brand names in the consumer staples and pharmaceutical sectors. Stockholder returns are driven by the difference between actual and expected earnings growth, the impact of which is magnified by dividends; it is assumed that all dividends received have been reinvested in stocks of the paying company. This line of reasoning will find its supporters also in the camp of value investors who reason that brands with worldwide reputation will translate in strong moats for their owner allowing them to increase prices and show strong profitability increasing their market shares.

However interesting it may be to know which approach has been successful in the past and which ones were not, the interesting question is whether the past winners and losers will keep their positions over the next 50 years? This is far from sure. Just referring to the Jeremy Siegel studies mentioned above which concluded that companies with strong brand names in the consumer staples and pharmaceutical sectors were the best investment over the last 50 years or so. It would appear that one of the effects of the internet is to weaken the power of brands. The behavior of large retailers has the same effect, for instance by setting up their own brands. These transformations are certainly one of the reasons why over the last 5 years or so Berkshire Hathaway is no longer as successful as it used to be in the past. Also consumer staples companies, which traditionally could rely on strong brands, say, General Mills, Kraft-Heinz, Procter and Gamble are no longer as profitable as they were 10 or 15 years ago.

Herd Thinking

The principal tenet of contrarian investing is that crowds are frequently (maybe even generally) wrong. If we consider only financial markets, and specifically stock markets, it may be said that this is clearly not true. The market is generally right, at least about 80 to 90% of the time, for instance during a long bull market, or an extended bear market. This means that most of the time it is advisable to ride the wave with the crowd, be it only for the reason that the crowd has one mighty argument on its side, namely it has the buying and selling power: going against this capital power is dangerous. However, the moment comes when the crowd gets it wrong by relentlessly pushing up stocks to bubble territory or beating down stocks in a bear market: these are the so-called inflection points, the tops or bottoms of the market.

To understand the mechanism underlying market inflection points, one has to consider that a market top is reached when everybody is bullish and nobody is there to join the party to push the shares to still higher levels. At that point it is sufficient that a very small number of shareholders turn bearish or simply need money to lead to a market turn. A similar development occurs at a market bottom: excessive bearishness makes sure that all those who wanted to sell have already done so and at a time where daily activity in those stocks is extremely low it suffices that a very small number of buyers finally push stock prices higher.

All this means that, especially at these market turning points, herd/group thinking is at its maximum, and it is at these moments that following the herd is most dangerous. At these inflection points the smart investor has to leave the crowd and to adopt a contrarian approach. The difficulty is to get the timing right. Getting it exactly right is impossible: the best the investor can do is to build up, or down, their positions in a number of steps over an extended period of time, say, several months. For example, in the internet bubble of 1999 – 2000, the investor, in order to preserve their capital, had to sell their grossly overvalued internet stocks or even go short on these same stocks before the bubble popped in March 2000.

Growth Stocks in General

According to a very vague definition growth stocks are those expected to increase their earnings at a significantly faster rate than the rest of the market. As such they are often opposed to value stocks defined as those that trade at a discount to the market according to different fundamental criteria (P/E ratio, Price Sales ratio, book value, etc.).

If you ask investors following the Wall Street circus on a daily basis which companies they prefer when faced with the following choice: company A is growing at 4% annually, company B grows at 8% and company C is growing at 12% many would conclude this is a no-brainer and choose

256

company C as it is the fastest growing company. However, in fact this is an unanswerable question as nothing was said about the price, neither was it specified whether the growth is profitable or not. If the 3 companies could be purchased at the same price, C would probably be the best choice. However given Wall Street's currently prevailing attitudes (which heavily favor growth over everything else) this is unlikely to be the case and company C will be sold at a hefty premium over B and A. The magnitude of this premium is reflected in the substantially higher P/E ratio. Investors should be extremely cautious and only reluctantly pay a significant premium for companies which, based on past results, *promise* higher growth also in future. Promises are not always kept.

Chapter 5: The Process of Investing

Wall Street often tends to oppose value investing to growth investing. This is an odd distinction. As often underlined by so-called value investors, growth is part of value investing: a company with high growth, all other things equal, is obviously more valuable than a company with low growth or no growth (assuming the growth is profitable). The only issue with such so-called growth companies is that they frequently do not come cheap, growth being frequently overvalued, or in other words they do not provide the investor with an adequate margin of safety, which represents the fundamental tenet of the value investing method of investing.

An Important Dichotomy: Price and Value

As the expression goes, price is what you pay, value is what you get. Many inexperienced investors do not really understand that the stocks they are buying are not securities which follow a life of their own (like birds in the sky) but that ultimately they represent the ownership in a business undertaking without necessarily almost following strictly the value of the underlying business. Instead of closely following the economic and financial evolution of the business, many investors prefer to simplify things by disregarding business developments altogether and by only closely following the movements of the stock prices for instance by 200-day moving averages. This tendency is pushed to its extreme by the so-called chartist investors (who deduct the future movement of stocks from the stock's past charts) pretending that they do not even care to know the name of the company as they only need the ticker symbol to initiate a trade.

If price did always coincide with value, things would be a lot easier and the only thing to follow would be the daily price fluctuations. This is actually what many investors do: they are in no way interested in the fundamentals of a business and they will (at best) just look at the stock price charts. These investors (better called speculators), whether they know it or not, adhere to the doctrine of "Efficient Markets" meaning they believe the "price is always right"

Truth be told this attitude is somewhere understandable and makes some sense for very short-term traders like day traders. If the holding period of stocks is at a maximum several hours or even several days, fundamental factors do not play any role at all. Over such short time spans any discrepancy between price and intrinsic value of the shares cannot really correct. Such corrections do take time and in reality nobody knows how much time is needed and it cannot be said when the correction will actually start and when it will end, being understood that this "ending" is only provisional because sooner or later it will be followed by other divergences either in the same direction or in a different direction. Furthermore, there is no reliable way to find these things out. Investing is a business which is dominated by many uncertainties of all kinds: anyone not having the character to stand this type of uncertain environment should not invest in stocks.

The implications of the fact that price and value do not always correspond are far-reaching. The discrepancy between the two is at the basis of the so-called value investing investment method. It is only because price and value may widely deviate that a "margin of safety" is at all possible. If price and value did always correspond no margin of safety could exist.

For most investors any increase in the stock price is cheered as a positive sign as it is implicitly considered as reflecting a higher value of the shares. A decrease in the stock price is viewed as a decrease in the value of the stock. Such attitude is extremely dangerous: investors which behave that way, knowingly or not, use the market as a guide instructing them what the values of the stocks are. The dangers of this attitude are demonstrated by the famous Mr. Market metaphor of Graham.

The Mr. Market Metaphor

This metaphor outlined in chapter 8 (called "The Investor and Market Fluctuations") of the Intelligent Investor describes the behavior of a partner (Mr. Market) with whom you are associated in a business in which you own a share which cost you $1,000. Everyday your partner gives a quote for the value of your share in the partnership and he offers to either buy your share or to sell you additional shares on that price basis. As your partner is a very emotional person his quotes vary greatly from reasonable to ridiculous. Graham advises not to let these funny quotations influence one's opinions on the value of the business but to feel free to profit from those quotes when they are beneficial, meaning to buy if the quote is very low and to sell if the price quoted is high.

Reality is as follows: the price of the stock will eventually reflect the value of the business (its intrinsic value) and more precisely the driver of the stock price is the earnings (or better still) the cash flow per share. In the short run, there may be a more or less substantial difference between intrinsic value of the business and its stock price. Stock prices are influenced by emotions like fear and greed as well as a lot of macro-economic factors, like the monetary policy of the Fed, GDP growth, the labor market, etc. If these last aspects do undeniably have an impact on business in general they may not directly influence the business of the company having issued the shares.

It is pretty clear that the intrinsic value of the shares does only move very slowly and only in a pretty much linear way, at most say 5 to 7% per annum if we refer to a stable business. Stock prices on the other hand may evolve very erratically and in a somewhat lively stock market session the stock price of a given company may in one single session lose one percent before closing with a 2 to 3 per cent gain; this means that over the 6 and a half hours of the NYSE session the shares have moved by 3 to 4 per cent peak to bottom, which is half the typical annual movement. It is obvious that the value of the business over that short time span has remained virtually unchanged just as the value of any building cannot be recognized to have moved in any respect over a period counted in hours or days.

For the investor, the best thing to do would be to disregard these movements as noise and just view them as offering interesting prices for either buying or selling shares but not to consider them in any respect as indications with respect to the intrinsic value of the stock.

Any investor should make their own calculations concerning the value of the shares but not deduce that value from the stock exchange prices. These prices may either be ahead of intrinsic value or lagging behind them (and only exceptionally truly reflect them). Sometimes, the relations between price and value is likened to a pendulum which would consistently either overvalue or undervalue the actual value of the stocks. Only when the pendulum crosses the horizontal axis does it reflects the intrinsic value of the shares. This image does suggest a kind of regularity which in practice is far from existing. A better analogy is the one of a man walking his dog and using a long leash. The dog's master (who represents intrinsic value of the shares) advances regularly although sometimes at a quicker, sometimes at a slower speed. The dog on the other hand represents prices and either lags behind his master or runs ahead of him and sometimes walks just aside of him: only at those rare moments do value and price exactly correspond.

Markets do not move in a linear fashion which is also demonstrated by the record of best and worst days in markets.

Best days and worst days

It has been repeatedly stated that a remarkable small number of days count for a very high proportion of total gains and losses experienced by stock markets over a very long period. It is more difficult to draw a meaningful conclusion from this fact. It is correct to say that an investor who has missed the 30 best days of a 30-year period would have missed about half of the net gains experienced by the market during that period. If some investors had missed the 10 strongest days of the period they would most certainly also have missed the day following all of these high-movement days, and during which the market gave back a more or less important chunk of the gains of the previous day. Taking these corrective movements into account as well would make the calculation a lot less spectacular.

Perhaps the best conclusion from these "best days" and "worst days" assessments is that the markets are unpredictable and the investor should simply not try to time the market: trying to do this will only result in frustration (if one or more of the strong days are missed) and high turnover costs (fees and taxes). Nobody is able to consistently time the market successfully.

Taxes and Long-Term Investing

"For all long-term investors, there is only one objective – maximum total real return after taxes."

John Templeton

Taxes and costs (which are both part of those leakages the investor should try to reduce to the absolute minimum as they directly hurt the investment results) are part of the very few elements which the regular investor is able to control. Most authors of investment books do scarcely talk about the taxes due by investors, and in fact do as if they did not exist at all. This is a big mistake. Taxes, if let uncontrolled, may be a major drag to the regular investor's performance, and they will often account for a high multiple of trading expenses.

Incidentally, if John Templeton in the above quotation refers to "real return after taxes" this specification is also very largely ignored by Wall Street which typically does not take the effects of inflation into consideration. Again especially for the long term investor this is a big mistake as their results are hugely impacted by the seemingly negligible current inflation rate of roughly 2%.

That Wall Street prefers to ignore taxes is highly understandable for the reason that taking them into consideration leads to lower yields. Wall Street prefers to avoid anything which makes its performance appear pedestrian. Taxes, trading costs just as stock options expenses (until recently) are simply ignored. New performance measures are introduced for instance in the form of EBITDA, pretending that this concept better reflects a company's performance whereas their only merit is to make management's performance look better than it actually is.

However, it is not by ignoring them that taxes will go away.

In fairness, it is true that the fact that the tax status strongly varies from one investors to the next (according to its legal status for instance in case of legal entities) in addition to their tax status (some companies are set up in tax havens, like Bermuda, Barbados, etc. and as such do not pay any local income taxes). This diversity of situations does complicate the taking into consideration of tax aspects.

It is furthermore true that a number of individual investors are legitimately able to ignore taxes (at least temporarily): this is the case for all those who invest through an IRA account in its various forms. For these investors it is perfectly OK not to calculate with a tax levy. But all the others, while drafting their IPS (Investment Policy Statement) should thoroughly reflect on the incidence taxes may have on their investment strategy: indeed, taxes are far from neutral with respect to the investment strategy chosen: the prevailing tax rules clearly favor a buy and hold strategy, and they penalize a very active trading policy, the extreme incarnation of which is the so-called "day trader". Although this may not really be a deliberate policy of the tax lawmaker but it is the result of two rules which exist not only in the US but in most other jurisdictions:

1) Non-realized capital gains remain temporarily untaxed (or said differently capital gains are taxed only when realized),

2) Short-term capital gains are taxed at higher rates than long-term capital gains.

The first rule is of paramount importance here: as this rule does apply not only to individual investors but also to corporations, it means that someone whose preferred holding period is "forever" can defer indefinitely the moment taxation of the latent (unrealized) capital gains occurs. Although deferral does not mean elimination of taxes, the result is that a deferral of taxes by, say, several decades is equivalent to a substantial decrease of tax rates.

In this way, Berkshire Hathaway has been able to defer the capital gains on the Coca Cola shares or the American Express shares held by Berkshire Hathaway for decades and still counting. Although on the balance sheet of Berkshire Hathaway the shares are recorded at market value, a provision is made for covering those tax costs in the financial statements of the company. The said provision represents a so-called "provision for deferred taxes" which in essence is a loan from the IRS to the shareholder (to Berkshire Hathaway), a loan with two interesting features: first it is interest-free and secondly its maturity is determined unilaterally by the debtor who will fix the maturity date by selling the shares, which is the trigger event for the tax levy. The amount of deferred taxes is not incidental only as they represent $32.13 billion on the consolidated balance sheets of December 31, 2019. (Unfortunately, the value of such interest free loans is no longer what it used to be in times of "normal" interest rates).

Maybe scrutinizing taxes due by the company (as opposed to taxes due by the investor) is one useful element for selecting stocks or to put it more accurately to avoid some blatant fraud cases. Reference is made here to some emerging markets where accounting standards sometimes are not very high, meaning that it happens that companies are showing high income but as these high results are blown up fraudulently they pay little or no taxes. On such markets it may be advisable to check which companies do actually pay taxes and to avoid those which do not, although they show healthy profits, as these profits might be only fictitious.

Perhaps more surprisingly this did also work in the US in the first years of this century. Enron, World-com, Global Crossing did hardly pay any taxes. It is certainly true that there may be valid explanation for discrepancies between earnings as shown by commercial books and taxes paid as shown by tax accounts. But if such huge discrepancies exist, they represent at the very least a huge red flag for the analytic investor.

Investing for the long term has the obvious advantage to minimize costs in terms of brokerage fees and in terms of spread between bid and ask ("the difference between the bid, or what someone is willing to pay for a stock and the ask, or what someone is willing to sell the stock for"). These costs, although they have come down considerably over the last 20 years or so, are still not negligible despite what brokers and bankers will make you believe. Spreads are actually very low for big capitalization stocks but they may be prohibitively high for small cap stocks included for instance in the Russell 2000 Index.

Taxes are another area where long-term investors enjoy huge advantages which are consistently overlooked by the media for instance and which are best demonstrated by the following example.

Assume two investors, investing in the same shares generating a constant 15% annual return and capital gains are taxable at a 15% rate (no dividends for the sake of our example). The short-term investor will sell their shares each year (with a capital gain of 15%) and hence will generate a 12.75% net result after taxes. The long-term investor will hold their shares for 30 years and on the eventual sale will suffer the 15% tax rate applicable to their net capital gain: after having paid their taxes, they will enjoy a 14.4% net result after tax; the effective tax rate (of 15% which is suffered by the short-term investor has in this way been reduced to 4% (0.6 to 15 equals 4%). In other words, it is as if the long-term investor had paid an annual tax of 4% (instead of the nominal rate of 15% which was the rate paid by his short-term peer).

The difference in rates compared to the short-term investor is 1.65 percentage points (or 165 basis points) which may not seem to be a big thing. However, it is well known that even minor differences in growth rates, due to the exponential character of compounding of income, create huge differences in results when these growth rates are applied over a long period of time. On a $1,000 investment the result is $36,601 at the end of the 30-year period for the short-term investor and $56,595 for the long-term investor, which is a result higher by 54.63% compared to the one of the short-term investor. In other words a difference, in rate of returns of 12.94% (14.4 compared to

12.75) has produced a difference in capital of 54.63%. This is the magic of compounding. How is this possible? The reason is that whereas the short-term investor will each year pay part of their funds to the Treasury in the form of taxes, the long-term investor is able to keep more iron in the fire because they will hold their assets together and be fully invested over a 30-year period before paying a one-time tax. Compared to the short-term investor, it is as if the Treasury had made them an interest-free loan for investing in shares.

Please also note that the above calculations do not take into account the additional transactions costs suffered by the short-term investor; also, tax rates are the same for the short-term and the long-term investor whereas, as mentioned above, very often tax rates for long term capital gains are often lower: taking these elements also into account the comparison would even be more favorable for the long-term investor.

Leverage

Leverage is nothing else than financing by debt. The expression comes from the fact that by using debt to finance purchases of stocks (or any other assets) there is an effect of levering which unfortunately is a double-edged sword. Where does the levering effect come from? The easiest way to explain this effect is by an example.

Assume you own a stock portfolio of $100,000 which generates a capital gain of 10 per cent per year. Now, imagine that your internet broker is allowing you to buy shares on margin for another $100,000 at an interest rate of 5 per cent. It is easy to see that the use of leverage will significantly increase the rate of return on your equity from 10 p.c. to 15 p.c. (after deducting the interest cost from the investment result): $100,000x0.1 + $100,000x0.1 − $100,000x0.05 = 15,000 or 15% on equity of $100,000. This positive result occurs as long as the yield of your investment exceeds the debit interest incurred. Concretely, in our case, if the return on investment falls from 10 per cent to 2 per cent, the return on equity will decrease to minus 1 per cent (the $100,000 investment financed by loan does in fact give a negative yield, $2,000 - $5,000 = ($3,000) which after deduction from the amount earned on the equity-financed portion of the portfolio will generate a result for the year of $7,000. In other words, leverage has decreased the yield on invested equity from 10 per cent to 7 per cent.

The conclusion is that leverage, is a two-edged sword which leads to increased volatility in the results of your portfolio. But this time increased volatility also means increased risk. Leverage is the riskier the higher the interest rates payable on the debt incurred and the higher the proportion of debt to equity.

A second form of leverage (which is of a completely different kind) is the so-called "operational leverage." This expression refers to the cost structure of the business, namely the level of its fixed costs as compared with its variable costs. Those businesses requiring big capital expenditures have high fixed costs, meaning costs which are incurred in any case, even if there is no turnover at all. Variable costs are costs only incurred if there is turnover and which are more or less proportional to the turnover realized by the company. The consequence is that companies with high fixed costs will have more volatile results than companies with a lower proportion of fixed costs. Just as with financial leverage, a 10 per cent increase in production may entail a 50 per cent increase in profit, just as in the opposite case a moderate decrease in production may lead to a disproportionate decrease in profits (or even lead to a loss).

Companies with operational leverage which in addition are financially highly leveraged do not have favorable business economics and are really risky. This combination describes a potentially lethal cocktail, examples of which may be find in cyclical industries, for instance of the automobile, steel, aluminum and airline sectors. These are not the most interesting places to find suitable stock investments.

Is leverage advisable for the long-term investor? Warren Buffett has consistently warned against leverage which he considers as dangerous and expensive. It is true that Berkshire Hathaway does not need to use much banking debt or debt in the form of bonds and notes issued in as far as it has ample interest-free resources at its disposal (the insurance float which on December 31, 2019 amounted to $129.42 bn to which provisions for deferred taxes of $32.13 bn have to be added). It is this unique combination of an insurance company and of a fund which makes one of the dominant characteristics of Berkshire Hathaway which is extremely difficult to reproduce by somebody else (which corresponds exactly to the definition of a moat).

On the other hand, Graham in The Intelligent Investor advised that investors should consider their investing activity as a business activity of its own. Such investment activity (unlike any business activity, for instance a manufacturing company) has limited liability only, as for the investor holding stocks means they may "only" lose the amount invested in shares, not more: share prices cannot go negative. Given this fact, a conservative use of leverage is in my opinion not to be criticized, provided that the investor makes sure that he will never come into a situation where margin calls will force them to sell at a moment where this would be exactly the wrong thing to do which, of course, is in case of a market panic.

Casino Capitalism

In a capitalistic market economy the function of the stock exchange is double: firstly, companies may finance themselves by the issue of new securities, shares in this case, on the so-called primary market. Secondly, by assuring a daily trading in all the shares noted on the stock exchange, holders of shares (whether newly issued or not) are sure that, in case of need, they may dispose of their shares on extremely short notice and at minimal costs. It may be noted that here a virtuous circle comes into play: "trading begets more trading." As the number of traders increase it gets easier and less costly to exchange shares: as a consequence more trades occur which again will increase liquidity, etc. This liquidity which is the result of a well-functioning secondary stock market, open on any workday, is a huge advantage for shareholders and which is far from being given for other asset classes, e.g. real estate, antiques, works of art, precious stones, etc. Another effect of stock market is that stock exchanges render free valuation services to the public and that the evolution of stock indices "act as a leading indicator of economic activity." Unfortunately investors generally speaking tend to make poor use of these free valuation services as they get tracked into inconsiderate activity for instance by selling as prices decrease or buying as those prices increase strongly.

The term casino capitalism was introduced by J.M. Keynes in "In chapter 12 of the General Theory, commenting: "When the capital development of a country becomes a by-product of the activities of a casino, the job is likely to be ill-done...." In other words, Keynes warned against the situation where the above named functions of the stock markets are eclipsed by mindless speculation. Generally speaking these warnings are still entirely justified in the 2020s as it is beyond doubt that for many traders active on stock markets these markets are viewed as a kind of game of luck. The frequently used expression "play the market" also reflects that reality.

Calculation of Intrinsic Value

Intrinsic value is one of the cornerstones if not of all investment strategies at least of some types of strategies and certainly of value investing. Day traders, chartists and momentum investors do not care about intrinsic value. Their holding times are so short that fundamental factors are of little or even no relevance at all. Things are completely different for fundamental investors, meaning those who are determining a stock's value on the basis of "underlying factors that affect a company's present business and its future prospects."

For so-called "value investors" a margin of safety which is the difference separating price from intrinsic value of the company divided by the number of shares outstanding is absolutely required. Hence, you may rightly wonder what is intrinsic value and how to calculate it?

Intrinsic value of a stock starts with determining the value of a business based on all the facts, including all quantitative and qualitative factors, like assets (tangible and intangible ones) and liabilities (both assets and liabilities are shown by the company's balance sheet), present and future earnings, business perspectives, competitive position, etc. The income figures are extracted from the profit and loss account of last year but it is certainly useful to also have a look at the evolution of income over a longer period, for instance over the latest 10 to 15 years in order to check whether the company is subject to some cyclicality. The Value Line Investment Service in its "Reports and Ratings" (R&R) section contains a one page summary on each of the companies covered going back some 15 years with data on Revenues, Cash Flows and Earnings, Capital Spending and Book Value (all calculated per share), Average Annual P/E ratio, Relative P/E ratio, Average Annual dividend yield. Furthermore the R&R section details total Revenues, Net Profit, Working Capital, Long Term Debt, Shareholders Equity, Return on Total Capital, Return on Shareholders' Equity. In the case of Value Line, all this information is displayed on one page, in a standardized format which gives a detailed picture of the company, including the current and the next year's estimated figures, as well as an estimation of the average figures for the future 3-to-5-year period.

It should not be lost out of sight that the value of a company lies in the future not in the past and hence cannot be assessed on the basis of a rear-view-mirror approach only. Hence, investors are confronted with the following problem: past information is available, in a precise and quantitative way but that information is of limited value only. On the other hand future data, which is the only one which really counts is not yet available and it can only be estimated: at the moment the investor assesses the future earnings of the company, they do not know for sure which scenario will actually play out: take an investor in Tesla trying in 2020 to invest in the company: they have to make assumptions on the future size of the electric cars market (TAM), on the actions of the legacy car producers, on the cost structure of the various competitors. On each of these points different scenarios may come up: to each of these scenarios a certain probability rate will be allocated which at the end will allow the investor to come up with an Expected Value of future earnings, to which value a certain growth rate (again a value ponderated by different probability rates) will be attributed. Needless to say that this process does lead to a value which is highly uncertain. The truth of this statement is confirmed by the analysts' estimations of the future values of stocks of any companies, take Apple as an example. If 40 analysts are following the company no two analysts will totally agree on the key determinants of the future stock price: earnings per share, growth rate, number of iPhone sold (even the number of iPhones sold in the past is no longer disclosed by the company), growth in Services, etc. Given these very diverging opinions on all these points it is clear that the investor is well advised not to take the results of these forecasts as reliable figures. At the same time, if the investor is going long on a certain stock they should be very conservative in their calculations and they should be knowledgeable of the fact that there are very well established biases which tend to push in the direction of high valuations, namely over-optimism, overconfidence (in their own ability to forecast future earnings and other future events) and finally the tendency to fall in love with one's stocks (the endowment effect). These biases are real but by being aware of their existence the investor may try to avoid or minimize their effects by adopting not the most optimistic case but a more conservative one, lower assumptions, a higher discount rate, etc.

Regardless of the difficulties of this process there is no way around it: intrinsic value is as a rule calculated on the basis of an estimation of future earnings flows. These future flows are then discounted by an adequate discount rate. The most basic approach is to estimate future cash flows (earnings increased by non-cash items like depreciation and amortization and decreased by capital expenditures) and to choose a constant growth rate applicable to these annual cash flows. These annual cash flows are then discounted by a suitable discount rate which is decreased by the growth rate applicable to the annual cash flows.

$$V = \frac{CF \text{ (next year)}}{d-g}$$

This formula applies in case of a growing perpetuity, meaning. a cash flow which is growing at a constant rate forever. It has to be noted that the growth rate "g" must strictly be lower than the discount rate, otherwise the denominator in the formula gets zero or negative and the formula stops working.

If the annual cash flow is 100, the discount rate (d) 8%, and the growth rate (g) 3%, V would amount to:

$100/(0{,}08-0{,}03) = 2000$.

Very often a so-called "two-stage discount model" is used which consists in using a certain growth rate during a first period (of for instance 10 years, but that period may be shorter or longer) and a different growth rate (a permanent, generally lower, growth rate for the time beyond).

The discount rate used does not only take into consideration the time value of money but also the degree of risk involved, meaning the uncertainty of the future cash flows. Investors should not always use the same rate but adjust the rate to the company under review. The higher the risk, the higher the discount rate. Anybody who has ever played around with different discount rates to calculate the Present Value of future cash flows knows how highly sensitive the results are in relation to the discount rate used.

At this place, one question needs to be addressed: what exactly are the earnings flows which are to be estimated and then discounted back? The choice is at least between three concepts: earnings (as published quarterly by any stock exchange noted company), cash flows (which refers to net earnings increased by depreciation, depletion and other non-cash charges) and so-called owner earnings (which is the amount which the owner may withdraw from the business without jeopardizing its long-term prospects); this last metric is favored by Warren Buffett.

These three concepts merit some discussion. Annual earnings are determined on a net basis, after deduction of all expenses (cash outlays) and charges (non-cash outlays) which the company incurs in its ongoing operations. Capital expenditure (e.g. trucks purchased by a logistics company) are not treated as an expense. The trucks are capitalized at their acquisition costs and these costs are depreciated over the useful lifetime of the asset, for the good reason that it would be incorrect to treat these costs as an expense of the year of acquisition; a correct allocation of costs to income requires these costs to be spread over the useful lifetime of the asset: this means that if the asset is depreciated over, say, 8 years, the acquisition costs are spread over 8 years through annual depreciation allowances which decrease annual earnings.

Cash flow is the second concept which is useful in this context but it is also dangerous as it generally simply discards capital expenditure on the grounds of the reasoning that capital expenditure is taken into consideration via depreciation, amortization, etc. which are non-cash charges and hence do not decrease the cash flow of the company. This is an unacceptable distortion of reality: far from being non-cash expenses which could simply be neglected, capital expenditures (or capex) are expenses of the worst kind imaginable as they are pre-paid, i.e. the expense occurs in year one and the income is then only generated over the next 5, 10 or 30 years. Economically this is more burdensome than employment expenses or rental costs as these expenses only occur later on namely in the month the income is generated. Accordingly, it is not acceptable to just neglect capex.

The concept of owner earnings is meant to take care of this task as they are defined as cash flow less the amount of capex and additional working capital needed in order to take care of the increased working capital due to the company's projected growth.

It depends on the nature of the business whether there are or not important differences between earnings, cash flows and owner earnings. For instance if capex are low and not increasing, then earnings are a reasonable proxy for owner earnings and may be used as income flow to be discounted.

Let's work on a real life example of the two-stage discount model.

The following table shows the earnings of company X which in Year 0 amount to $40,03 mn and which grow at a rate of 12% (g1=12%, the rate applicable during the strong growth period of 10 years, by assumption).

A	B	C	D	E
Line Nr	Year	Profit	Disc. Rate (d)	Disc. Profit (Y)
1		40.03	11%	
2	1	44.833	0.9009	40.390
3	2	50.213	0.8816	40.754
4	3	56.239	0.7312	41.121
5	4	62.987	0.6587	41.492
6	5	70.546	0.5882	41.492
7	6	79.012	0.5299	41.865
8	7	88.493	0.4774	42.243
9	8	99.112	0.4301	42.623
10	9	111.006	0.3874	43.007
11	10	124.327	0.3490	43.395
12		g1=2%	Sum (E2-E11)	418.386 (1)
13		g2=4%		
14			Disc. Profit Y11-Yn	694.322 (2)
15			$\sum$(1)+(2)	$\sum$= 1112.708
16			Nber of shares:42.3 mn	
17		Value of 1 share:	$\sum$/Nber of sh.	**$26.3 (sh. val.)**

Some explanations are needed. This valuation model is typically suited for companies with a strong growth rate, called g1, during a certain initial period of say 10 years (with the possibility to choose a shorter or longer period) followed by a period of slower growth, at a rate called g2, (typically somewhat in line with the growth rate of the economy increased by the rate of inflation).

The discounted amounts corresponding to the first 10 years are outlined in the last column.

In a second step, we calculate the profit at the end of year 11 which is the profit of Year 10 increased by the reduced growth rate g2 (4%) which is then capitalized by the discount rate decreased by the growth rate (i.e. 11%-4%=7%). The figure in cell E14 is the result of the following calculation: the profit of Y10 is first increased by g2 (the growth rate of the slow-growth period) which gives the profit of Y11: to this figure we apply the capitalization rate of 4% and discounted by the discount factor of Y10. (The explanation is here that the present value of a perpetuity is given by the formula : PV= C/i, where C= annual payments, and i = discount rate.) As this PV is calculated at January 1, of Y11 this value has still to be discounted back to Y1 by applying the discount rate of cell D11. Finally, cell E16 represents the PV of one share, obtained by dividing the value of the company by the number of shares outstanding.

Financial Solidity

Any equity investment should start with an assessment of the financial stability of the company. Given our long-term perspective, this point takes a predominant importance. A day trader couldn't care less about a solid balance sheet. Long-term investors want to make sure they do not invest in a company with a shaky balance sheet position, for instance high debt, low equity, a low current ratio, chronical lack of liquidity, etc.

A weak balance sheet could mean that at the next unforeseen event (for instance the next pandemic) the company could be in serious trouble which may even jeopardize its very existence. For example, assume a court case is initiated against the company by a supplier or a client, a probe by the SEC, etc. The mere announcement of these events will of course lead to an immediate decrease in the stock price. A financially solid company will just sit this out and maybe even react by purchasing back its own stock; just the announcement of this buyback will again support the share price, just as the actual repurchases will do as well.

For a financially weak company the scenario could work out in an entirely different way. Analysts looking at the company's balance sheet (and also, as it is usual for them, at the stock price!) will point at the weak position and downgrade the company. This will lead more or less inevitably to a further decrease in the share price, decrease which will make new headlines, new downgrades from analysts and possibly make suppliers and employees even more nervous, etc. This downward spiral dynamics may have as a consequence a further decrease in the stock price and finally make the company a take-over target: a vicious circle dynamics has been triggered

The conclusion from all this is that a financially weak company is an additional risk factor which is relatively easy to avoid (or at least to be minimized) as it can be assessed based on currently available data, its present financial statements: no guessing of the future is involved at this point. That said, even the most solid balance sheet will not protect against deep-rooted changes in a company's business fundamentals; take newspapers, books or TV networks. However, such changes are mostly long term and very gradual. A financially weak company is exposed to more sudden and short-term surprises.

Income Reliability

The long-term investor looks for investing in a company which has a good business, with reliable income, with a constant , albeit moderate, growth rate. Reliable income progression is a huge advantage in practice and especially if there are no loss years. In practice, income will always be expressed not in global figures but on a per share basis. This makes sense for the reason that if expressed in absolute amounts, the number of shares which do participate in this profit will not be taken into consideration. However, this number of shares is far from constant: a company which proceeds to a lot of acquisitions financed by issuing new shares may be able to increase its consolidated profits by 20 percent per annum but if this increase is accompanied by an increase in the number of shares by a higher percentage, then the profit per share will decrease. Conversely, a lot of companies have as a policy to massively repurchase their own shares with the result that the number of shares decreases by 1 to 2 percent per year. This might seem negligible but if repeated over 10 or 20 year the effect may be dramatic. For instance, AutoZone Inc., a retailor and distributor of auto replacement parts and accessories, over the period 2003 to 2019 has reduced the number of shares outstanding by nearly 75% (from close to 89 million to about 24 million).

The long-term investor will look at past earnings per share which the company has realized over a long period of time, say, 10 to 15 years. Obviously, the pattern over the most recent 3 to 5-year period is somewhat more relevant than the one of the preceding 10 year period.

Such a look at the rear-view mirror is important but does have serious limitations. It is important as it will tell us a lot about the business of the company: growing earnings (not interrupted by loss periods) over a 10 to 15-year period show that the business is a stable one, that the company is in a good competitive position, perhaps it shows that it is gaining market share. It does however not tell us what the company's position will be in 10 to 15 years from now. The usual warning in annual reports "past performance does not guarantee future results" is applicable here as well. The important element which is to be included into the equation is what about the competition? Who are the competitors and how are they behaving? It may be that the competitive landscape is unchanged or it may be that it is in the process of completely changing: for instance, due to mergers the number of competitors is decreasing but in the same time it created one over-mighty dominant market player. Or, it could be that although the competition did not change but due to a management change at one of these compteting firms a price war was triggered as that management intents to double its market share in a slightly shrinking market. Without competition, business and investing is easy: if there is no competition then the company is a monopoly and it can increase prices nearly at will. But this is very rare and if it happens at all it will not last for very long, except for monopolies instituted by law, say, utilities.

If the economics of a business are such that it takes a market share corresponding to some 55-60% of the total market to recover all the costs (or to put it differently to reach break-even) then what is the number of competitors which can be in this market? The answer is one and only one.

This reminder to not forget about a company's competitors is very useful but unfortunately it is often neglected in practice.

Nowadays everyone and everything is rated all the time. These ratings are published with great fanfare and although those who publish them will always take care to issue the standard warnings of the kind mentioned above, they know (and probably hope) that the public at large does believe that in fact the future will resemble the past. And the public does believe so. When Morningstar publishes the performance of investment funds they know the high-performing funds of the last year will attract a significant amount of new capital which is the case only for the reason that investors believe that successful managers of the last year will repeat their recent performance this year and the following years.

All this said, a company with a moderate but stable growth rate is generally preferred to a company with a totally erratic progression, including two multi-year loss periods over a 15 year time span, even if the progression of the second company is quicker over the same period. This is at least the view of Wall Street which definitely prefers a smooth progression, which is an important sales argument to be used towards investors. The problem with this attitude is that this preference of the market may induce bad behavior from the side of companies: knowing that Wall Street prefers shares with constant income progression, management may help a little bit by "smoothing" earnings, meaning that the earnings of profitable years will not be fully recognized and booked into some reserve accounts or into provisions which may then be released in less profitable years in order to show the smooth progression Wall Street adores. A nice example of this tendency is shown in Bryan Burrough's and John Helyar's novel "Barbarians at the Gate" where a meeting was set up between KKR's (the potential buyer) Raether and Nabisco's (the seller's) Greeniaus and according to confidential remarks made to Raether, Nabisco could easily increase its operating income by 40 percent in a single year, if necessary, by increasing profit margins from 11 to 15% but their mission was to run the company on a steady basis at a margin of about 12%. If that level was exceeded he would have to expense all that cash in order to prevent earnings to go too high ! This discussion is just confirmation that volatile earnings, as characteristic of some businesses are not rewarded by Wall Street, which, above everything else values consistency of earnings.

Goodwill

One of the concepts frequently used in business is goodwill. Goodwill is an intangible asset the buyer of a company records in their own books if the price paid for the target company exceeds the going concern value of its assets decreased by its liabilities. Often analysts or journalists explain that goodwill has been shown because the buyer paid "too much" for the company it purchased. This is an incorrect or at least biased presentation of things: the buyers of a well-functioning and very profitable company does not only pay for the tangible and intangible assets on the balance sheet but they also pay for all the other elements which explain the success of the living organization which the company represents (for instance the competence of its employees, its business connections, its know-how in specific technical processes, the positive image it conveys in the eyes of its clients and of the general public, etc.). These items have value for the reason that if they did not exist it would be extremely costly to create them, assuming this were at all possible, which is far from certain from the outset.

In financial theory a business sells at a premium if it has a high return on capital. In any case, the seller is not ready to sell their business for a price which would not adequately compensate for all these items which are difficult to identify and even more difficult to valuate individually. In practice, such individual valuation is not necessary for the reason that goodwill is calculated by deduction. Buyer and seller negotiate a price which will take as key value the earnings power of the company. The annual future earnings will be estimated and by using a suitable discount rate (the rate which reflects the future of the business) buyer and seller will agree on a certain price.

Assuming this price is $1,000 and assuming that the going-concern value of all the assets purchased is $900 and the liabilities amount to $300 the net value of all assets decreased by the liabilities will be $600 and goodwill represents simply the difference between this value and the price paid: goodwill of $400 will be recorded on the balance sheet as an asset.

What happens to goodwill after acquisition of the target company? On this point the rules have changed over time. Traditionally goodwill was treated as any other asset with a limited lifetime: this means that goodwill was written off over its useful lifetime, just like any car, computer or production equipment. Then, in June 2001 FAS 142 was issued and goodwill was no longer amortized but companies were required to assess the fair market value of the unit and compare it to its book value (book value of assets minus liabilities).[36] If the fair value is less than book value as reported in the balance sheet, then an impairment has to be booked in order to make book value and fair value correspond: this booking corresponds to a loss in the income statement.

If such impairments occur, management will generally explain that this represents a non-cash item which does not impact its cash flow. This is true but nevertheless misleading: the cash flow impact occurred in the past already, at the time the purchase was made. If impairment of the book value is made it is just the recognition in accounting terms of a mistake which happened years before. The bottom line is that shareholder value was destroyed possibly on a massive scale and it is not infrequent that such acquisitions bring the acquirer into great difficulties.

It has to be emphasized that this treatment of goodwill is controversial. Impairment of goodwill (which needs to be made only if fair value of the purchased entity decreases under its book value) is very subjective and as practice sufficiently shows, is only done reluctantly and with substantial delay. The result is that in fact since the abolition of the rules that goodwill has to be amortized systematically over its useful lifetime if a company acquires another company in a transaction giving rise to accounting of goodwill then the income of the purchased entity will be recorded on the books of the acquirer whereas on the other hand the cost of the purchase (as far as there is a goodwill whereas other tangible or non-tangible fixed assets are depreciated or amortized which means that annual earnings are impacted) is simply ignored whereas for non-public companies it would be depreciated over 10 years. This means that such publicly traded company would show higher income than its smaller non-publicly traded competitor. If later on the financial situation deteriorates in a way that the impairment can no longer be avoided then goodwill might be written off *en bloc,* entirely in one go. In this way the volatility of the annual results is increased.

Ratios in Finance

A very useful and commonly used tool in analyzing the economic and financial situation of companies and in comparing companies among themselves consists in using ratios. Different types of ratios do exist and hereafter the most common ones are shortly described.

These ratios have different purposes as they measure different things.

Liquidity

A company needs to have constantly sufficient resources to face its obligations as they become due. It is furthermore understood that short-term assets should cover short-term obligations. Whether this is or is not the case is measured by the so-called current ratio.

Current ratio = current assets/current liabilities

If current assets (those which can be converted into cash within a year) exceed current liabilities (those which become due within a year) then the current ratio is higher than one and the company is in a comfortable position in respect of liquidity. If this is not the case, then assets are not sufficient to cover all (current) liabilities over the next 12 months and some action is probably required. Such action may for instance consist in taking up long-term debt which may be used to pay current liabilities.

A second liquidity ratio is the widely-used quick ratio which instead of using all current assets, does not include inventories in the numerator.

Quick ratio = Cash + accounts receivable + marketable securities/current liabilities

The rational behind the exclusion of inventories is that inventories might not be really liquid as they may be difficult to sell. Still the quick ratio should be higher than one.

Solvency

This type of ratio analysis relates to the capital structure of a company. The first ratio under review simply compares total debt to total equity.

Debt to equity ratio = Total debt / Total equity

A high ratio means that a company is highly leveraged which may be good in case return on assets is higher than interest expenses but will be negative in case of an economic downturn when leverage will negatively impact results.

The absolute amount of this ratio does not mean very much as there are enormous differences from one business sector to the next one. Generally speaking, a healthy rate is 50% meaning that there is $2 of equity for every $1 of debt. Financial companies like banks do tend to have extremely high debt to equity ratios: for major banks like JP Morgan Chase, Citicorp or Wells Fargo, assets are financed by equity only by 10% on average, which is one reason for investors to be very cautious before investing in these companies as low equity may very quickly translate into high risks.

Debt to capital ratio = Total debt / Total assets

This ratio expresses the proportion of a company's assets financed with debt (short-term and long-term). A high ratio indicates a high degree of financial leverage, and consequently, financial risk.

Interest coverage ratio = Operating income (or EBIT) / Interest costs

A high interest coverage ratio means that debt is a low burden to the company. As interest has to be paid out of operating income (in this case Earnings Before Interest and Taxes) the ratio should always be comfortably higher than one. If the ratio falls under one this would mean that the company is in a loss position.

Return of the Business

This type of analysis compares inputs and outputs and assesses how profitable the company is. The first of these ratios is the Return on Assets ratio. The important point is that profitability is not measured on the basis of the share price (which management cannot control) but in comparison to the assets used (which are entirely under management's control). A high ratio means that management is doing a good job and does use the company's resources in an efficient way. Again there are considerable differences from one industry to the other.

Return on assets ratio = Net Income/Average Total Assets

Whereas ROA does not take into consideration how assets are financed, the situation is different for the next ratio called Return on Equity ratio.

Return on equity ratio = Net Income / Average Total Equity

ROI and ROE analyses are commonly used in forecasting future earnings. A high ROE may mean that a company has a strong competitive position allowing it to continue to enjoy above-average profitability; however, it may attract new competition to the industry and drive down profits for all the competing companies. Conversely, low ROI may be evidence of overvalued assets and inefficient management, or it may be an indication that the business has a large amount of unused resources that give it a margin of safety and the wherewithal to expand the company's earning power.

Obviously this ratio is highly influenced by the capital structure of the company, by the amount of leverage it uses. Suppose that a company does not have any debt, then the ROE will be equal to its ROA. Now suppose that the same company will finance half of its assets by debt, then the ROE will substantially deviate from its ROA.

Profit Margins

Different kinds of profit margins exist. They measure different level of profits relative to sales. They are always expressed as a proportion of sales and will always be lower than 100%; profit margin ratios express how much of every dollar of turnover the company is able to keep as earnings.

Reinvestment of free cash flow in a manner that continues to earn above-average returns is seen by many as the most important point for finding companies which become x-baggers in a small number of years. Ideally such company will not pay out dividends and not buy back shares as both will decrease the amount of equity to be reinvested.

Gross profit Margin = (Sales – Cost of goods sold)/Sales

If two competing companies charging the same prices do have substantially different gross profit margins, the one with the higher margin is more efficient as its costs of goods sold is lower.

According to some studies made it would appear that gross profit margins tend to be rather sticky, meaning not to be subject to mean reversion. In other words companies which show high gross profit margins tend to continue to do so over long periods of time. The same holds true for companies with low gross margins which do also tend to be lasting. Gross profit margins are at the end determined by the market position of the company: a competitive moat acts as a means to avoid reversion to the mean of profit margins. The very fact that one company has higher gross profit margins than its competitors and that it is able to maintain these profits margins for a long time period shows that this company probably has a solid moat.

On the other hand, the situation is different for net profit margin which are determined by SG&A expenses. The volume of these costs which are generally rather volatile can easily be influenced by management decision. In other words, companies with high expenses in this category could relatively easily be turned around.

Operating Profit Margin = EBIT / Sales

This ratio measures the operative performance of a company and it tells us how much the company earns per dollar of sales after deduction of variable costs of production as wages and raw materials, but before debt interest and taxes. The company's operating profit is divided by its net sales.

Net Profit Margin = Net profit after taxes / Sales

Unlike the preceding ratios, this one takes into consideration all the costs incurred by the company in order to perform its sales. The net profit used in the numerator is the one corresponding to the bottom line in the P&L account.

As expected, gross and net profit margins vary widely from industry to industry (which tells us something on the quality of a given industry) and also from company to company within the same industry. For instance, supermarket chains have very low gross margins (roughly 25 %, operating margins of 6% (WMT) or 30% and 11% (TGT). The same holds true for the airline industry (operating margin of 10-20% on average) whereas software industry boasts gross margins of 90%.

Balance Sheet Versus Earnings Statement

A long-standing debate among analysts is what matters most: earnings data or balance sheet data? When watching the financial news channels one clearly gets the impression that the only thing which counts are earnings (sometimes only turnover when looking for instance at stocks like internet stocks in 2000 or nowadays the ride hailing companies like Uber or Lyft). This may be a good approach for some investment strategies but it definitely is not the case for value investors. They should be mindful of the saying that balance sheets don't matter until it's all that matters. This statement refers to near-bankruptcy situations where anyone will, maybe for the first time, look very closely at such mundane things as the type of assets on the balance sheet, how liquid they are, long-term debt, etc. in order to see whether suppliers will continue to sell goods to the company and bankers decide to extend their credit lines for one more month.

Value investors know that they are in for the long term which requires them to be more demanding than others (say those who have an investment horizon of one three months as a maximum) when it comes to financial safety issues.

As value investors usually have a longer time horizon than most investors, they have to allow for the possibility that the reasons why a certain stock has a margin of safety might disappear. They are aware of the fact that the future is unknown and even unknowable and that among the various scenarios which may play out there is also always a worst-case scenario and that means nearly always bankruptcy.

It is generally easier to forecast <u>what</u> will happen than <u>when</u> it will happen, meaning that transformations, restructurings and turnarounds (whatever that may mean in a concrete case) generally speaking take a lot longer than expected. At this point, a strong balance sheet may have its value in gold: it buys time for things to happen whereas a weak balance sheet will not grant the company such luxury as the time which may be needed for planned adjustments to take place might not be granted to the company by nervous creditors. In this respect it may be useful to mention that behavioral studies show consistently that humans have a constant tendency to grossly underestimate the time it takes for realizing a certain job. Investing with a margin of safety means by definition that stocks are bought at a depressed price and the implicit assumption is that, at least most of the time, that undervaluation will correct sooner or later. Nobody knows how much time this will take and it may well take more time than expected as totally unforeseeable events (Fukushima, coronavirus...) come up which act as set-backs delaying a price recovery. With a weak balance sheet that time might simply not exist. Conversely, a strong balance sheet buys that time and the company will be able to play another day, month or year in this way increasing the chances to navigate through the years needed for a complicated restructuring to unfold successfully.

Berkshire Hathaway

For some market commentators, Berkshire Hathaway is an index fund, which means that it represents a diversified portfolio of stocks of predominantly US companies including such household names as American Express, Apple, Bank of America, Coca Cola,Wells Fargo, etc. These shares have mostly been bought many years ago and, you have guessed it, at substantial discounts compared to today's prices. For instance, Berkshire owns 400,000,000 shares of The Coca Cola Company. The cost at which these shares are recorded is $3.2475 per share compared to a market price of some $50. If these shares were sold at present prices substantial taxes on capital gains would become due. These taxes, which are a huge reason not to sell the shares are booked as deferred taxes the amount of which was significantly reduced (by $29.6 billion)[37] due to the Tax Cuts and Jobs Act (TCJA) end of 2017 and as of December 31, 2019 reached $32.134 billion. In essence, these deferred taxes represent an interest free loan of the US government to the company. This loan will become due only when the shares in the companies will actually be sold... don't hold your breath!

These deferred taxes are not the only interest-free resource of the company. The second resource of this kind is the all-important "insurance float", represented by premiums cashed in and which will be paid out only if and in as far as a disaster occurs. The amount of this insurance float has reached some $130 billion at the end of 2019.

The qualification of an index fund applied to Berkshire Hathaway is not accurate and in fact it is less and less true as time goes by: the reason is that, especially over the years following the Great Recession (2008-2009) Berkshire Hathaway, in lieu of purchasing minority positions in large capitalization stocks (of the types mentioned above), has changed strategy by buying majority positions in large companies: major acquisitions of this kind have been BNSF (Burlington Northern Santa Fe a railroad) purchased for US$26 billion, ISCAR (a toolmaking Israeli Company) purchased in 2010, MidAmerican Energy Company (a utility in the meantime renamed to BH Energy), Precision Castparts Corp. a manufacturing company making complex metal components for aerospace and industrial markets purchased in 2015.

These acquisitions of majority holdings (often 100-percent holdings) have consequences on the bookkeeping of these holdings. The financial statements of these companies are consolidated into the books of Berkshire Hathaway. This means that, unlike for minority holdings in publicly traded companies, there is a difference (a substantial one in most cases) between real value of the companies and its book value. With time, this difference will only increase. This means also that the token traditionally used by Warren, Buffett for valuation of Berkshire Hathaway, namely book value, consistently, and increasingly as time went by, underestimated its real value. As an example, for this growing divergence between book value and intrinsic value let's take BNSF, Burlington Northern Santa Fe. This company has been purchased in 2010 for $26 billion. At the end of 2019 book value of the stocks of Union Pacific, another railroad company of similar size and importance which is still publicly traded, was $28 per share whereas the share price for the year was around $185, which is more than six times book value. The same divergence is certainly true for other important acquisitions, like ISCAR, Lubrizol, Marmon Group, BH Energy, etc.

The accounts of Berkshire Hathaway do not show the assets and liabilities of BNSF separately. It is absolutely certain that the book value of those assets have over time increased substantially but as market value has increased as well, an important gap remains between book value and market value of BNSF.

In recognition of this inadequacy of book value as a valuation tool for Berkshire the column "Per-Share Book Value of Berkshire" which has been reproduced in the Annual Reports of the company since 1965 was for the last time appeared in the 2018 Annual Report. At that final appearance the cumulated growth rate of book value over the 1965-2018 period was a compounded annual gain of 18.7% whereas the growth of the stock price showed a compounded annual rate of 20.5% increase. Again this "only" 1.8% difference translated into a huge difference overall: 1,091,899% compared to 2,472,627%. Compounding, over long periods translates small differences in growth rates into huge differences in results.

It is true that over the most recent years (from 2016 to 2020) the acquisition of entire businesses (of significant size) has come to a halt, the reason being that Warren Buffett considers that the prices quoted on the various stock exchanges do not allow for any margin of safety. Being as patient and as consistent in his investment policy as he is, Warren Buffett will not buy such businesses at prices which he considers excessive. Hence, no significant acquisition of whole companies has been done over the last 4 years. The Covid-19 crisis may well lead to changes in this field and give rise to or the other purchase of entire businesses of a very big size, although so far this does not seem to be the case as stock prices corrected very quickly after reaching market lows on March 23, 2020. However, beginning of July 2020 Berkshire announced the purchase of 7700 miles of natural gas transmission and storage assets along with 900 billion cubic feet of gas storage from Dominion Energy for a price of some $10 bn.

The evolution from a portfolio of substantial stock holdings (representing less than 10% of the share capital) to a conglomerate of entirely-held businesses also means that the transition to the post-Buffett era may have less incidence than the markets seem to believe. Indeed, it is well known that neither Buffett nor anybody else based at Kiewit Plaza in Omaha interferes in any respect with the management of its fully-owned subsidiaries. Incidentally, even if they wanted to do differently, with a total staff of 25 people or so, whereas the conglomerate employs some 380,000 employees, they would not be in a position do so. Buffett's role has been limited to capital allocation without any interference into management of the fully-owned subsidiaries.

It came as a surprise to many "Berkshire watchers" that during the virtual shareholders' meeting held on May 2, 2020 Warrren Buffett informed the audience that Birkshire had not used the company's huge cash pile to invest either in certain portions of stocks purchased on the stock exchanges or to make public offers for buying whole businesses. Neither did Berkshire buy back their own stocks beyond negligible amounts.

The reason for this abstinence as indicated by the CEO himself was that prices are not that attractive and that the possible economic outcomes, at that moment, were extraordinarily diverse. However, during the more than 5 hours which the shareholders' meeting lasted Warren Buffett had repeatedly insisted on the mantra: Don't bet against America. This was the real message. Buffett's philosophy is as clear as consistent: he says he is unable to forecast what the markets will do tomorrow, in a year, etc., to forecast when planes will fly again, when the Covid-19 virus sanitary crisis will be over.... but he knows one thing: America will prosper.

What to think about Berkshire as an investment?

It is a fact that value investing in general (and Berkshire Hathaway in particular), for the time being, are not really faddish on Wall Street. Market commentators consistently insist on Berkshire underperformance over the last 10 years and increasingly many of them suggest Buffett "has lost his touch." These conclusion requires some comments.

1. In the first place, and by referring to p. 2 of the Annual Report 2019 of Berkshire Hathaway this "underperformance" if it does exist it is minimal only. Calculating the arithmetic mean, the cumulated gap in favor of the S&P 500 (dividends included) is 1.8%. This result is due to the huge discrepancy between the BRK/B share price and its benchmark which came up during 2019: whereas the Berkshire stock price increased 11%, the S&P 500 (dividends included) did increase by 31,5% a difference of 20.5%, which represents the highest underperformance since 1999 (when the underperformance was 40.9%).

Over the last 20 years (before 2019), Berkshire outperformed the S&P 500 (cum dividends) by 59.9%. Over 15 years by 7%. Over 10 years, as already mentioned, we have an underperformance of 1,8% (meaning we have a result of -1.8). If we do that same calculation for 5 years we have outperformance of Berkshire for 2010 and 2011 (by 19.2 and 4.1 respectively), underperformance in 2012 and 2013 (-18.3 and -13.8 respectively), outperformance in 2014 (+13.9) underperformance in 2015 (- 6.3) outperformance in 2016, 2017 and 2018 (+11.9, 11.2 and 18.1 respectively, and underperformance in 2019 (-15.7). These figures, on a cumulated basis, show two things: firstly, the comparative results are increasingly close, secondly, the fact that there are alternative periods of underperformance and outperformance is not new but goes back already to 2012 already.

2. It is undeniable that the ten-year period to which reference is made here was an uninterrupted bull market, which is precisely the most unfavorable scenario for Berkshire. This point has always been stressed by Warren Buffett himself who has repeatedly insisted on the fact that Berkshire will likely underperform compared to the benchmark in rising markets but beat that same benchmark in contracting markets. When holding some $130 billion in cash or treasury bills, which at current interest rates produce hardly anything for Berkshire, whereas the S&P 500 is "fully invested", outperforming the benchmark gets close to impossible in a rising market. In a falling market this cash cushion would work in reverse.

3. Another unfortunate aspect of the current situation is the low-interest environment which we are currently experiencing. Berkshire's balance sheet is characterized by extremely high liquidity, a war chest of $137 bn ready to be invested. Whereas such liquidity in normal times is a worthwhile advantage, in a situation where interest rates are high and banks and investors are cautious and risk averse, this is not the case in the current situation where basically any business receives liquidity grants at very low costs under government economic aid plans, or central bank investment schemes exceeding the X$ trillion mark. The result of this situation for Berkshire has been that unlike what happened during the Great Recession when numbers of banks (Bank of America, Goldman Sachs) and industrial companies (General Electric, Mars, Dow Chemical and Harley Davidson) took up huge loans from Berkshire, this is not the case during the current Covid-19 pandemic.

Furthermore, the principal structural advantage of Berkshire compared to most other conglomerates which consists of its insurance float, the funds which insurees pay to Berkshire, their insurer, and which will be paid out as indemnities many years later if an insurance event occurs (currently some $130 bn), bears a significantly lower value in low-interest and high-liquidity times.

4. A further reason for the relative underperformance probably lies in the fact that the FAANG stocks (however defined with precision) being as successful as they currently are (and as they have been over the last 10 years), value investing looks stodgy in comparison.

5. Another point is Warren Buffett's notoriety: he is extremely popular even on a world-wide scale, particularly in China, which, together with his age, is a combination which is currently a liability for Berkshire. It is totally unusual to see two nonagenarians occupying the two top positions of a S&P 500 company with one of the highest capitalization of that index.

Having said this, what is there to like about Berkshire (as an investment)? Hereafter I mention a non-exhaustive list of points.

1) Any shareholder of Berkshire is sure that their interests are aligned not just on paper but in reality with management in place. Buffett annual compensation does not exceed $200,000 and no stock options are allocated to any manager or employee of the company.

2) Central management is not interfering with management of the numerous subsidiaries. Management of the various operating subsidiaries are invited to adopt a long-term view without being distracted by the numbers which will be shown by the next quarterly accounts (such figures if they are supplied on a quarterly basis to Omaha, they are not published separately). Accordingly management of each company

may concentrate on developing the moat of the businesses they manage.

3) Intrusive bureaucracy is not taking over at Berkshire: no regular meetings are held, no budgets (at head office), etc.

4) No aggressive accounting, no serial restructurings, no ongoing mergers or acquisitions of companies at excessive prices, no hazardous tax planning. In case acquisitions are made, these companies keep their management and there are previously applicable procedures. This means that in case a new CEO replaces Buffett there is no change whatsoever in the way subsidiaries are run and these entities will continue to prosper as they presently do. Any successor could just take no decisions at all on an ongoing basis for a number of years and if he does not have ideas to invest the considerable cash flow from the operating entities he could simply decide to pay substantial dividends and/or proceed to share buybacks (especially if prices are depressed).

5) No inconsiderate stock buybacks.

6) An overall conservative approach privileging the conservation of what is there when compared to chasing the most profitable expansion evidenced by a speech Buffett made to an assembly of utilities managers which he opened by saying: "You do not invest in utilities to get rich … but to stay rich."

Doubtlessly the stock price of Berkshire is penalized by the age of its CEO and of its vice-president. As the example of Apple shows, the loss of a dominant and iconic CEO does not necessarily spell trouble for the company or its stock.

Whoever the new CEO will be, it has to be assumed that he has been carefully chosen and that he will be a perfect fit with the corporate culture of Berkshire Hathaway. Even if he wanted, he would not be allowed, for instance by the board of directors and/or by the shareholders, to substantially deviate from the guidelines set in place by Buffett and Munger. This element of corporate culture is not sufficiently taken into account by most analysts (although Buffett himself continuously stresses its importance in his annual Letter to Shareholders). For instance, a successor would not be allowed to follow a Ross Johnson management style (as described in the remarkable book "Barbarians at the Gate, The Fall Of RJR Nabisco" of Bryan Burrough and John Helyar) made of partying, travelling and entertaining on account of the company, RJR Nabisco in that case. The head office of the company was transferred from Winston-Salem a small town in Virginia to Atlanta. This will certainly not happen with Berkshire: the seat of that company will not be transferred to any other place. The same will hold true at least for a very long time for compensation policy, hiring (or better, not hiring) outside consultants and lawyers for this and that issue the CEO wants to implement, etc.

Buffett is fully aware of the importance of his statements in this respect. In my view, this is the reason why he puts this enormous effort in the chairman's letter published in the annual report of the company where he informs the shareholders (his "partners" as he calls them) of the company, and corporate America in general, how a corporation should be run: in my view, part of these writings is a kind of testament through which he puts pressure on his successors and for a very long time those successors will not be able to deviate substantially from what these guidelines laid down during decades did require.

Looking into the future it may be said that as long as the FAANG stocks, and, by extension a large chunk of the technology sector, are doing well (the Covid-19 crisis has even given them an additional boost) the chances for a value investing approach to shine are small. In this respect things could change if these high-flying stocks lose some of their luster, for instance due to increased costs: it is a fact that these companies do have to invest heavily mostly into data centers and they no longer are companies without capex. Under the combined pressure of higher capex and exploding compliance costs (resulting in exponentially growing payroll expenses) it may be that these groups of stocks may know the same fate as banking stocks after the Great Recession: whereas they escaped trust legislation consequences ("too big to fail"), higher costs destroyed profits margins.[38]

Beyond these aspects of higher costs, which the companies concerned might well overcome without meaningful damage, it gets increasingly clear (in mid July 2020) that the FAANG stocks themselves may be heading for some trouble and if those problems realize, value investing could easily receive an upgrade compared to so-called growth investing.

On February 11, 2020 the Fortune magazine published an article entitled "5 Companies now make up 18% of the S&P 500. Is that a recipe for a crash?" The 5 companies concerned were Amazon, Apple, Alphabet, Facebook and Microsoft which collectively as Ben Carlson noted added 4.4 trillion of market cap since 2013.

Now, what is in store for the FAANG stocks? On the price front it has to be noted that valuations at which these shares are traded do look increasingly "bubble-like", or at least disconnected from the economic reality of the Covid-19 crisis. Apple at $450, Amazon at $3,300 etc. seem to me to represent very rich valuations, not to talk about TESLA at currently $1,800 after having multiplied its price by 4.5 since beginning of the year 2020.

Although prices may always go higher still, the trade-off between upside and downside gets dramatically negative: risk is sky-high at these valuations and the foreseeable yields over the next 5-10-year period appear very modest at best. Sooner or later markets will get this.

Another potentially even more dangerous development for the FAANG stocks is that the business model of these stocks in jeopardy. This model consists essentially in collecting data on users (who falsely do believe to be the clients but who in fact are "the product"[39] or "the means to others' ends"[40]) and without respecting their users' privacy are monetizing these data by selling them to the most-offering advertiser. As mentioned elsewhere, it may be that the existing anti-trust legislation might not be adequate to target such questionable behavior of those companies (principally Facebook and Google but also Amazon and Microsoft) but the likelihood of new legislation has increased on both sides of the aisle in the Capitol where consensus has grown that the behavior of the companies mentioned above cannot anymore be unchallenged at the risk of destroying democracy (meddling with the Brexit referendum in the UK in July 2016 and the presidential election in November 2016 in the US), dividing the population by opposing one part of it to the other (by creating filter bubbles) in addition to significant collateral damages, namely increasing inequality.

Readers who want to have a critical look at the business models of these companies and their dire consequences which led those companies to become the stocks with the highest capitalization of the world should read the following books: "Don't Be Evil: The Case Against Big Tech" by Rana Foroohar, "Zucked: Waking Up to the Facebook Catastrophe" by Roger McNamee, "The Black Box Society" by Frank Pasquale and "The Age of Surveillance Capitalism: The Fight for a Human Future at the New Frontier of Power" by Shoshana Zuboff.

Valuation of Berkshire Hathaway

Valuation of Berkshire Hathaway is not that easy and this for several reasons. Berkshire Hathaway Inc. is a conglomerate including more than one hundred different businesses and accordingly it cannot be allocated to one specific industry. Value Line, for instance, puts it into the "Insurance (Property/Casualty)" industry. Although insurance and reinsurance are very important parts of Berkshire's activities in terms of underwriting results (the difference between premiums received and amounts paid) it generates (insurance float, which amounts to currently some $130 billion), in more recent years other sectors have been added which have led to a far more diversified conglomerate. Over the last 17 years, (from 2003 to 2019) the company has shown an underwriting profit in 16 years and earned a total pretax amount of $27.5 bn.

Due to the silo approach followed by most investment banks which do run research departments, this conglomerate situation has consequences: only a handful of analysts are following Berkshire Hathaway compared to at least 40 following Appleor Alphabet for example.

In addition to a number of smaller businesses which have been owned for several decades already, like Nebraska Furniture Mart, See's Candies, a number of "elephants" have more recently been joining the zoo: BNSF, BH Energy (formerly named MidAmerican Energy), IMC, Lubrizol, Marmon Industries and Precision Castparts Corp. in January 2016 at the cost of $37 billion. These entities frequently enter into bolt-on acquisitions which increase their assets and their income.

Another important contributor to the assets and results of the conglomerate, in the category of minority-held businesses (between 20% and 50% of shares or voting rights), we find Heinz which after the merger with Kraft represented a high proportion of the securities portfolio of the company ($26 bn on 30 June 2016). However, as of December 2019 the carrying value of this participation had decreased to approximately $13.8 bn due to very significant impairments ($15.9 bn and $1.9 bn respectively) booked over the years 2018 and 2019. Contrary to the majority-owned businesses (more than 50%) Kraft Heinz Corporation shares are recorded according to the so-called "equity method" meaning that the non-distributed profits of the subsidiary are each year added to the cost of the participation recorded on the books of the parent company.

In addition to being an insurance group as well as a conglomerate of industrial and commercial companies, Berkshire is also a kind of investment fund which holds a huge portfolio predominantly, in large stock exchange noted companies in which the insurance float as well as the retained profits are invested. These holdings are mostly valued "mark-to-market" which means that on any balance sheet date the shares are recorded at the stock exchange prices of the last business day of the record period. This also means that tax provisions are calculated on the latent gain which would become due in case the shares were sold on the day the balance sheet is drawn up.

The result of these accounting rules combined with the business reality of holding such a huge portfolio of stocks is that income fluctuations from one quarter (or year) to the next one are very significant and tell us little to nothing about the evolution of the various businesses held by the conglomerate: net income is not a meaningful figure in Berkshire's case. To demonstrate this point it suffices to have a look at the annual results of 2018 and 2019: in 2018 Berkshire showed a measly profit of $4 bn followed by a gargantuan result of $81 bn although in both years the operating result was practically the same, at some $24 bn.

Berkshire Hathaway being a conglomerate composed of literally hundreds of different business undertakings, valuation according to the standard model of discounting future profits (or cash flows) is in practice impossible at least for investors without inside knowledge. The profits of the individual companies are not disclosed. In other words, an alternative tailor-made and simplified method of valuation is needed.

In his shareholders letter of 2010, Buffett has for the first time given the elements allowing any shareholder to do a simple calculation of the intrinsic value of Berkshire (and hence of A-shares and B-shares issued by the company). Buffett did not give his own calculation but gave the two per-share figures (only two) permitting the intrinsic value calculation. The first element of value is the market value of Berkshire's investments in securities, cash and cash equivalents (including all the dividends and interest income earned during the financial year). The second element is earnings coming from other sources than investments and insurance underwriting which refers to earnings (pre-tax) from non-insurance subsidiaries. As Buffett explains, these two figures allow anyone to appreciate the value of the two parts of Berkshire the day the company were split into two entities: a portfolio of marketable securities (including cash) and an operating company which bears all the operating costs.

It should be noticed that this calculation in 2010 completely disregarded the profits from insurance underwritings. The reason as given by Buffett was that "the value of our insurance operation comes from the investable funds it generates, and we have already included this in our first bucket." In older shareholders' letters, Buffett insisted on the fact that underwriting results are erratic and that they may be negative for a large number of years.

In 2014 Berkshire was looking back on an uninterrupted series of 12 years during which total pre-tax profits of $24 billion have been accumulated. In clear, this meant that annual pre-tax profits of $2 billion (on average over a 12 year period) were totally neglected in Buffett's valuation of Berkshire Hathaway. As a consequence, starting with the letter on 2015 Buffett has included underwriting profits into operating earnings calculation.

For putting a value on Berkshire Hathaway shares there is only one missing element: the multiplier to be applied to pre-tax profits generated by the non-insurance businesses. In 2014 the shareholders' letter states (p. 7) in a very lapidary sentence what should be the most important passage for any Berkshire shareholder: " Here is an update

303

of the two quantitative factors: In 2014 our per-share investments increased 8,4% to $140,123, and or earnings from businesses other than insurance and investments increased 19% to $10,847 per share."

Over the 40-year period 1970 to 2010 the pro-share investments have increased from $66 to $94,730, a compounded annual rate of 19.9%. Over the same period the second element, in other words the pre-tax non-insurance gains have increased from $2.87 to $5,926 in 2010, a compounded growth rate of 21%.

Unfortunately the chairman's letter to shareholders of later years do no longer indicate these same figures.

Which multiple (which means the P/E ratio applicable to operating businesses) shall we apply to this profit figure?

The easy answer would be to take the average current market rate. The danger of this approach is that the market might be over-valued at the beginning of 2020 which might very well be the case given that the indices have tripled since the bottom of 2008 and that in July 2020 all of the major indices are close to all-time-highs, which appears the more unjustified as the Covid-19 pandemic is far from over, to the contrary. A look-back to the not so distant past shows how perilous this method is: during the technology bubble of the 1998-2000 it was tempting to conclude that an internet company with a P/E ratio of say 35 was a steal, simply by comparing it to other similar companies which were even more overpriced.

Concretely, a P/E ratio of 15 (applied to after tax income) would not appear excessive especially when we consider the low level of interest rates and which has increased at a growth rate of 20.3% over a more than 50-year period. Another noteworthy point is that if admittedly Berkshire's growth rates have decreased since the 1970's, the risk of the business has considerably decreased as well. The likelihood of Berkshire showing a loss-year (in operating earnings) is extremely low and is further decreasing over time. By way of example, although profits decreased substantially in 2008 (compared to the previous years), Berkshire did remain strongly profitable whereas many major companies were in dire straits at that time. This "loss resistance" will only increase over time.

In the 2015 annual report (p. 11) Buffett explained that even if, at some time in the future, the insurance industry did suffer a mega-catastrophe with a $250 billion loss (about triple the highest amount experienced so far), Berkshire would still show a significant profit because of its numerous businesses showing substantial profit streams. In a previous chairman's letter to shareholder, Buffett mentioned that on average if a major catastrophe occurs the share of the loss covered by Berkshire ranges from 3 to 5%. A rate of 5% applied to an amount of $250 billion equates to $12.5 billion which is far less than the annual increase in net worth generated by Berkshire over recent years.

Losses with respect to operational income in Berkshire have over time been exceptional and should even be more exceptional in the future. On page 2 of the 2019 Annual Report figures the usual presentation of the results starting with 1965. During these 50 years, it was only during 2 years that book value per share did not increase, and that was in 2001 (-6.2%) and 2009 (-9.6%): those years, which were the years of the terrorist attacks of 9/11 and of the financial crisis respectively, were not due to the fact that Berkshire's operating companies showed losses but were due to the fact that Mr. Market lived up to his reputation. In 2008, for instance, pre-tax earnings of non-insurance companies fell only slightly from $4,093 billion to $3,921 billion whereas investments per share fell from $90,343 to $77,793, a decline not caused by net sales of securities but by a decrease in market prices. Because of the magnitude of Berkshire's stock portfolio and of the magnitude of the fluctuations to which it is subject, Buffett has in various chairman's letters to shareholders advised readers to concentrate on operating earnings instead of net income.

Another element of considerable weight, which is also neglected by Berkshire analysts, is that the earnings of the company are consistently understated when compared to other companies and this for reasons of inadequate accounting rules.

As Buffett explained in the chairman's letter to shareholders of the year 2017 the GAAP rules applying to the treatment of unrealized gains have changed and as of the said year they have to be taken into account in the net income figures. The result is that the net income of Berkshire since 2018 has been subject to wild fluctuations as the ever-growing portfolio of minority-held stocks in publicly traded companies have a huge impact on the net result of the company. This fact explains that Buffett advises to concentrate on operating earnings instead of net income.

Another accounting rule of considerable relevance has to be underlined here: it concerns the treatment of retained earnings at the level of the various companies owned, either wholly or partially. This treatment is very different according to the importance of the participation held.

As indicated above, and as very largely known, Berkshire holds a huge portolio of stocks in minority-owned companies. This is not the result of a deliberate policy from the part of the CEO, who would prefer to acquire entire businesses but which was not able to do such acquisitions at reasonable prices over the last twelve years or so. Contrary to majority-held participations which are fully consolidated in the financial statements of the parent, meaning that the profits of, say, BNSF are entirely counted as operating profits of Berkshire, the situation with less than 20% holding is different in as far as the profits of the subsidiaries will not fully go into the operating earnings of the parent but they will be included therein only in as far as they are paid out as dividends to the shareholder parent company. Until 2018 the same was the case for realized capital gains in case such minority held stock holdings were realized by Berkshire. It is true that those thesaurized profits are not neglected altogether but they are taken into consideration in as far as they increase the market value of the stocks of the company.

For participations of less than 20% of the shares issued by the companies only dividends go to net income. Retained earnings of the target company are disregarded. Arguably this is a misalignment of the accounting rules applicable to the different types of participations held. In case of majority-held participations there is a full consolidation of the assets and liabilities of the subsidiaries into the account of the parent, meaning Berkshire Hathaway Inc., with the consequence that the results are fully part of the results of the parent company. For participations of 20% at least but not exceeding 50% the equity method may be applied which, although not requiring a full consolidation of the subsidiary's assets and liabilities, will entail full integration of the subsidiary's result in the result of Berkshire, the parent company. However such inclusion is not possible for stockholdings smaller than 20% for which only dividends paid out by the stock issuing company will be included in the operating result of the parent company, whereas retained earnings are neglected. In case of Berkshire the amount of these retained earnings reach enormous proportions which I try to estimate hereafter at the date of December 31. 2019 based on the indications given by the company in the Annual Report 2019, p. 5, where a table indicates the amount of dividends received from Berkshire's 10 most important minority-held companies, and in a further column the amounts of the retained earnings for each of these companies. In total, these companies paid dividends of $3.798 bn in 2019 and the retained earnings amounted to $8.332 bn. As this table only refers to the 10 most important holdings it may be interesting to extrapolate from these data the total amount of retained earnings. It is easy to determine the market value of these 10 holdings based on the figures given on page 10 of the same Annual Report. These 10 holdings represent $197.989 bn out of $248,027 bn, or to extrapolate from these 10 holdings to the total portfolio we have to multiply the smaller figure by 1.2527. This means that 8.332 x 1.2527 = $10.437 bn represents the estimated amount of retained earnings of all minority-held (less than 20%) stocks of Berkshire.

This calculation assumes that the proportion of retained earnings to dividends is the same for the smaller holdings as for the 10 largest ones. This assumption seems reasonable and the actual result should not deviate much from the one determined here.

Anyway, operating earnings of Berkshire would be higher by the amount of $10.437 bn (pretax or $8.245 bn after tax) if the same accounting rules as those applicable to majority controlled companies applied also to participations lower than 20%.

1) This will lead us to adjusted operating profits of $32.245 bn or $19,733 per A share ($13.156 per B share). If to this earnings figure we apply the P/E ratio of 15 (which is low by today standards and even disregarding relative pricing is extremely conservative at a time of zero interest rates) we obtain an intrinsic value of $197.34 per B share (which is only slightly lower than their present price in the market). In other words, the proportionate share of the companies' liquid assets and securities portfolio is nearly for free).

2) At the end of 2019 the total amount of cash and cash equivalents, Treasury bills, fixed maturity securities and equity investments reached $391.865 bn or $159.934 per B share.

Total intrinsic value of a B share: $197.3 (1) + $159.9 (2) = $357.2. This looks like a solid margin of safety for a stock currently traded at some $213.

This calculation is based upon a number of assumptions which may be questioned. The figures driving this result are the operating earnings and the assets taken from the Annual Report 2019. It is true that in the meantime these figures are no longer up-to-date: whereas the prices of the securities held by Berkshire have nicely corrected when compared to the lows reached on March 23, 2020, operating earnings of the current year will be lower than those of 2019. Intrinsic value calculations, especially those of a conglomerate like Berkshire, should be based not upon one specific annual or quarterly results but on a "normal earnings capacity." It is this earnings capacity which the operating earnings figure of 2019 (as a relatively normal year for Berkshire) is deemed to approximate. In other words, it is implicitly assumed that Covid-19 is only a transitory phenomenon which sooner or later will be put behind us.

Another question is whether it is legitimate to adjust the earnings of Berkshire by adding the proportionate share of the retained earnings to Berkshire's income? Some might argue that counting the retained part of the subsidiaries' earnings as income of the parent company while at the same time valuing the stocks of the subsidiary's at market value might be viewed as counting those retained earnings twice as those earnings are shown on the balance sheet of the subsidiary and are doubtlessly a part of the net asset value of the subsidiary and increase the value of the stock issued by the subsidiary. Those readers inclined to consider that there is actually such an issue of double-counting may want to adjust the value of the stock portfolio: my suggestion would be to adjust that value by the amount of the retained earnings, meaning $10.437 bn (pretax or $8.245 bn after tax) or $4,26 per B share ($6,931 per A share).

The figures concerning the equity investments as shown by the balance sheet of end-2019 have also been taken over without any adjustments, which may again be criticized as too high. Although market indices at the end of 2019 have definitely been at historically high levels, this is not the case for all sectors of the markets and certainly not for the majority of the shares held by Berkshire. Concerning Apple, the most important single position held by Berkshire, although prices were high at end of 2019, they have even increased significantly since that date.[41] In aggregate, the finance sector represents the majority of stocks held by Berkshire and these stocks are not at historically high levels, quite the contrary.

In a nutshell, the calculation here above is suitable for a long-term investor who intends to hold stocks over a long time and who willingly accepts to patiently wait until markets correct their over-reliance on momentum stocks.

Anyway, it is up to the reader who considers the assumptions made are not accurate, to adjust the calculations made here, either by inserting another value for the securities portfolio, the amount of operating earnings and/or the P/E ratio applied here. Given the simplicity of the calculations suggested here, such adjustments do take a minimum of time. In any case, intrinsic value calculations, by definition, and especially in case of conglomerates with hundreds of operating businesses should not fluctuate significantly over a short period of time, not more so than the water debit of the Mississippi will change hugely from one day to the next. Wildly fluctuating values are the distinctive feature of stock market quotes, delivered every working day by Mr. Market, but should not be the one of intrinsic value calculations assessing the value of a multitude of inherently stable businesses.

Margin of safety

The keystone of any cautious, risk-minimizing investing method (and not only of value investing) is to only buy if the investor is able to benefit from a "margin of safety." Why? The reason is that the intrinsic value of a stock, as it is based on the future flow of profits generated by the issuing company, which nobody may forecast with any reasonable certainty, cannot be calculated with mathematical accuracy. The margin of safety is meant to protect the investor against calculation errors (at least to a certain extent). Assume for example that an investor, a month ago did consider that a share of company X (which realizes all its income in the US) is worth $75 but due to a sudden market correction due to political tensions in the Middle East those shares may be purchased at $50 currently. This makes a margin of safety of 50% for the investor. It may very well be that the calculations of the investor were excessively optimistic, and that on the basis of the adjusted data the intrinsic value is to be adjusted downwards, say to $60. The investor will have to admit that in reality his margin of safety is considerably less than what he assumed it to be, but in fact it does still exist and a purchase of the shares at the adjusted level is still justifiable.

The margin of safety has still another extremely useful function and which this time relates to the rate of return on the investment. The profit lies in the purchase price as any value investor knows. A short example will show what this means. Let's assume that an investor purchases a share at $50 whereas the intrinsic value is $75. This intrinsic value will increase over time, for instance if the EPS (earnings per share) will increase as time goes by. Let's assume that intrinsic value over a 5-year period increases from $75 to $100. If over the same period market value of a given stock will close the initially existing gap with its intrinsic value, then the investor might hope for a doubling of its investment over a period of 5 years whereas intrinsic value has only increased by a third.

Of course, there is no guarantee that this gap will be closed over the said period but it may as well be closed over a shorter time span. The important thing is that the investor is aware of the existence of the margin of safety: once they know that undervaluation exists, they just need to be patient and wait for the moment when the gap will eventually close down.

What does the investor do when the gap is closed (meaning when market value and price do correspond)? The answer is that at least they should consider to sell not that they should necessarily do so. This issue will be treated in more detail in Chapter 6.

What is the minimum margin of safety required? Very few authors or practitioners have given a precise answer to that question. By exception, Steve Morrow has asked for a minimum of a 35 percent discount to their current estimate of intrinsic value.[42] Such margin is relatively high and it means that there will be a more than 50% upside if market price meets intrinsic value. Obviously, the magnitude of the margin of safety may be somewhat lower if your calculation of intrinsic value has a high degree of reliability, say, in case of a regulated electricity utility.

When and where to find such shares trading at a discount? You will certainly not find them in the last phase of a raging bull market especially not in those industries which are highly visible and fashionable.

This means that an investor should have a somewhat contrarian attitude by looking for companies in sectors which are not the latest fad and probably also during periods when stock markets go down or at least are in a boring sideways move. In other words, the investor should look for shares nobody wants (under the additional condition that the intrinsic value is substantially above the market price).

It may not always be easy to find stocks with an adequate margin of safety. Especially in times of bull markets this may not be the case. If a large number of stocks with a decent margin of safety can be identified the margin of safety calculation may serve as an instrument of selection: if, all other things equal, three stocks have a margin of safety of 30, 40 and 50% respectively, the investor will logically purchase the one showing the highest margin of safety, in other words the one with the highest relative margin of safety.

Any margin of safety on an invidual stock (even a very high one) will not guarantee that the investment will ultimately show a profit; it only means that the likelihood of earning a profit is higher than the one of making a loss. The higher the number of such trades in which the investor is involved the more certain it will become that the total amount of profits will exceed the total amount of losses. Diversification which will result in a higher number of holdings increases the chance of gains compared to the chances of losses.

Value of Brands

One or the other media or management consultancy firms do from time to time publish studies made by a ranking of brand values, For instance, Forbes magazine, as of 2018 came to the following results for the 5 top ranked brands:

Apple: $182.8 billion

Google: $132.1 billion

Microsoft: $104.9 billion

Facebook: $94.8 billion

Amazon: $70.9 billion

As usual in case of valuation questions, different methods are used which do all have their merits as well as their shortcomings. A detailed description of these methods is beyond the scope of this publication. Anyway, these rankings are not very useful: at best their relative ranking of these large company generate some added value: if we concur that the value of Apple brand is higher than the one of Google which trumps that of Amazon, etc. it does not mean that the Apple brand is more resistant to change than the ones of the other four companies mentioned. In fact the statement that the Apple brand has a value of $182.8 billon is pretty much pointless. That value will appear in no accounting records or financial statements. Furthermore, this brand does not represent an asset which the eponymous company could dispose of. Apple will never give up its name to adopt another one; conversely nobody will pay $180bn to acquire the right to use a certain name without acquiring the Apple business at the same time. The brand will follow the business in the unlikely event that that business would be sold or otherwise disposed of to somebody else (in a merger for instance).

The internet age and more specifically e-commerce have also impacted the value of brands in the economy of the 21st century. Brands do no longer have the same weight with consumers and retailers alike. This means that companies with what used to be strong traditional brands are no longer traded and the same premium prices as they were one or two decades ago. Kraft-Heinz held for a substantial part by Berkshire Hathaway is a case in point here.

Commodities and Franchises

Products and services sold are not created equal. Most of the products and services offered fall into the commodities group which means they are virtually identical to those offered by the competition. Belong to these categories: oil, gas, steel, copper, aluminum, computers, cars, power and water and in the field of services, banking and insurance services, airline transport, etc. These businesses are obviously very difficult ones and in fact they have only low profit margins. As the products (services) sold are identical to those offered by competing firms, competition can only happen on the basis of price cutting, in this way immediately hurting profit margins of all market participants. Although trying hard and with sky-high advertising budgets, the companies producing these products/services are unable to differentiate their products from those of the competition.

The concept of franchise is ambiguous as it is used with different meanings in investing and in business life. Legally a franchise is a contract by which the franchisor grants a license against a fee to a person or company (the franchisee) permitting the performance of specific economic activities.

In investing, a franchise refers to a business having favorable characteristics based on the fact that a product (service) does not have a direct substitute which allows the company to increase prices without having to fear a loss of market share. The reason for such franchise-business status may be a strong brand, a technological advantage, a cost advantage which is difficult to copy by the competition, etc.

It is noteworthy that the fact to have a franchise has consequences on the requirements on management of the company. A franchise does not necessarily need to have a very competent management. In a commodity business on the other hand, a competent management is an absolute must as in the absence thereof the company will in all likelihood not prosper.

The qualification of franchise or commodity business may change over time. The newspaper industry has evolved from being a strong franchise business to a commodity business (under the influence of the internet). Similarly, retail outlets which, at least in some areas, have been franchises, also have mostly become commodities businesses due to the development of e-commerce.

Chapter 6: The Selection of Stocks

As investors may either take a long position (in view of benefiting from an appreciation of the stock) or a short position (forecasting a decrease of the stock price), the kind of stocks investors are looking for are quite different depending on which type of position they intend to take. In a first step some considerations on taking short positions.

Shorting of Stocks

Short sales of stocks consist in selling stocks which the seller does not own and that they first have to borrow in order to be able to deliver the shares to the buyer. Short sellers assume that the stocks they sell short will decrease in price and when they later buy back those stocks in order to close the borrowing transaction they will be able to do so at a lower price realizing a profit equal to the difference between the higher (short) sale price and the lower repurchase price.

Under the EMH (Efficient Market Hypothesis) markets may be efficient only if in a situation when stock prices increase relentlessly some investors start to consider the increases as excessive and take action by selling their holdings which lead to a market correction. If the said skeptical investors consider that Tesla's stock price is excessive they will sell the Tesla stocks they hold. But that may not be enough to correct the sky-high prices as the shares held by these investors and sold by them may easily be bought up by other investors showing a bullish attitude, especially if a stock has a kind of cult status, as is the case with Tesla. However, even investors who do not hold Tesla stocks may intervene in order to correct the (assumed) bubble in Tesla stock prices if they are allowed and willing to short sell those stocks. This means that short sellers do play an important role in the effective functioning of stock markets.

There are several fundamental differences between long and short operations of which the potential short seller should be aware before engaging in this type of operations.

1) Whereas the potential gains of an investor taking a long position are unlimited (in a way: "the sky is the limit"), their potential losses are limited to the capital invested. The short seller's situation is exactly the opposite one: their gains are limited to 100% of the investment made (as the shares cannot go lower than zero due to the limited liability granted to investors in corporations), whereas their losses are unlimited. This element needs to be accounted for by short sellers, either by using stop loss orders or by stock options trades resulting in hedging their positions, because the short seller could be wiped out if their investment (even if it involves only a minor position) unexpectedly increased substantially in value.

2) Short selling is treated as a margin account which means that if the shorted stocks increase in price the broker will require additional funds. If the short seller is unable to put up these additional funds short sellers are exposed to receive margin calls from their brokers in case the stock price goes against them. The short position is closed as the broker buys back the shares on the market and returns them to the lender.

3) Short selling of stocks is essentially a short-term activity: if Buffett's ideal holding period is "forever", this cannot be so for the short seller: given that their upside is limited to 100% of their investments, any long-term holding (say, 10 years or more) will result in mediocre

returns only: the longer the holding period, the lower the return generated even if the investment goes well, meaning the stock goes to zero. An investor with a long position, especially in dividend-paying stocks, may be patient as long as they are confident in relation to the fundamentals of the underlying business. The short investor is in a completely different position: they have no income (if his investment pays dividends, they in fact do even have expenses, see above) and only limited upside potential. If time is the best friend of the investor holding long positions, it is the enemy of the short seller.

4) The tax treatment of capital gains from short sales is generally speaking (which means in most countries) less favorable than the one applicable to long positions. In the US, capital gains are treated as short-term gains, entailing the application of higher tax rates. As mentioned under point 2) a long-term deferral of the tax liabilities will normally also be excluded for the reason that successful shorting requires a quick realization of gains (as these gains cannot exceed 100%).

5) Shorting is more costly than taking long positions. By definition short selling consists of selling a stock without owning it. Hence, in order to make sure that the transaction may be settled within the short delays prevailing on stock exchanges (the 2-day rule) the seller has to borrow the shares they have sold and which they have committed to deliver, which gives rise to a securities lending transaction, a service remunerated by a lending fee to the benefit of the lender (at the expense of the short seller). The amount of this fee is generally rather low: less than 1% per annum (which will increase if stocks are difficult to borrow as is the cast with stocks favored by short sellers).

6) In case the stocks shorted are paying dividends the short seller has to pay the dividends to the stock lender. Whereas an investor taking long positions may select high dividend stocks (for a number of reasons which are

318

explained elsewhere), a short seller should avoid high-dividend stocks because the costs of the short sale increase dramatically.

7) Short sales are of a more limited scope than long trades. The short seller needs to find first a lender of the securities (which is not always the case). Furthermore, shares with a price lower than US $5 generally speaking, typically cannot be shorted.

8) As the normal tendency of share prices over the long term is to increase, the short seller, betting on decreasing prices goes against the base rate. It is a fact that most of the time (in fact two thirds of the time) equity markets are rising. Including dividends, stocks have risen roughly in nominal terms at the rate of some 10 percent per year over the 20th century. This is the base rate. The short seller has to overcome that hurdle. In addition, beaten down stocks are often takeover targets: such takeovers will result in sudden big increases of the depressed stock price leading to unexpected losses for the short sellers. In case the short interest is very high, this situation may lead to a so-called "short squeeze" occurring when hard-pressed short sellers are running to the exits and try to cover their short positions which have turned against them. Such a short squeeze happened in 2008 when Porsche in order to take control of Volkswagen had acquired 70% of the shares of Volkswagen driving up its share price. A lot of hedge funds considered that these prices would quickly corrected once Porsche would have obtained control of Volkswagen. However due to the scarcity of the shares publicly traded, stock prices increased from €200 to more than €1,000 in several days' time only (and in this way making Volkswagen the company with the highest capitalization in the world … for a very short time only!). Short sellers getting nervous they covered their positions at extremely high prices which eventually corrected massively.

The here above listed factors explain why short sales are a significantly different ball game from taking long positions. This is a loser's game with the odds heavily distributed against the investor.

As mentioned above a short sale is a wager with limited upside but unlimited downside and as such it represents a fundamentally bad bet which investors should avoid.

The chances of shorting successfully in rising markets are low. The number of consistently successful short sellers is very low (the only name which comes to mind is Jim Chanos, who became famous when he publicly forecasted Enron's fall a full year before it's actual collapse) which would seem to indicate that this is not a game where easy money can be made.

Although this point is not decisive, short sellers are not very popular and from time to time some politicians and/or regulators are changing the rules in order to render shorting of stocks more difficult or more onerous. During the Great Recession shorting bank stocks was prohibited for some time. Although generally misguided these efforts may hurt investors taking short positions.

For all these reasons, my personal recommendation is to avoid shorting shares as a general rule. This does not mean that it is impossible to be a successful shorter. It only means that when you are shorting shares, the odds are heavily stacked against you (when compared to taking long positions). Exceptions should be made only in rare circumstances in which weak shares in weak sectors can be identified in an environment of very weak equity markets (in a bear market).

Examples would be most of the internet shares (those without any turnover) in 2000 during the internet meltdown or several banking stocks (Bank of America and Citicorp) during the Great Recession of 2008-2009. In such situations, profits can be considerable in a very short time.

However, investors should be aware that timing is extremely important and that stocks having fallen quickly and significantly may rebound very rapidly. Stop-loss orders may be useful in these cases.

But once again, timing being so important, make sure you do not miss the moment to stop shorting.

Short sellers should never forget that a ridiculously overvalued stock is not synonymous with an imminent substantial decrease in its price. As famously stated by Lord Keynes, markets can stay irrational much longer than anyone can stay solvent...

The Use of Filters

Most experienced investors do use a preset list of filters they apply when performing their concrete choices. Such filters do have the priceless advantage to discard from the start large chunks of investments which allows them to save a lot of time and efforts: using filters results in significant gains in efficiency. Although it can never be excluded that in this way one or the other gold nugget may be missed, this possibility is more than compensated by the energy and time saved in this way, allowing these resources to be concentrated on other more promising areas. Which concrete filters precisely will be used in practice will vary from one investor to the next and will at the end of the day be determined by the precise investment strategy which will be followed. Examples of filters may be the following ones: no investment in companies with a P/E ratio exceeding a certain threshold, for instance 20 or 25, no investment in companies having a debt to equity ratio higher than 3, no investment in companies having a ROE or ROA lower than 10%, no investment outside one's area of competence (which area has then to be defined with precision), etc.

Such filters may be applied for instance, to initial public offerings.

IPOs

An IPO is an initial public offer of stocks through which a hitherto private company floats a substantial part of its shares in a public offering and becomes a public company. Such IPOs are strictly supervised by the financial regulators, the SEC (in the US). The regular investor without special connections to investment banks etc. should avoid such IPOs altogether. The principal reason for this conclusion is the timing of the IPO which is exclusively fixed by the company going public. Obviously, this guarantees that the shares are offered at a moment of extremely favorable market conditions. In fact, a big increase of IPO activity is a very reliable indicator that the market is at least heavily overbought, if not already in bubble territory, for instance the internet bubble of 1999/2000. In addition, the company in process of going public and the investment banks involved to assist it and its shareholders will do their very best to create the buzz which will give rise to the excitement (the "irrational exuberance") which will almost guarantee that the offer price will be on the high side. (As the joke goes, some investors believe that IPO stands for "It is Probably Overpriced.") Excitement is the enemy of shareholders. An extreme example is given by the IPO of VA Linux Systems (LNUX) which on December 9, 1999 opened with a price of $30, increased to $299 to close at $239.25, an all-time record increase of 698%. A year after that historic IPO the stock was trading at $8.49.

Of course, it is always possible to point to the few occasions which apparently contradict this very negative conclusion: the IPO of Google in August 2004 and more recently Facebook in May 2012, although that IPO of Facebook was, at the time, dubbed a "fiasco" by the Wall Street Journal.

This very small minority of counter-examples does not invalidate the conclusions given above: clearly, the base rate is that stocks purchased in an IPO do underperform during the period of several years following the IPO. The chances for the investor to identify the winners (the exceptions which confirm the rule) are close to zero. The examples to the contrary do not eliminate the difficulty that on the day of the IPO nobody knows for sure that Amazon, Facebook and Google will be trillion dollar companies one or two decades later on.

If my advice is to discard investments on their IPO this does of course not preclude to buy those stocks later on. Experience shows that once the hype of the IPO is gone, there may be excellent opportunities to buy those shares at a lot more reasonable prices several years down the road. Even if that is not the case, meaning that the IPO price was never reached again (as was the case for Alphabet and Facebook) this is not a sufficient reason to cast over board the rule to not buy on IPO's. On the moment of the respective IPO of Google (as it was still called at that moment) or Facebook it was not yet known (and it was in fact unknowable) that the two mentioned companies would be the undisputed stars of their respective industries: you might as well have been buyer at the IPO of Twitter or Snapchat as of Facebook. Another advantage of only buying several years after the IPO is that at that later moment it was a lot easier to decide that the company concerned would be a success, as for instance in case of Facebook it was possible to see that first the number of dayly and monthly users was still increasing at a surprising speed and even more importantly the company had proved that is was able to monetize its user base in a very profitable way: in other words the risk of the investment had decreased a lot over time.

Another possibility for the use of filters are cyclical companies.

Cyclical Companies

An investor in this type of companies is typically following the business cycle, trying to get in at a moment business is bad and before it will improve and getting out as soon as the fundamentals deteriorate. It is true that when choosing the moment to get in and out one should always be aware that financial markets anticipate these turnarounds by at least several months and very often by more than that. This anticipation explains why the P/E ratio will fluctuate wildly for this type of cyclical companies: when things are going well, the P/E ratio will be very low (for instance 4 or 5) whereas the opposite will hold true at the bottom of the business cycle. In both cases, the applicable ratio anticipates an imminent change of the profit outlook. With cyclical companies, timing is all-important. Unfortunately, market timing is a particularly difficult exercice and the proportion of unsuccessful transactions will inevitably be far from negligible. Furthermore, these cyclical companies, generally speaking, do not have favorable business economics: quite the contrary. They generally have high fixed assets (that is high fixed costs which is one reason why they are cyclical), high capital expenditure and they are selling commodity products. All this together means that these companies will suffer heavy losses over several quarters and possibly over years. These losses result in a decrease of equity so that the company's share price will not increase as rapidly as a company in a stable business (say the beverage business) having a moderate growth rate.

Insider Activity

The term "insider trading" is ambiguous and generally speaking it is used in the context of illegal behavior. This is however not necessarily the case and depending on the circumstances trading by insiders may as such be perfectly legal. Lawmakers did not want to pronounce a general prohibition against trades by corporate insiders in the securities issued by the corporation they are part of and they considered it preferable to allow these operations, provided, (1) they report the transactions and (2) they are not trading in circumstances that they have an undue advantage compared to the general public: in other words, insiders are not allowed to trade on the basis of non-public information. Accordingly, trades made by insiders are illegal if they are trading on the basis of still non-public information and in this way profiting from an unfair advantage against regular investors who do not have the same information. This also means that the same trades are legal if made once the information is public. In any case all trades done by "insiders" have to be disclosed to the public very shortly after their realization.

Following the activity (more precisely the purchases of sales) of insiders is one of the favorite games played by many investors who in fact are looking for a free lunch (or maybe a free ride). The reasoning is that those insiders, by definition, know their company very well and in any case way better than any analyst may ever pretend to know it. Hence, given that these purchases/sales of stocks by these insiders have to be published within rather short deadlines it is tempting to follow their market moves and buy if insiders buy and sell if they sell.

According to SEC regulations on insider activity the purchases and sales of company shares made by certain people with management duties must be disclosed. The reason for this rule is easy to see: insiders are in a privileged position compared to regular investors as they have access to information other people do not have or will only have later on: most information will sooner or later become public knowledge. When such is the case, the information will be worthless (in view of making a trading profit) as it is already included in the stock quotes. In order to level the playing field for all investors, insiders (although not prohibited to trade the shares of their own company) are compelled to inform the public of this type of activity.

In a first approach it would appear that insider buying represents a bullish signal whereas insider selling is a bearish indication. However, the situation is less simple. In the first place, there is a difference between purchases and sales of shares by insiders. An insider sale of stocks they own may have no other reason than that the seller needs the money... be it for purchasing a house, for pension contributions, for college tuition, you name it. This means that insider sales are as such to be taken with caution.

Insider purchases have a higher level of relevance: an insider, just as any investor has the option to choose among thousands of publicly traded stocks on the US and international stock markets. If any insider opts for buying stocks of their company then this can only mean one thing: they are bullish on the prospects of these shares (just as they are on any other shares they purchase).

However, things tend to be more complicated: knowing perfectly well that insider activity is closely followed by "the Street", some corporate officers tend to make believe that their shares are interesting for insiders by having them perform purchases of shares, often in small amounts. Such operations are not really bullish signals: if a CEO earning $5,000,000 per annum buys 15,000 shares at $30 per share then this operation should be discarded as void of any signification. Nevertheless, strangely enough similar transactions often make the headlines of internet sites following insider operations.

Value Line for instance, details the monthly insider operations in terms not of money amounts but in numbers of operations: "Buy, Options, Sell".

This way of accounting for insider operations is obviously far from perfect. If for the month of May 2016 company X has recorded 5 insider operations under the heading "Buy" this does not mean anything if on further investigations it shows that the CEO has given 3 buy orders for a total amount of $140,000 completed by 2 other buy orders of the CFO for a total amount of $70,000. Such trades may at best represent a red flag, inciting to do further investigations.

Wall Street does not view things this way. It is not unusual to read headlines that Mr./Mrs. so and so has sold shares for $12,389.46 of the shares of its company. This is ridiculous and absolutely meaningless.

One final comment on the usefulness of following insider trades: in an interview Joseph Kennedy (who had made a lot of money on the occasion of the Great Depression and who later on became the first President of the SEC, the Stock Exchange Commission) when asked if he thought inside information was a major problem for investors in the booming stock market of 1961 he made the following comment: "If I had all the money that has been lost on inside information I'd be really rich."

Top Down or Bottom-Up Investing?

Many investment advisors will frequently explain that any investment in stocks should be delayed for the reason that general economic conditions are currently not good enough, interest rates will increase, and a recession is around the corner, the Chinese economy is slowing down, or the EURO is falling apart and Europe with it. However, uncertainties of this kind will always exist. Furthermore, the picture given by economic data is rarely a clear or non-ambiguous one. On any given day, there will be some data pointing in a positive direction whereas others give bearish signals. Finally, assuming that the economic outlook is really gloomy, this fact will generally speaking be already reflected in the stock prices, which means that the price rebate more than likely will be quite substantial, maybe sufficient to compensate (and maybe overcompensate) the buyer for the possible bad results which the slow economy will foreseeably generate in the short to medium term. If the investor waits until the moment when all economic indicators are positive, assuming this will ever happen, then optimism will be widespread and the following economic expansion will be fully reflected in stock prices. Remember, the markets (or Mr. Market) have a tendency to get taken away by emotions which leads to overreactions in one or the other direction. In all likelihood share prices will more than reflect the forthcoming economic expansion and in fact the time for buying may be over already.

A further element is that these economic forecasts, all too often, are simply wrong and this by a long shot: according to an old joke economists have forecast 9 of the past 5 recessions. More seriously, during the 2008 financial crisis (also called the Great Recession), all the Central Banks of the major economies injected enormous amounts of funds into the economy to prevent the collapse of economic activity, these injections being financed by debt as already at that moment nearly all the major countries were confronted with heavy budget deficits. Whereas they generally approved these steps for lack of alternatives to end the economic chaos, nearly all of these economists, agreed that the inevitable consequence was to generate inflation of unseen proportions. Furthermore, such inflation could only be further enhanced by easy-money policies pursued by the Central Banks of all the major economies, most prominently the FED, the ECB, the Bank of England and the Japanese Central Bank.

Until now, at the beginning of 2020, these dire forecasts have not realized and the nightmare of some central bankers (the ECB being first in line, but followed by the Japan Central Bank) is not inflation... but deflation! Currently, as the Covid-19 pandemic is raging, the same forecasts of an inflationary tendency are again issued. Arguments that "this time will be different" may be made (say, a trend to growing nationalism which induces deglobalization, the whole fired by the pandemic) and they could have some merit. We will see but without being dogmatic we shall wait "watchfully."

The question is whether such general issues should at all be taken into consideration in the investment process?

This question refers to the investment approach the investor should follow, either a top-down or a bottom-up approach.

A top-down process seems to be the preferred approach of most large professional investors. For them, the starting point is to make predictions about the economy and possibly the political future and once this is done they deduct investment implications for different business sectors and the individual companies, and then acting upon them.

One of the disadvantages of this method is that those who are investing on the basis of such big trends do not have any quantifiable limit to the price they are ready to pay: if value investors will shy away from investing if there is no margin of safety, the question is what are the limits up to which such top-down investors are ready to pay up?

As opposed to this approach we have the bottom-up approach which does not require any forecasts: the essence of this method is to buy bargains, meaning shares at a price substantially under its intrinsic value (i.e. offering a substantial margin of safety) and then wait and see what happens.

Whereas a top-down investor has to make several successive correct forecasts the bottom-up counterpart just buys at an interesting price and waits for the market to correct its mistakes, it being understand that such correction may take much time and that the exact moment it happens is not foreseeable.

Competitive Position and Moats

Long-term investors should very closely follow the competitive position of the companies whose stocks they currently hold as well as those they intend to hold in the future. This statement refers to the concept of economic "moat" (literally a ditch filled with water and surrounding a castle), in other words a protection against competing companies which good companies have (or at least should have). An economic moat is the ability of a business to protect its market share and profits against its competitors.

The persistence of the economic moat is all about the behavior of the competition. It has been known for a long time that management of large groups (at the CEO level and at the board level) when making forecasts concerning the situation of their company over a long period of time, predicting revenues, profits capital expenditure, cash flows, etc. do concentrate on their own situation but what is consistently missing in their projections are the reactions of their competitors. The behavior of the competition is the 800-pound gorilla in the room which management all too often fails to see. Competition will act as a strong headwind which does prevent companies to make progress. However, it is not because these reactions are not known with certainty that they may confidently be ignored. If a company in a very stable industry with 4 major competitors which together represent 90% of the market decides to double its 18% market share over the coming 5 years, it can be certain that the major competitors will not stand still but they will react, for instance by reducing prices which, in turn will lead to price wars which at the end will, in all likelihood, be detrimental to all of the market participants.

It is good advice to avoid industries with rising competition. Not surprisingly it is precisely those industries with high ratios of return on investment and return on capital that attract new entrants which will trigger additional competition which will bring down the ROI and ROC ratios. Sometimes the bride is too beautiful and industries with high ROI and ROC ratios may be a harbinger for problems to come. Such large returns will attract competition driving the return rates down. The opposite holds true for a business selling at a discount: the low rate of return prevailing in the sector will lead to the withdrawal of competition together with the fact that no new entrants will lead to an improved situation and to higher return rates on capital.

In other words, investing in companies operating in sectors with low and decreasing competition should be one criterion for stock selection. Competition will have other consequences for companies with a competitive moat. In commodity industries such moats do not exist which means that profit margins tend to erode and stocks will produce mediocre returns. However, if competitors disappear (for instance because of mergers or bankruptcy) the financial situation of the remaining companies may improve, the more so for the reason that if the industry does have a reputation for low profit margins it is not likely that new competitors will emerge. This is what has happened in the airline industry which after having been an unmitigated disaster for shareholders since its very beginning, was subject to a number of changes which led to a completely changed environment with the consequence that as of the decade of 2010, as a group, the industry was for the first time profitable. The situation of the rental cars industry is similar: relaxed supervision led to mergers with the consequence that the market is dominated by very few players and it has become a lot less competitive.

The railroad industry has also been subject to a considerable number of changes and it has become a very favorable ground for investors, (at least for those who did not discard it upfront as being the past) and they could record brilliant returns, outperforming the S&P 500 over the last 50 years.

Consumer staples produced by firms with strong trademarks have been the big winners of the past 50 years (although things appear to change here as well) and it is far from sure that they will be the winners over the next 50 years. These consumer stables (which produce products which are basically commodities with low prices which are used on a daily basis) have by far beaten consumer discretionary products, like cars, consumer electronics, etc.

331

This is a surprise in itself as with the increase of income over the period after WWII it was discretionary income which increased which should have allowed consumers to expend more money for such high-cost items. However, this was not what happened: consumer discretionary products have been very difficult fields for investors as the industries producing this discretionary goods became commodity sellers with extremely high levels of competition and as consumers, thoroughly compared the products of competing companies and decided mostly on price.

The fallacy of composition

The concept of fallacy of composition refers to the erroneous assumption that what is true for the parts must be true for the whole as well. In the context of business and competition it means that if one business by adopting new technology which gives it a competitive advantage it may take market share from its competitors. However, if that same technology is freely available to everyone, at the same costs, the consequence will be that none of the competitors will eventually have any competitive advantage anymore: price advantages go to the consumers. In such circumstances technological progress is a blessing to consumers, but a curse to businesses. This result may be observed not only in manufacturing sectors but in other areas as well. If in a given city, in any country in the world, some hotels are offering free Wi-Fi connections to their clients then they may attract clients from competing hotels in their quarter. However, sooner or later all hotels will do the same and the initial advantage of the first offeror will go away, the clients are the winners and the hotels will just have additional costs without any increase in revenue.

If in a geographical area with hot summers where retail stores (including restaurants and bars) did not use to have air conditioning, if one chain of stores installs air conditioning then it may expect to attract clients from competitors and in this way increase its market share: The cost of the air conditioning for that company was a lucrative investment with its corresponding adequate returns. However, at the latest over several years' time competition will have followed the leader and air conditioning has become a must and it does no longer represent a competitive advantage. To the contrary, the fact not to have air conditioning would have become a competitive burden. The result is increased costs for everybody and the consumers are the winners.

Innovation and disruption

There is hardly any better example than Nokia to show how quickly a large and apparently well managed company and industry leader may get wiped out by market forces when innovation strikes in the high technology area. Founded in 1865 in Finland as a wood pulp mill operator, it eventually operated in the wireless communication market, and in 1987 it launched its first mobile phone. In 2007 it was the recognized leader of this market (with the consequence that in some countries "a Nokia" was synonymous with a mobile phone) with a market share of 40% worldwide and a market capitalization of well over $130 billion. The attack on its position came predominantly from two US companies which previously were not even considered as competitors, i.e. Apple and Google. In 2007 Apple, so far essentially a personal computer maker, launched the iPhone which only three years later had grabbled 60% of the upper-end smartphone market. The Android operating system launched by Google was destined to hardware and software developers allowing Samsung, Huawei, Xiaomi, etc. to take on the remainder of the smartphone market. The consequence was that as of 2012 Nokia's mobile phone business showed heavy losses, and as of 2013 the company declared it exited the handheld business. With the bright light of hindsight (hindsight visibility is always 20/20) it is easy to spot where Nokia did miss a trend and what it should have made differently. The bottom line however is that the real problem was not the actions of Nokia but those of the competing companies in the sector in which the company was active.

Market Share

Basically no company has a monopoly in a given market (although there are exceptions to this rule as public authorities sometimes grant such monopolies in sectors which are then heavily regulated, like utilities) so that any company shares "its" market with a more or less large number of competitors. Each of these companies seeks to increase their market share at the expense of the competition. Not surprisingly, one measure of the quality of a company is its capacity to gain market share. Such gains translate into high-quality growth, such growth being independent from market growth.

Gaining market share at the expense of the competition does frequently involve cutting prices so that this tactics harms the bottom line. In the financial sector (meaning notably banks and insurance companies) it is possible to increase market share simply by relaxing selection standards and/or becoming less risk averse. The dangerous point here is that such relaxation of standards may seem to be efficient for a number of years before losses will eventually show up with a vengeance. For the said sectors it may be said that "the profits of today will be the losses of tomorrow" if the loans made in the past are not repaid or when the insurances written at insufficient premiums give rise to indemnifications.

Media and the Internet

The interactions of the various existing media are a lot more complex than market commentators make us believe. Take for example the area of the internet and the traditional written media, books and newspapers; it may be said that books (unlike bookstores) may profit from the existence of the internet in the sense that sales of books may be enhanced by the internet. Even more importantly, the internet has been at the origin of the e-book which allows editors to offer their products not only in their physical form which has existed for centuries but also in an electronic form, which when appreciated objectively, has a number of advantages, for instance from a cost point of view (not to talk about the ecological advantages with respect to paper savings and transportation costs). It is a fact that prices of e-books are lower than those of their paper-format siblings which again pushes up demand. It also appears that whereas more people than ever do not read any books at all, a small percentage of the population reads a lot more than before the internet. Similarly, newspapers after having absorbed the chock of declining sales for many years, have taken a more proactive attitude by offering their content also on the internet. Some newspapers were even able to brave the forecast that as of 2017 all newspapers would have disappeared from the US. As the Financial Times wrote in April 2019 the New York Times has surpassed 4 m subscribers where as its peak circulation in 1994 has been 1.18 m[43]. Similarly the Financial Times has registered its millionth reader, the most in its 131-year history. However, these examples are the exceptions just showing that if some newspapers will survive, hundreds of local and regional newspapers have closed there doors already whereas others linger as their economic basis, the advertising money, has moved over to the internet, namely to Amazon, Google and Facebook. As a conclusion, whereas the internet will not ring the bell for books and newspapers it hugely impacts not only the growth rates of this media but even more so the valuations of the companies involved in these sectors.

With respect to the the smartphone it may be said that if it has a huge impact not only on the classical cellphone but also on the PC market, it will certainly not settle the death of these products.

Growth is Overrated

Probably one of the greatest mistakes made by inexperienced investors consists in falling into the trap of investing only in so-called high growth stocks (which nowadays means mostly high technology stocks including social media).

Such high-growth industries have always existed but sector rotation has happened here: the railroads at the beginning of the 20th century, automobiles in the 1920s, aircraft and carpets in the 1950s, electronics in the 1960s, computers in the 1980s, internet and telecommunications in the 1990, social media in the 2000, sharing economy shares in the 2010, etc.

Most of the companies dominating these sectors are good companies and as a group they have had, and still have, an enormous impact on society and on the way people live and work. As investments, the stocks of these companies have at least two problematic features: in the first place, the rate of change prevailing in these "hot" industries is so quick (and furthermore it is unforeseeable to know from the outset into which direction the journey goes) that it is not possible to know who will be the winners and who will be the losers of the fierce competition developing before the public's eyes. To make things worse, it is not infrequent that today's winners are tomorrow's losers. As an example, it suffices two mention RIM (Research in Motion, the producer of Blackberry) which was the undisputed champion of the smartphone (initially centered on the enterprise scene) before the whole industry was disrupted by Apple and Android (sponsored by Google). The second issue with high technology stocks is that as these companies are able to show high growth rates (for sales and possibly for earnings) they are fashionable and benefit from high media coverage, they are very generally overbought and hence overpriced. As we have seen before, overpaying for shares is not only detrimental to future returns but it furthermore increases risk (by substantially enhancing the chance of realizing a capital loss on the sale).

All these overhyped shares will sooner or later come back to earth (at least the likelihood for this to happen is very high, a lot higher than that they will stay overpriced forever). If this downward adjustment happens, the investor may experience the following uncomfortable situation which many investors have problems to understand: although earnings increase at a healthy pace, say at a high single-digit rate, the stock price goes nowhere for the reason that the increase in profits is accompanied by a continuous decrease in the P/E ratio: This decrease in the P/E ratio, also called "multiple contraction", is due to the fact that the market is in the process of reassessing the future perspectives of the company, meaning its future growth rate. In such a situation, investors may over a very long period of time (of a decade for instance) see their stocks going nowhere and their return on investment is limited to the quarterly dividend which for such companies is often pretty low (Microsoft, Apple) if they pay dividend at all (which is not the case for Alphabet, Amazon or Facebook for instance).

It may be added that if the investor buys the shares at a moment where the hype is at its peak, the overprice aspect is at its maximum as well and they will be particularly unlikely to generate a decent return on their investment. In terms of value investors' speak, the margin of safety is not there, or worse, it is negative, meaning that the investor is paying a price not below but above intrinsic value.

Many successful investors have known for a long time already that the way to profitable investments is to avoid the fashionable stocks (currently of the high technology scene) and to concentrate on more mundane sectors with no growth (or low growth). The reason is that these sectors are characterized by no significant inflows of capital (meaning no new competitors enter the scene), low innovation rates (over decades roughly the same products are offered to the markets), low capital expenditure requirements to be made just to stay in business and contributing little to the bottom-line. At the end, these capital outlets will only benefit to customers.

Generally speaking in today's markets growth is overrated which means investors are paying too high prices with the consequence, which for many investors may seem surprising, that low-growth companies (with low P/E ratios), do regularly perform better than high-growth companies with their overblown P/E ratios. It needs to be stressed that what counts is not the actual growth ratio but the only thing that counts is that the actual growth is higher than anticipated growth as embedded in the prevailing P/E ratio.

This is again a reminder that prices paid for stocks matter, that they always matter and big time so.

The easiest way to find out what are the earnings expectations which the markets have baked into the stock prices is to look at the P/E ratios. As there are a number of variables involved in these calculations, there is not only one set of assumptions which will lead to the specific P/E ratio applied by the market. If you are following the usual valuation method based on two-level growth rates (a certain rate for the first 10 years followed by a different rate for the following years up to infinity…)[44] using a discount rate of 10% will result in a present value, a stock price, with a P/E ratio of 20 with a first-period growth rate of 6% followed by a second-period growth rate of 4%. Substantially the same P/E ratio is obtained by a first-period growth rate of 8% followed by a 2% "permanent" growth rate. In fact this P/E ratio is slightly lower as it amounts to 19.87 compared to 20.17 in the first scenario (6% growth for 10 years; 4% for the following period).

At a higher discount rate of, say, 12% (which leads to lower present values) you will get to a P/E ratio of 17.63 with the previous growth rates of 6% and 4% respectively. This time the same alternative rates of 8% and 2% used above do not give a similar P/E ratio, but a significantly lower one. In order to obtain a similar P/E ratio it is needed to experiment with different rates: a first growth rate of 9% followed by a permanent rate of 3% gets us to a P/E ratio of 17.52, meaning very close to the previous rate of 17.63.

Another variation on this subject would be to assume a higher growth rate in earnings for the first 10 years and a lower rate for the following years (or do the opposite) and both assumptions may lead to the same P/E ratio, or the same stock price.

As always with these calculations the discount rate used plays an important role: the higher the rate, the more demanding the investor is with respect to the returns offered by their stock investments. For instance, in the first above example if the discount rate of 12% decreases to 10% the P/E ratio which applies will increase to 28.5. In the second example the discount rate which increases from 9% to 10% will lead to a P/E of 26.3.

High P/E ratios mean that investors expect above-average earnings growth. It is a proven fact that investors consistently err on the high side when it comes to estimating future earnings growth. Whether this is due to a tendency of over-optimism, to recency bias (consisting in looking to closely at recent growth rates which are simply extrapolated into the future) does not matter as long as the fact it is so is well established.

On the other hand, we have the stocks of companies which are considered as low performers, which are not highly viewed upon by investors, which have low expectations (as shown by their P/E ratios); it is relatively easy for these companies to beat those expectations and in fact they very often do exactly that.

Many investment scholars warn against simply projecting a favorable past growth trend into the future, and insist that competition, regulation, the law of diminishing

339

returns are as many powerful limitations to unlimited growth.

It is a fact that Wall Street is nowadays focused exclusively on earnings growth and in the absence of earnings, on sales growth. This approach completely discards the risk element in the investment equation which is a very dangerous aspect. Worse even, by concentrating on sales growth, it may even falsely conclude on investment returns: assume a company growing its sales by 20% per year at the cost of significant capital outlays made in order to reach these investment goals. If the cost of capital is 10% and the ROA (return on assets) amounts to 6% then the company might well grow but it will grow straight into bankruptcy.

Such myopic views of Mr. Market give rise to excellent opportunities for investors. It is not rare to see that a stock with earnings growth of 12 per cent with a dividend yield of 1 per cent is traded at a much higher price than a stock with 8 per cent growth and a 5 per cent dividend yield. Because of the focus on earnings growth, the smart investor may obtain a free lunch.

Another such rare opportunity were money was easy to make was the debacle of the Nifty Fifty in 1972 where blue chips had reached P/E ratios of 41.9 on average, double the one of the S&P 500 with a very low dividend of 1.1% only half the one of the same Index. In his book Stocks for the Long Run, Professor Jeremy Siegel analyzed whether the conventional wisdom that these stocks were hopelessly overvalued was in hindsight correct. Despite those high earnings multiples, he found out that many of these stocks were in fact greatly undervalued by the market when comparing the 1972 P/E ratios with the earnings actually realized up to 1996. For instance, Philip Morris with its 1972 P/E ratio of 24 was cheap as based on its performance over the following 25 years would have warranted a P/E ratio of 76. For Coca Cola the corresponding figures are 46.4 and 92.2, for Pfizer 28.4 and 54.9, etc. See Table 7-1 p. 107.

The crucial point here is whether these companies are able to deliver high earnings growth rates during a long period of time: if that condition is met, high P/E ratios may be entirely justified. However, even if with hindsight the said P/E ratios were not excessive, this does not mean that investing in these stocks would have been smart investing at the time. It only means that the investor did run high risks (for instance by betting on the growth rates to be long-lasting) and that they got away with it. Furthermore those excellent results were only attainable if the investors actually did reinvest the high dividends they received (for instance from Philip Morris) in shares of that same company, which in reality very few people did you. By taking these risks investors went against the base rate, which is that such stocks are on average not good investments as they only rarely live up to the high expectations built into their sky-high prices. Investing in stocks with very high P/E ratio is certainly not risk-averse investing: as it is often said, such stocks are priced to perfection. A lot of things have to come together to justify such high prices. The base rate is that such P/E ratios do produce low yields and this should not be forgotten by investors: to deviate from the decision which this base rate suggests, they should have very compelling arguments… and they probably also need a lot of luck.

Nassim Taleb, the well-known author of a number of bestselling books (Black Swan, Fooled by Randomness, Skin in the Game, Antifragile, etc.) admonishes market observators (as well as historians) to avoid the danger of focusing only on the scenario which actually realized and to neglect the countless other alternative scenarios which could have happened as well but did not realize. Instead of using hindsight the historian should look at the events from the perspective of the historic actor who had to act on the basis of the information available at the moment their decisions were taken. From this angle what happened to the stock of Altria was perhaps just a lucky outcome: in any case given the avalanche of litigation which occurred against that company it is clear that other scenarios could have occurred as well and these more harmful scenarios, had they realized, would have had less favorable outcomes for the stock of the company.

Technology Stocks

It is not doubtful at all that nowadays the sexiest stocks, the ones that are the most prominently treated in the media are technology stocks, this term includes social media. Obviously, these companies, e.g., Apple, Google, Amazon, Facebook, Qualcomm, Tencent, Samsung, etc. are great companies. Everybody and his brother will come to that conclusion. Having said that, the real question is whether these companies are also great investments. Doubts are allowed and the odds are, and at least generally speaking, that the answer is probably no (unless, by exception, the purchase price has been depressed when the investment has been made).

Investors have to always remind themselves that great companies do not necessarily make great investments. Why is that so? The reason is obvious: great companies, especially technology companies, are nearly always richly priced and generally overpriced. This is the base rate and as seen above, that base rate should not lightly be discarded.

To check whether this is the case or not, the most readily available tool is the P/E ratio which incorporates an implicit guess on the future growth rate of the company. If the P/E ratio is 25, then investors, at a discount rate of 12%, are forecasting that the company will continue to grow at a rate of 13% for 10 years followed by a growth rate of 4% thereafter.

Especially if these great companies are part of so-called growth sectors which for some time were labelled to be part of the so-called New Economy before this label became somewhat disfavored during the Internet Bubble meltdown.

If it is stated here that the investor should distinguish the stock from the company this is not really contradictory with what was said in Chapter 1., namely that the investor should be aware that they do not buy a piece of paper but an investment into a living organism, a co-ownership in a company with a real, a living business. What is meant here is that the investor should watch out and not overpay for the stocks: investments in great companies may be great investments (that is great stock investments) but only if they are acquired at a reasonable price. In fact, most of the prices at which these stocks are traded do not offer any room for error or for profit. To belabor this point: there is no such thing as a stock which is a buy at any price. Prices as those quoted during the Internet Bubble era, resulting in P/E ratios of 200-300 are not justifiable, period! Even if (by exception) in a given case, a company ends up of being a big success after having been traded at stratospheric P/E levels with the result that ex post we could conclude that those high prices compared to earnings were in fact even too low, this still would not mean that buying at those high levels would have been a smart decision, to the contrary! It would have been a dumb decision and the investor has been just lucky, as at the time there was no way to know that this company would be so successful. Furthermore, frequently P/E ratios could not even be used at all as valuation tool for the reason that these companies did not have profits and sometimes did not even have any revenues.

Because of all the media attention these shares with high visibility, with even higher promises of future success stories, are getting, the condition of a sensible price is only met in exceptional conditions, for instance at the end of the 2008 financial crisis (also called the Great Recession), at which time all the shares, including technology shares, were trading at a huge discounts compared to any traditional metrics of value.

If price is the most important reason for being extremely cautious when it comes to high technology investments, there is another more fundamental reason for that as well. The reason is that this business sector is characterized by continuous change which implies that, whereas it is easy to find out who are the winners today, e.g. in the smartphone markets Apple and Samsung as well as Google are the winners (at least for the time being), whereas Blackberry and Nokia were the losers, there is no foolproof method to find out who the winners of tomorrow will be. The said companies, to survive and to go on prospering, will have to take countless strategically important decisions jeopardizing their future. Looking back to the beginning of the 2000s, NOKIA and Blackberry (RIM) did certainly not look as losers, just the contrary.

In other words, while betting on one of today's winners you are not sure that you will be betting on a winning horse for the long run.

It is not advisable to stick to a stock through thick and thin meaning to keep the shares even if the fundamentals of the business deteriorate dramatically.

Value investors, with their long-term approach, look for sectors where change is either nonexistent or, in the worst case, extremely slow. They are looking for stability of the economic sector to which the company belongs. Stability means resistance to change and hence greater dependability for the results shown in the past."

In a stable sector the results achieved in the past may be projected into the future with a lot more confidence than is the case in other sectors which are more prone to change. Furthermore, the fact to be in such an unstable sector does also have consequences on the costs of the firm and directly on its profit margins and its results. Companies which are under continuous pressure to innovate will have higher R&D expenses and higher capital expenditure than is the case in more stable sectors.

Take a company, like Coca Cola, which is able to produce the same product (or basically the same product) for more than one century. In addition, this product is easy to manufacture which means that the investments in industrial plants and installations is minimal in the first place and they will only be replaced when they are completely worn out, which will be decades later only. Compare this to an area like the semiconductor industry, dominated by Moore's Law which is the standard rule applied by all those active in this sector. Moore's Law, named after Gordon Moore, together with Robert Noyce founder of Intel Corporation, implies that the power of semiconductors doubles about every 2 years. This "law", first stated in 1965, applies until the present time.

This doubling of the capacity over a ridiculously short period of 2 years means that a company like INTEL has always to plan and develop not only the next generation of chips but already the generation afterwards and the third generation following the one currently under production. This involves huge R&D expenses and "capex" (or capital expenditure) meaning tremendous costs for retooling the production lines; all this means that R&D costs and capital expenditures are gigantic.

Investors should be aware of the fact that capex does not appear in the profit calculations. In other words, among two companies having exactly the same profit, preference should be given to the one having the lowest capex. Indeed, the economics of the one which does not need high capex, like Coca Cola (or the breweries) is by far more favorable: the sums which do not go into capex may be used to pay back the company's debts (and in this way enhancing future profitability) or be returned to the shareholders, either through dividend payments or through buying back shares and in this way boosting the profit per share figures accruing to the remaining shareholders.

It is beyond any doubt that what happens in these ultra-competitive sectors (like semiconductors, etc.) is nothing else than Joseph Schumpeter's "creative destruction" by which competitors are continuously eliminated and their resources (capital, equipment, human resources) which were used sub-optimally by the losing firms will be taken over by the dominating firms and used in a more efficient way. In such very competitive businesses the quality of management has a predominant role. If a firm needs a superstar as manager in order to produce decent results then the business cannot be deemed to be great.[45]

The investing public invariably overreacts to unfavorable developments. This creates special opportunities when you are dealing with blue chips: bad news is good news because it makes strong stocks cheap.

If share prices are all-important, one should not assume that price declines do automatically represent buying opportunities. Although markets are far from always being efficient, they are mostly efficient which means that generally speaking share prices decline for a reason. It is the duty of the investor to find out why a stock price declines and make up his mind whether the reason is a valid one or not. If the conclusion is this is not the case then a buying opportunity may actually exist.

Investing in Foreign Markets

To any investor having funds available for investment, the task to select different stocks for composing a diversified portfolio (composed of 10 to 30 securities) may appear overwhelming. In the US alone there are close to 4.000 publicly traded companies, the number of which having decreased since the beginning of the century. With globalization, the number of shares available for investment has increased dramatically and nowadays the number of equity securities available exceeds the figure of 100,000.

This being said it is not really the same thing whether investors invest in shares of their home market or whether they opt for a foreign market. The first difference, and it is far from being a minor one, is that investing in a foreign market usually involves exchange rate risk meaning that in addition to the inherent volatility involved in stock investing, the investor will have to suffer exchange rate risks. In plain English this means that if a US based investor opts to buy shares in a UK company at £50 per share and if some time later they are able to see that those shares are now quoted at £60, this represents a 20 per cent gain but only if the UK £ did not change in value compared to the US$. If such change has happened then the actual capital gain will be mitigated by the exchange rate variation. Obviously, this is a two-way street which means that the stock price gains may be enhanced by exchange gains so that instead of a 20 per cent gain the investment in the UK shares may translate into a 40 per cent overall gain (if the UK £ has appreciated by 20 per cent over the investment period). In summary, investing in foreign markets does increase volatility of the investment results.

Each investor has to decide for themselves whether this is a valuable goal to follow but they should not forget that converting $ into £ and maybe later on, £ into $ will involve currency exchange commissions.

It has to be added that foreign markets are different than national markets not only by the fact that the shares are generally quoted in a different currency. There are countless other differences from one national market to the other one and many of these are far from being visible at first glance: although globalization has doubtlessly decreased these differences over the last 10 or 20 years they still do exist and they will continue to do so in future. These differences may pertain to accounting rules, corporate law, corporate governance, or simply local habits, these last ones being the most difficult to track.

I will just give two examples in this context: the first occidental fund investors and fund managers to get really interested in the Japanese stock market after WWII in the 1050's soon found out some significant accounting differences between the US and Japan one of which concerned the accounting of shares and earnings of subsidiaries. Whereas in the US the financial statements of a group parent company reported the consolidated earnings of the entire group this was not the case in Japan where the financial statements of the parent only encompassed the income directly earned by the parent company in addition to any dividends received from its subsidiaries. The consequence was that earnings of the subsidiaries not paid out as dividends to the parent company were not included in the parent company's earnings. Accordingly it was possible a simple analyses of the financial statements of the subsidiaries held by the largest conglomerates searching for those with the highest amount of retained earnings compared to the earnings of the parent company it was possible to find companies with an apparent P/E ratio of 15 but which in fact was only 4 or 5 when the profits of the subsidiaries where als taken into consideration.

Beyond any difference in applicable legislation it may be that the local habits may simply differ from one country to the other one. Whereas a US company which has consistently paid dividends for many years will not easily reduce dividend payments, European companies do not have the same hesitations: if business conditions deteriorate the company will probably slash dividends before turning to other measures like for instance decreasing payroll expenses or slashing capital expenditure.

In other countries accounting standards may first be different (see the above example of Japanese accounting rules) and beyond their precise content they may have a substantially different degree of reliability which means that the content of its annual report and of other mandatory publications may not be trusted to the same extent as this may be the case in the investor's home country.

The conclusion on this subject is that investors should not engage on a blind flight. Either they have the time and other resources to familiarize themselves with foreign markets or this is not so. In the second case, they simply should leave their fingers from markets they do not know and are not willing or able to go the extra mile to really get knowledgeable of the particularities of the said markets.

The resources of the individual investor are limited; institutional investors located in the US may have a Japanese desk, a UK desk, a Eurozone desk, etc. which they will staff with several analysts hired for having many years of relevant experience in those markets. The individual investor cannot compete on a level footing with these players and in my view they should not try to do so.

The individual investor should anyway avoid to get involved in a large number of markets: such involvement will result in higher costs (especially if those markets are using different currencies) which will inevitably result in exchange fees and mean higher research and documentation costs, inevitable for the investor who wants to keep themselves up-to-date with the said foreign market(s). In any case, the number of markets in which an investor is active should be very limited and should not exceed 2 or 3. In my view, it is clearly better to know one market well than to superficially know half a dozen. It may be different if the local market of investors (which they may view as their natural market) is clearly in a very bad shape, does not have a sufficient choice of stocks in numerous business sectors out of which to choose, so that this market has to be eliminated: in such case it may make sense to select a foreign market as first choice market.

If such a choice has to be made, the first market of choice should be a market with excellent accounting standards and corporate governance, rule of law and with an extensive choice of securities in a comprehensive number of business sectors.

Given this huge selection of stocks, how to choose the stock to invest in?

BRIC and BRICS

The acronym BRIC, the authorship of which is generally attributed to a 2001 publication by a Goldman Sachs asset manager, named Jim O'Neill, stands for Brazil, Russia, India, China (to which list South Africa has been added later on, which then leads to a modified version, namely BRICS). This acronym is meant to identify a close link between the four (or five) countries concerned as emerging and fast growing countries. This is a very simplifying view and investors should be very cautious in using this acronym in that sense. Gideon Rachman a book author and frequent columnist with the Financial Times has undertaken the task to identify the common feature between these countries and he came to the conclusion that the dominating unifying factor, far from being quick economic growth, in fact is... corruption on a wide scale.

The above mentioned Jim O'Neill is said to have paid a visit to only one of the four BRIC countries (a two week journey to China). Had he taken the time to visit all of the four countries I doubt that he would have concluded that these four countries have much in common. China is definitely an economic powerhouse, the other three (or four) are not. Brazil (which is frequently associated with the following statement: "Brazil is the country of the future and always will be") and Russia are mostly pure natural-resources plays. India is of course on track of soon becoming the most populous country in the world and in India it is mostly taken as a foregone conclusion that this will automatically have as a consequence that it will also have the largest economy in the world around 2050. On this point doubts are allowed: When China under Deng Xiaoping opened its economy as of 1980, per capita income of China and India were about the same. In 2019 per capita income in China was 4.5 times the corresponding income in India. Of course, many economists will point out that growth India's rates are now higher than the Chinese ones (even if that difference is really small). However doubts have recently been issued about the accuracy of the figures produced by the Indian state. In a paper on the post 2009 crisis slowdown co-authored by Arvind Subramanian[46], a former chief economic advisor, it is noted that whereas every important economic indicator like investment, credit, profits, tax revenue, industrial output, exports and imports decreased sharply since the crisis years, economic growth has apparently risen. The authors conclude that official growth rates over the years 2011 and 2016 have been overestimated by some 2.5% which, if true, would reduce the actual growth rates to 4.5% which would be *lower* than those of China over the same period.

Will India be able to close that significant gap over the next 30 to 40 years? Everything is possible of course but those who have read the book "The Billionaire Raj", authored by Jim Crabtree's (an Englishman, who has lived in the Mumbai for many years where he has been the India correspondent for the Financial Times) will have some legitimate doubts. Similar doubts concerning the future of Russia will come to the mind of the readers of the Sergei Medvedev's book, "The Return of the Russian Leviathan." Anyway, and to take up again the initial statement of this section, investors should be very cautious and not be led to believe that whereas China since 1980 has been an incomparable economic success story that the same is true (or will be true) for the other 3 or 4 countries concerned: such conclusion is far from obvious.

Uncertainty

Investors, just as anybody else, are flooded by overall economic appraisals, by the views of analysts, central bankers, chief economists, and so on. In the forecasts of these so-called experts, just as in any forecasts, there is always uncertainty, which may or may not be underlined by the forecaster. Investors listening to these forecasts will resist acting until the prevailing ambient uncertainty will have cleared. The problem with this approach is that such uncertainty is actually the investor's best friend as it makes sure that prices are depressed (the uncertainty is priced in) whereas if uncertainty is resolved (or better is *deemed* to be resolved), the chances are that prices will have risen substantially. By the way, the fact that the dominating opinion is that the future is extremely bright has never prevented events like 9/11, the Brexit and even less the devastating earthquake and tsunami which hit Japan on March 11, 2011 or the Chernobyl nuclear meltdown of 1986.

Paraphrasing Mark Twain it may be said that it is not what we do not know which brings us into trouble but what brings us into trouble is what we thought we knew for sure but which simply ain't so. The examples confirming this statement are legion and I will just give one at this place: Walter Isaacson in his Jobs biography relates that when Apple introduced the iPhone the senior representatives of Microsoft Bill Gates and Steve Ballmer both "knew for sure" that a smartphone without a physical keyboard will be a flop. We all know how this movie ended, namely that the iPhone (despite the absence of a physical keyboard) dominated the smartphone market (which largely contributed to make it the most valuable company in the world) whereas Microsoft plays no meaningful role at all in that competition.

Other examples showing the same "knowing-for-sure" attitude may be seen on a daily basis on a forum like Seeking Alpha where market commentators are preoccupied to talk up (or down) a certain stock defending a certain thesis leaving little doubt that this is the one and only one scenario which may play out.

It is extremely dangerous to act on the basis of such groundless statements because the chances that they are wrong are in fact higher than that they are right, as there are many different scenarios which may realize and not just two. If they are wrong, the investors who have acted based on them will be caught on the wrong foot and they may have gought a stock which they should have sold (or vice versa).

352

Concrete Choices

Whereas traditionally economists have considered that the fact of having a large panoply of choice is always beneficial for consumer as it allows for maximizing the value of a specific objective, recent scientific studies have shown that a multitude of choices may be negative for customers in the sense that a high number of alternatives may have a paralyzing effect on them and will inhibit sales. Instead of offering customers 20 different types of marmalade it is preferable to offer 5 only, which will drive sales.

Such a plethora of alternatives is representative of today's financial markets on which the stocks of thousands of companies are traded. In addition, the Internet makes sure that on most of these companies, including those with no or only low media coverage, it is possible to obtain reliable financial information.

The most advisable way to handle this problem is to attack it from the other end or to invert it, meaning to start determining what one should not invest in. One first element is exchange risks: maybe the investor does not want to take a bet on exchange rate fluctuations so that they will simply discard any securities other than those of their home country currency. The population of stocks available will be reduced accordingly.

The prudent investor will eliminate those shares that everybody (analysts, the media, etc.) consider an excellent investment at the moment of their purchase. As everybody considers those shares to be excellent (this qualification is mostly the result of the past performance of these shares), these shares are in all likelihood richly priced, probably overvalued. In other words, the advice is that one should never buy popular stocks: those are the stocks the herd is buying. This means that the price asked will be justified only if the very positive forecasts on the business's future are correct (generally speaking, these forecasts are excessively optimistic). Even if this is the case, the investor will just avoid realizing a loss; in order to make a profit, these optimistic forecasts would have to be beaten by a significant margin… which is very unlikely given the excess of optimism which is underlying the forecasts made and baked into the stock prices.

If, however, these forecasts are not met and the business gets into trouble, the share price will correct and in all likelihood it will correct in a massive way. Hence, the advice to investors is to concentrate on shares which nobody wants, not because they are fundamentally bad (for being part of a bad business or for having incompetent management) but for reasons of market misappreciations.

Investors should always be aware of the advice given by Kenneth Fisher according to which money can be made only if one knows   something which others do not know. This advice should not be taken too literally however. It does not mean that the investor would need to have some kind of inside knowledge (for instance that the company has developed a new compound or discovered oil somewhere) the knowledge of the investor might simply be to interprete some public knowledge in a different way, for instance that cloud computing will be the future of the business at a moment when this conclusion was not widely shared.

Investors, especially long-term investors, should avoid shares in businesses which are cyclical by nature. Cyclical businesses are characterized by frequent periods of expansions and contractions in their turnover and even more so in their profits. It also means that companies active in these businesses will regularly show periods of losses. Such cyclical businesses are not suitable for making the magic of compounding work properly. Nothing will hurt such compounding more than if over, say, a 10-year period there are 2 or 3 years of losses. These losses may wipe out the positive effect of 2 to 3 profitable years. This means that a 10-year period will actually, in terms of growing net worth, count only for a 5-year period. The conclusion is that cyclical businesses should be avoided and beyond those businesses, companies even in good businesses which tend to regularly have loss-making years. As Wall Street cannot deny that some stocks are cyclical by their very nature their advice will then be to buy those shares once they are in their cyclical trough and sell them when they reach their cyclical peak. In theory this makes sense. The problem is that it is only with hindsight that it will be obvious when the market's troughs and peaks are reached. In business the rear-view mirror is always clearer than the windshield.

Another pitfall which inexperienced investors should avoid at all cost is the following one: towards the end of the business cycle (at the moment before profits will decrease) cyclical stocks do have very low P/E ratios and appear to be particularly cheap, which falsely could appear to be a "screaming buy." This low P/E ratio is however everything but that: in fact it is an extremely bearish signal which tells us that the market expects a steep fall in the future profits: once this decrease in profits has occurred, the P/E will adjust as well by decreasing significantly. It might very well be that the company is now loss making and the P/E ratio is no longer of relevance.

Some big investment ideas touted by analysts and media are based on the realization of some catalysts: if a certain catalyst realizes, then a big rise in stock price will be the unescapable consequence. These ideas are risky. The first problem is that the catalyst, if it is widely accepted to occur, will already be priced into the stock. If the catalyst doesn't happen, the stock price will correct severely. As an example, I will just mention the forecast that handheld devices will replace the PC as the primary way consumers interact with one another and with businesses (for instance to do their e-commerce operations). The second risk is that even if the catalyst occurs it might not produce the forecast effects. Taking the general tendency of exaggeration into account, it is normally fair to guess that the effects will be overrated. During the 1998-2000 stock market bubble the general view was that the internet will be "huge." That forecast was basically correct but that did not mean, and it still does not mean, that any internet company (however defined) will be highly profitable. Due to the usual exaggeration and excessive optimism, the effects will very probably by far lower than those foreseen. By the way, this is a quite usual scenario: just think of how the proliferation of car traffic has changed society or how airline travel has changed the world and the way we travel, we spend our holidays and so on. And still very few car producing companies have become good investments for their shareholders and the same is even more the case for the airline industry. The important point is to decide whom significant innovations actually profit: the consumer or the company? In many cases the answer is that consumers are the beneficiary.

Let's have a closer look at the airline industry. Over the period covering 1919 to 1939 there were 300 US companies active in aircraft manufacturing. The number of those that survived are probably in the single digits only. Over the twenty years covering 1984 to 2004 more than 120 airlines filed for bankruptcy in the U.S. It is only during the 2010s that the airline companies as a group are making profits. This development was heavily influenced by the fact that fuel prices have come down to historically incredibly low levels and nobody knows how long these exceptional circumstances will go on to prevail. In any case, the airline business in general is still not a good business which investors should privilege. Recently the general attitude of investors with respect to the airline industry has changed and this has been the case for the reason that its basic economics have changed, due principally to concentration of airlines, low fuel prices, the absence of terror attacks on airplanes over the latest ten or so years.

Recently this situation has again changed as the Covid-19 pandemic unfolded: since spring 2020 the airline industry has basically been grounded so that the airlines including the aircraft manufacturers, namely Boeing and GE, did need state support in order to avoid becoming insolvent.

It is amazing to follow on a day-by-day basis how some stocks get talked up and written up whereas others are talked down and written down in a totally surprising manner. Some stocks have a positive connotation whereas others are just viewed as being pariahs which should not even be touched with a ten-foot pole. Among the obvious glamour stocks of the first type one may find Uber and Beyond Meat which represent something new. These shares hold very lofty valuations: such valuations may be justified only in case of relatively small high growth companies which still do have the opportunity to grow at very high rates for a very long time that is for decades. If we compare these valuations with those of a number of high growth stocks of one or two decades ago like Facebook and Amazon one might conclude that those companies were able to keep up the high growth ratio for a sufficiently long time to justify their high valuations. However, there is a big flaw to such reasoning: it is based on survivorship bias. This term refers to the logical error of concentrating on those (individuals, organizations or things) which succeeded in some selection process and ignoring those who did not make it. Such elimination of the non-successful ones will lead to wrong conclusions, generally to over-optimistic ones. In the case at hand of Amazon and Facebook, these are part of the few lucky survivors of the hundreds of companies which were incorporated over the last 20-30 years and which succeeded, the countless competitors which were either absorbed, liquidated or do just linger are simply ignored. Nothing allows as to conclude that Uber and/or Beyond Meat will be in that lucky group of successful survivors as well.

The important point is that once a company is either in the anointed stock camp or in the stock graveyard camp any news will be viewed through a very colored filter:

objectively good news will either be viewed as eminently positive factors which will lead to a bounce of the share price or as just noise which will at best delay the eventual and inevitable demise of the company and of its shares. The opposite holds true for inherently bad news.

The market's attitude to a certain stock may change over time and does so very rapidly. An example is Microsoft which for a very long time did have a very negative connotation for being too closely associated with the PC and not enough connected to mobile in the form of smartphones and tablets. However, recently especially, with a change of management at the CEO level (as Satya Nadella replaced Steve Ballmer) and as cloud revenues of Microsoft have taken off, it is quite clear that the markets' attitude has changed and the stock price increased in an impressive way. Once again the principal factor of this change of attitude is not difficult to find: price action. Whereas from 2001 to 2012 the stock price did move mostly in the range from \$22 to \$38, as of the beginning of 2013 it increased from \$26 to 190 at the year-end 2019.

Market observers are confronted with a chicken-and-egg conundrum here: it is clear that the anointed stock camp coincidentally is populated by stocks whose prices have substantially increased over several years, the reverse being true for the graveyard camp. The question is now whether, for the anointed stocks, the mood is positive for the reason that the share prices have increased or the other way round?

In the first case we would have an occurrence of the so-called halo effect which refers to the human tendency to generalize from one characteristic to all others. As described by Phil Rosenzweig in his book "The Halo Effect", consists in the fact that humans tend to generalize excessively and to conclude from the fact that someone is good (or bad) at a certain skill they should be good (or bad) also at other things regardless of the fact that those various skills are totally unrelated one to the others.

The existence of the so-called halo effect has long been recognized. It is the phenomenon whereby we assume that because people are good at doing A they will be good at doing B, C and D (or the reverse—because they are bad at doing A they will be bad at doing B, C and D). The phrase was first coined by Edward Thorndike, a psychologist who used it in a study published in 1920 to describe the way that commanding officers rated their soldiers. He found that officers usually judged their men as being either good right across the board or bad. There was little mixing of traits; few people were said to be good in one respect but bad in another.

The most likely answer is that it is a mixture of the two: the share price increase creates a positive mood (or if it already pre-existed, enhances it) whereas price decreases either create (or enhance) a negative mood. Either way, investors should take these fluctuations at their fair value: they are distractions or just noise. The real investors, those who do not just pretend to have forecast the latest crash or the previous five bull markets, do ignore such fads altogether unless they view them as contrary indicators.

Investors should never forget that shares represent a participation in a business and as long as the company having issued those shares is doing well (for instance increase its profits by 5-8 % a year) it does not really matter if the shares decrease 5% during a given year. If the market has in the past always applied a PE of 15, it will most certainly go on to do the same in the future as well and shares will catch up sooner or later so that the market value which has been lost in a given year will be gained back at that moment.

Hereafter I give just a brief selection of ivestment methods which have been developed mostly by investment professional used over the past and which go on to be used by a more or less important group of investors. Most of these methods have been tested and back tested over large number of years and most showed good results over the past which is certainly a good starting point but everything but a guarantee for future success. Any investor has to decide which method (s) they trust the most and which one they will apply or alternatively whether they prefer to remain totally opportunistic.

Dogs of the Dow

The "Dogs of the Dow" is a very well-known investment method based on selecting annually a certain number of underperformers of the Dow Jones index. It has been introduced by Michael B. O'Higgins who has back tested the proposed methods over a 26- year period; in fact the method exists in several variations. The "Basic Method" consists in selecting the 10 Dow Jones stocks which over the preceding 12 months had the highest dividend yield.

What is the rationale behind this concept? Companies of the size of those of the DJIA do not intend to pay dividends in the magnitude of 4 to 6% of their stock prices. The highest yielding stocks of the Dow do however pay such high dividends. The reason for this fact is that companies who in normal times pay a 2-3% dividend but for one or the other reason have their stock price divided by two or more will see their dividend yield multiply by at least two (to 4-6%) and hence they will join the group of the Dogs of the Dow.

A more successful variant of this method consists in selecting the 5 lowest-priced stocks among the 10 most high-yielding stocks.

A third method consists in selecting just one share, the so-called "Penultimate Profit Prospect" (PPP) which invests exclusively in the second lowest-priced high-yielder stock. Whereas the Basic Method has beaten the Dow Jones Index over the period 1973-1998 by 3 times, the 5 stocks, high-yield and low-price portfolio has done so 5 times and the PPP method 17 times.

These figures are impressive but in order to have any chance of repeating them in future one has to be able to find out a solid rationale behind this method. The method has a solid basis not only because of a contrarian bent (it is focused on the high-yielders, the reason for this being that their prices have taken a beating), and lowest-priced stocks. The method does not consist in just selecting problem-stocks but by focusing on dividend-paying stocks it is made sure that the companies are still in decent financial shape. If this financial situation does deteriorate then dividends will be slashed or cancelled and the stock does fall out of the Dogs of the Dow selection. The PPP-method is based on the finding that the lowest priced stock may be in real financial difficulty and its price tended to be hit "before dividend action is taken." Such was for instance the case for Johns Manville, Chrysler and Westinghouse.

The method also bases on the premise that American companies and especially Dow Jones Index companies (unlike European companies for instance) want to avoid dividend cuts by nearly all means.

Other reasons why the Dogs of the Dow method may work are that Dow Companies are big companies with a capitalization of at least $50 billion, tens of thousands of employees, multiple flows of income, and multiple facilities in many states and countries having often considerable political weight. This means that these companies are resilient and hence not extremely risky. Furthermore, these companies are not really profit maximizing as you might expect this to be the case for smaller, younger and hungrier companies. In other words, these companies have some room in order to easily, and without cutting deeply into the flesh, save costs, and boost earnings in case temporary problems come up. In other words, these companies have staying power and in all likelihood will overcome the temporary difficulties which have recently afflicted them. By virtue of sheer size and strength – call it raw staying power – blue chip companies tend to be survivors.

A slightly different version of the Dogs of the Dow has been introduced by Chuck Carlson (www.dowunderdogs.com) whose focus is the worst performing Dow Jones Index stock. The stocks with the worst price performance in a given year will easily beat the Dow in the following year. Dividends are not taken into consideration at all with this variant.

The Magic Formula

This concept refers to a very famous stock selection method which has become famous by a book named "The Little Book That Beats the Market (Little Books. Big Profits)" by Joel Greenblatt, Andrew Tobias) published in 2006. This method requires a significant data base and it applies a separate ranking to all stocks based on two criteria: the earnings yield and return on capital. By screening the data base all stocks get two numbers allocated based on their level of earnings yield (based on last year's earnings) and on their level of rate of return on assets. The earnings yield is dependent on the market price of the stocks. The return on capital does reflect how efficiently the company operates regardless of its stock price. A company with the combined lowest number will make the top of the list, preceding the one with the second-lowest number, etc. Suppose company number 1 for earnings yield holds ranks 18 for return on assets: Its total rank number will be 19 (1+18). The lowest combined rank will be the top choice for the magic formula followed by the stock with the second-lowest number, etc. A selection of stocks is bought over one year and each stock will be held for one year before being sold (either shortly before the one year anniversary or shortly afterwards, based on US income tax considerations). The results of this investment method has been outstanding (as described in the book to which the reader is guided here). This is not a long-term strategy and accordingly tax aspects (capital gains taxation) have to be taken into consideration as well by the investor.

Deep Value Investing

Deep value investing is simply a variant of value investing. It has been first developed by Graham and it consisted in valuating stocks at a level corresponding to their net-net current assets. Current assets (cash, inventories, creditors) are added together and then reduced not only by current liabilities but by all liabilities. Shares were bought only if they could be purchased at a price lower than net-net current assets. Current assets other than cash were not valued at book value: creditors were corrected for doubtful accounts and inventories taken at liquidation value.

This approach is asset-based; it even neglects fixed assets and does not care about a company's earnings. The main problem is that under normal circumstances this method does not give many stocks to purchase and especially so over recent years and certainly not in sectors which are nowadays favored by investors, for instance technology. In these sectors, share prices are a multiple of book value which is always higher than the net-net current assets value.

Spin-offs

It happens relatively often that large companies and especially conglomerates do have quite interesting divisions which have undeniably value but which are not part of the core business of the entity (for instance Eastman Chemicals was spun off from parent Eastman Kodak in 1994 and it survived its parent which went bankrupt in 2012). In order to unlock "shareholder value" a clearly defined division may then be the object of a spin-off which trades as an independent company on the stock exchange. Shareholders of the company will get shares in the spin-off: generally such spin-off operations are tax favored meaning no capital gains taxes are due on the transaction (neither in the hands of the company nor in the hands of the shareholders). Often these spin-offs are an interesting opportunity for the following reasons: institutional investors prefer to get rid of these new stocks they received in such a low capitalization company as they do not offer a sufficiently high liquidity.

Frequently there are no analysts which follow the spin-off (which may be active in a very specialized field very there is a lack of knowledgeable analysts) so that the shares will not be followed by the Street or as these companies generally have low capitalization only they will only generate low trading volume meaning that the implication of analysts is hardly justified.

One study completed at Penn State, covering a twenty-five-year period ending in 1988, found that stocks of spin-off companies outperformed their industry peers and the Standard & Poor's 500 by about 10 percent per year in their first three-years of independence.

A 2018 study by S&O Global confirms that spun-off companies did spectacularly outperform, by close to 30% over a period of 3 years, businesses of the same industry. However according to the same study parent companies lagged behind the market by 10%.[47] These results are somewhat astonishing as they would suggest that companies would spin-off their crown jewels: as the CEO and other top managemers do generally remain with the parent company this would seem surprising at first glance.

X-Baggers

The expression of "x-baggers" is owed to Peter Lynch the famous money manager and top investment book writer (together with John Rothchild) who frequently referred to stocks as 10- baggers, 25- baggers, etc. in this way expressing the fact that a given stock price has been multiplied by 10, 25, etc.

There is no investment method allowing to reliable identify stocks having the potential of becoming one day 100-baggers. Nevertheless it may be useful to say a few words on the subject and identifying some of the points which might lead in to the right direction and at the same time avoid those decisions which certainly do not get the investor there.

Two books published on 100-baggers" have to be mentioned here namely Thomas W. Phelps From *1 to 100 in the Stock Market* and Christopher Mayer *100 Baggers, Stocks That Return 100-TO-1 And How to Find Them*.

Such outstanding investment results are not that exceptional even if very few investors can boast themselves of actually having personally realized such 100-baggers in their investment lives. Obviously, making such killings requires a long-term attitude (although not that long as one might think) and the strong resolution to hold on despite market corrections of 20 to 30% or even 50 to 80% as many of those 100-baggers have actually experienced. This capacity to hold on through thick and thin is the most difficult part and the principal reason why so few people did actually experience such outstanding investment returns.

Some advice from the above named authors of the said books on 100-baggers may be useful here. Let's start with quotations form T. Phelps. "The basic reason so few of us have ever made $100 on a $1 investment is that we have never tried to do so. In a sense we have been brainwashed into looking for and acting on types of information that have little or nothing to do with multiplying one's investments one hundredfold." T. Phelps, 100 to 1 in the Stock Market, p. 221.[48]

The principal advice given by Phelps is never to take an investment action for a non-investment reason, which means principally price movements (which should simply be ignored altogether). Sales of stocks are rare and should only occur if it is clear that the purchase was a mistake.

When selecting potential 100-bagger stocks, the most important point is to identify companies with a very high Return on Capital which can be maintained for many years.

This allows to put in move the principal engine of high growth, namely earnings per share. In many cases this first engine is helped by "multiple expansion" which means that the P/E ratio will grow over time: the two points are obviously connected: once investors understand that the high earnings growth is a lasting phenomenon they are ready to apply higher P/E ratios to these earnings. If P/E ratios are constant then a 100 bagger requires per share earnings to grow by 100 (which does not happen over a 5 or 10-year period unless if at the starting point earnings where very low). However, if earnings have been multiplied over, say, a 20-year period, for instance by 50 and if over that period P/E ratios have doubled, then we would have our 100-bagger because 50 (earnings per share multiplier) times 2 (P/E ratio multiplier) would give 100.

If the P/E ratio did decrease over the holding period of the shares this would result in an important headwind on the voyage to 100-baggerdom: imagine shares are purchased at a P/E ratio of 20 and the P/E ratio decreases to 10 then an increase of earnings per share of 100 times would not be enough: this profit multiplier would have to increase to 200 in order to reach the target.

Are there many 100-baggers? The answer is yes. It may be said that basically all the large capitalization companies around are at least 100-baggers, some even several times: the FAANG stocks, Microsoft, Cisco, Coca-Cola, Pepsi Cola, the pharmaceuticals, many consumer staples....etc. Of course, this is a hindside view with survivorship bias. The challenge is not to identify those companies which in the past would have been good investments (but which are too big now to repeat that performance starting from their present level) but to identify those companies which are small now but which will be the 100-baggers of tomorrow. The pond at which to look then would be principally those companies which have been offered in IPO's over the past years (but certainly not to buy at the moment of the IPO, see under IPO). Beyond Meat, Impossible Food, Peloton, Uber, Lyft, Airbnb; Zoom, etc.

Acquisitions of Companies

"Mega-mergers are for megalomaniacs."

David Ogilvy

Wall Street reacts in bullish fashion to mergers and ... to its exact opposite, divisions. As Graham/Dodd noted sarcastically: "Putting two and two together frequently produces five in the stock market; and this five may later be split up into three and three." The same authors explain these reactions by the psychology of the speculator who wants "action" and is willing to contribute to this action if he can be given any pretext for bullish excitement." (Graham/Dodd, p. 590). This statement reflects the situation of Philip Morris (nowadays renamed Altria) which after spinning off Philip Morris International (at a cost of $55m) has recently been said to envisage to remerge again the two entities (at an estimated cost of $200m).[49]

The long-term investor looks for stability, knowing that any aggressive acquisition strategy will inevitably lead to instability and maybe more importantly even, to a non-transparent situation. A company endeavoring in serial acquisitions (e.g. Cisco) acquiring dozens and sometimes hundreds of companies over several decades is evolving in permanent chaos. Tyco acquired 600 companies over 2 years ! Does anybody believe that such a large number of companies may really be integrated in a sensible way into the acquirer's organization?

Furthermore, there is more than a strong likelihood that these acquisitions will be overpaid. Once a large acquisition (meaning that the target company is large compared to the bidding company) is announced, the reaction of Wall Street is that the shares of the target will increase (which is quite normal because a premium beyond the share price has to be paid in order to incite investors to sell their shares to the acquirer), but more interestingly the shares of the acquirer will typically *decrease*, and this because financial markets consider that the deal is biased in favor of the target company (and will harm the acquiring company and/or its shareholders).

Serial acquisitions constitute a huge obstacle to the transparency of financial statements with the consequence that it becomes nearly impossible for any investor or analyst to determine the exact profit situation and patrimonial situation of the company. Profits of the previous year, which in a normal situation represent the benchmark against which this year's results may be compared, do in general have no significance at all. A split-up of income (turnover) of the old operations of the acquirer and the new operations of the acquired company are generally not made (and if they are made they are open to manipulation) and hence a reliable growth rate cannot be calculated.

For unscrupulous managements such acquisitions are welcome occasions to proceed to a bloodbath via so-called restructuring expenses (which are qualified as non-recurring and hence will in some way be viewed as not really relevant as they will not impact the long-term earnings capacity of the company). This attitude of Wall Street vis-à-vis so called restructuring costs explains the inclusion of operating costs of future years into restructuring costs, which will allow management to show inflated results during the coming years. For instance, by writing down assets below their actual value (those impairment costs are ear-marked as restructuring costs), future depreciation allowances are minimized which will boost future earnings. This procedure is followed as long as management has a vested interest in short-term increases of the share price, which is in fact always the case as they get stock options allowing them to acquire their company's stocks.

Finally such acquisitions are extremely expensive and not even a zero-sum game between the shareholders of the acquirer and of the target company. A lot of "helpers" are involved which will participate not in "shareholder value creation" (although they may claim to do exactly that) but in "shareholder value destruction." Auditors, consultants of all shapes and colors, lawyers, M&A specialists, investment bankers will do their very best (trust them!) to rip off a sizable chunk of the value of the transaction. Of course, these same helpers will not have any problem to show by inch-thick reports that those costs are incidental and will be recovered in a very short time through the tremendous synergies inherent in the deal and which will accrue to the business of the acquirer.

You may ask if such operations are so negative why are they still so frequent in practice? The answer is double:

1) It is in the self-interest of management and their helpers to promote such operations. Management is often remunerated not on the basis of growing the profits of their company but on growing its size.

2) Such operations are sexier for testosterone-driven managers. As Peter Drucker once reportedly said: "Deal making beats working. Deal making is exciting and fun, and working is grubby. Running anything is primarily an enormous amount of grubby detail work... deal making is romantic, sexy. That's why you have deals that make no sense."

All this means that investors might perfectly consider to use such multiple acquisitions as a negative filter meaning that such company will be eliminated from the potential target list.

Accounting of Merger and Acquisitions

In the field of mergers and acquisitions accounting rules play a not insignificant role which has to be explained. During the 1950s mergers were most generally booked under the so-called pooling-of-interests method. Under that method the assets transferred from one entity to another were recorded at book value so that acquiring companies did not have to write off premiums (in other words goodwill) paid for their acquisitions. Whether that was the correct method to apply was however debated and finally the FASB adopted FAS 141 which ruled that the so-called purchase accounting method had to be used as of June 30, 2001. Under that method premiums paid for acquisitions above market value of the different assets acquired, had to be booked as goodwill which had to be amortized, which resulted in lower income than the previously applicable pool accounting method.

Not surprisingly companies doing numerous acquisitions, say Cisco or Enron felt the results. The AOL Time Warner merger resulted in accumulated losses of $100 billion in 2001.

In 2007 the FASB adopted another significant change by amending the purchase accounting method and replacing it by the so-called purchase acquisition method which does not require a systematic amortization of goodwill involved in the merger. This mandatory systematic amortization was replaced by an impairment test: amortization was required only if the fair value of goodwill was lower than its book value in which case the impairment did hit earnings.

Synergies

When managements of two or more companies have agreed to join their forces this proposed merger, which has to be approved by its shareholder basis, will be explained to the financial world via its usual media channels. One big argument put forward to justify the merger will be that shareholder value will be uncovered. One of the channels through which shareholder value is uncovered is synergies: the idea behind this concept is easy to explain as it may be summarized as follows: 2+2 = 5, the result of the combined companies will be higher than the sum of the parts. If such synergies are a perfectly possible result of a merger many research studies show that these synergies exist more often in theory than in practice.

In fact, numerous studies show that synergies induced by acquisitions and mergers are by far exaggerated and finally most operations of this type are simply flops. Just think of the Daimler- Chrysler merger which resulted in a disaster for shareholders (but not for the helpers or for managements involved). According to a 1999 KPMG study analyzing 800 mergers the rate of failures is roughly 80%.

In the 1960s conglomerates developed on the grounds that a diversified company is worth more than the sum of its parts as the various divisions complement each other operationally whereas they would benefit financially from the support of the entire conglomerate. Conglomerates were also deemed to represent a management philosophy in the sense that by making divisions responsible for the parent company's return on investments, divisions would become autonomous and accordingly the entrepreneurial spirit could be held up in such big conglomerates.

The market's attitude to such conglomerates has fundamentally changed over the latest decades. Wall Street blames the intransparency and the lack of focus of such conglomerates for a lack of profitability and asks for a breakup of the conglomerate in order to enhance shareholder value.

The reasoning is that nowadays investors seek exposure to specific sectors of activity and reject the accumulation of diverse sectors in one single company. One might say that specialization trumps diversity and risk spreading. The bottom line of this change of attitude with respect to these conglomerates, which were mostly formed in the 1960s and 1970s, is that instead of a conglomerate bonus nowadays there is a conglomerate malus meaning the total is worth not more but less than the sum of the parts. Such valuation differences do clearly lead to the request to break-up the conglomerate in its parts in order to "break up shareholder value." Such claims are easy to make but the acid test is to show later on that they actually do realize and if so that they have been the result of the break up operation (and not of something else).

Berkshire Hathaway is one of the examples of the undervaluation of the total compared to the value of its parts. The stock price is stalling for some time already it is probably remaining depressed as long as stock prices remain at the present high levels, it should not be forgotten that currently (that is in Sempter 2019) the level of the three large US stock indices is within 1 percent of the historical high water mark. Buffett without saying that markets would be overpriced (even if he did think that he would avoid to say so for the reason that such statements would certainly heavily weigh on market prices) has not only said that prices are at levels at which he does not find interesting targets with the result that he has not done a major acquisition since 2015 (acquisition of PCP in January 2015) and the cash pile has increased to some $135 billion. It is obvious that when roughly a quarter of the capitalization of a company is held in cash (which yields close to nothing at present interest rate levels) the chances to beat the index which serves as a benchmark (the S&P 500 in this case) are very small.

It is to Buffett's credit that he is not bulging and does not the least deviate from his principles: if the prices which Mr. Market throws at him do not allow for a decent margin of safety then he will not buy, even if the cash pile goes on increasing. Those investors who have the patience to resist the temptation to just buy before rationalizing their choice are very rare and they deserve a lot of admiration. Here again this is a habit which he has in common with many other billionaires who attribute a large part of their success to precisely this ability to say no nearly all the time (before, on rare occasions, swinging for the fences when by exception all the conditions are aligned for making a killing).

Buffett has shown over many decades that his discipline is unmet by anybody. In 1969 he dissolved his partnership as he did not see any way to invest his capital in the overpriced market then prevailing. He waited until the Recession of 1974 (which started end of 1973 and lasted to the beginning of 1975) and then to invest heavily. Again more recently Berkshire's cash pile increased to some $130 bn at the end of 2019. When the Covid-19 crisis hit in the first quarter of 2020, a lot of people thought Berkshire would massively invest. This is not what he did (so far at least) and instead of buying many stocks Buffett surprised more or less everybody by announcing that he had sold all the airline stocks in the four US airlines in which Berkshire had recently built up a significant shareholding.

Corporate Governance

Corporate governance may be defined as "the system of rules, practices, and processes by which a firm is directed, managed and controlled." The concepts of corporate governance, corporate culture and corporate ethics are heavily interwoven as all three influence corporate behavior. One important point in corporate governance is to design rules in order to balance the rights and obligations of the different categories of stakeholders of the company, among which the shareholders, the board of directors, management (principally the CEO), employees, clients, suppliers, banks and other suppliers of capital like bondholders, the State, the community, etc.

One of the issues of corporate governance is whether the tasks of chairman of the board and of CEO should be performed by the same person. If we consider that one of the dominant tasks of the board of directors is to control the day to day management of the company than this task cannot be properly performed by a board of directors headed by the CEO. Accordingly, it is nowadays considered best standards in corporate governance that in order to avoid an almighty person at the steering wheel the two roles should be separately held. The UK corporate governance code advises against combining the two roles and in fact only one company part of the FTSE 100 does have a one person at its head. All over the world, but at the fastest pace in Europe, did the number of combined CEO – chairman of the board decrease.

Does separation of the roles enhance performance? Some studies done on the subject suggest so but their results may be debatable as very often troubled companies which change management do hire a joint CEO-chairman to improve performance. On the other hand, it may be assumed that to separate the two roles may give a better chance to avoid a major scandal. Here as always the warning applies: "High correlation doesn't mean causation, but causation means high correlation." The rooster's crow, although highly correlated with the sunrise, doesn't cause it.

Notwithstanding this warning, to suggest that any kind of weak correlation means causation, is exactly what journalists of all kinds of media are doing the whole day long, year in and year out. Headlines stating, for instance, that children doing this or that have a 15% higher chance to get one or the other disease are totally meaningless as this increased likelihood to get the said disease may be explained by dozens of other factors which arbitrarily have been left out of the scope of the study made.

One has to look at things as they are in all their diversity. Sometimes a certain result is caused by one and only one cause which is then necessary and sufficient. Such is the case for the cholera disease which, as was discovered in the 19th century, is caused and only caused by a bacterium called "Vibrio cholera" which develops in water containing feces. Unfortunately such one to one causality chains are extremely rare. Even if they do exist it might not be certain which one is the cause and which one the effect. Take for example the relationship between illness and fever. For a long time it has been discovered that there is causation between fevers and illness but it was not sure which one causes the other. Is fevers the cause of illness or is illness the cause of fevers? As is known nowadays it is the latter: illness causes fevers and not the other way round.

Dubious Accounting

In 1996 in order to boost its earnings, AOL did not deduct as expense the marketing costs incurred for acquiring its customers. These costs were treated as a balance sheet asset and booked as "deferred subscriber acquisition costs." Over a 12-month period ending mid-1996, AOL had spent some $360 million on promotion which corresponded to a third of its total revenues. Only $126 million were charged against profit. The remainder of more than $230 million far exceeded the net earnings of $65 million. In other words, if all these costs had been treated as an expense the annual result of the company would have been negative by some $165 million.

Finally, responding to those who criticized its accounting, AOL in the third quarter of 1998 booked a charge of $385 million writing off part of the marketing expenses incurred over the years and booked as an asset. Although this was the admission that the critics were right and that the profits shown over the years were in fact not real, the markets seemed to like what they saw and the stock increased by 12%.

When talking about "dubious accounting" it cannot be avoided to refer to the most egregious scandal in corporate America since World War II, namely Enron.

In a very remarkable book "The Smartest Guys in the Room: The Amazing Rise and Scandalous Fall of Enron the authors Bethany McLean, Peter Elkind relate the part accounting rules, concretely mark-to-market accounted, played in the pervasive deceit which Enron engaged in.

Mark-to-market accounting

Whereas under traditional "historical-cost" accounting, profits are booked as realized, mark-to-market accounting allows companies to book the entire profit (by assessing the estimated value of these long-term contracts) at the moment the contract is signed. Over the lifetime of the said contract, changes of that estimated value are booked either as losses or as profits. In the case of Enron, one of the consequences of relying on this accounting method was a very dangerous discrepancy between the moment of recording and their actual realization, in other words between booking profits and cash realization: whereas profits are recognized upfront, cash is only gained gradually over the lifetime of the contract. For this reason, reliance on mark-to-market accounting allowed Enron to show high growth rates initially but this fact put it under enormous pressure to maintain this growth rate in the future.

Whereas under historical-cost accounting long-term contracts of last year contribute to the profit of the current year and of all future years until the end of the contract, this is not the case under mark-to-market accounting where in order to show growth of 10%, the company has to conclude not only the same amount of contracts as last year but they had to conclude 10% more of those long-term contracts.

Another issue was the benchmark for valuating these contracts, the market to which contracts are "marked-to", which was far from giving investors any guarantees of reliability. This difficulty which is quite general for all situations where assets traded are non fungible ones. In this respect energy contracts are not comparable to stock markets.

On this subject McLean/Elkind comment:

"Individual traders could tell the trade press anything they wanted—and they did. Sometimes, they made up spreadsheets showing pricing for trades that never happened. They did it to make their own books look better, and they did it because everyone in the industry thought everyone else was doing it."

Other methods used to pump up profits were the sale of assets which were non recurrent but not mentioning this but simply including such capital gains in their operating income. Another far more dangerous way was to hide a significant part of the company's debts originating from numerous failed deals and projects, in partnerships, so-called special purpose vehicles.

Trading Advice

Hereafter the reader may find some hopefully useful pieces of advice in connection with their buying and selling of stocks.

Once the decision to buy a certain stock has been taken, the next question is how much of one's capital should be invested in that specific position. The so-called Kelly formula may give some highly useful insights here.

Kelly formula

Named after John Kelly, who in the 1950's was employed by the famous and successful AT&Ts Bell Laboratory the formula was first published in 1956 under the name "A New Interpretation of Information Rate." Although meant to address a technical problem pertaining to electronic transmission of signals the formula has become known for helping gamblers to assess the optimal amount they should place on a given bet: a certain number at the roulette table, a given hand at poker, etc. It may also be used to calculate the fraction of a portfolio to be invested in a certain stock or market sector.

The Kelly formula, which calculates the the percentage to be invested in any stock position (K%) has two variables, namely the probability of a profitable outcome (W) and the ratio of gains compared to the losses, the gain/loss ratio (R).

These two factors are then put into Kelly's equation which is:

K%=W−(1−W) / R

Let's suppose your winning probability is 55% and that your Win/Loss ratio (the proportion of your average win divided by your average loss) is 2, meaning you win twice as much on winning trades than you lose on losing trades.

K%=0,55 - (0,45)/2=0,325 or 32,5%

By following the Kelly formula you would invest 32,5% of your capital in a single position,

It is interesting to give some values to the above formula to see how it works out in practice: for instance, if in a coin-tossing experiment (with the probability to win at 0.5) in case of loss the money amount of the loss is identical to the amount of gain, with the result that R equals 1, K% would equal 0 [K% = 0,5 − (1-0,5)/1 = 0] which means that one should reject this bet and not play at all.

Another conclusion is that a positive K% may arise either by a winning probability higher than 0.5% (which means you are right more often than wrong) or a Gain/Loss ratio higher than 1 (on average your winning bets are higher than your losers). You may be wrong more often than not and still reach a positive K% provided your R is high enough: think of option traders which may have a low W and still be profitable as their few big winners will more than make up for their many relatively small losses (a high W).

When applying these principles outside of the world of gambling (where the probability of gains and losses is well known and fixed once for all) in order to use them in stock trading some adjustments need to be made. The first thing to do is to establish the Gain/Loss probability which requires that the investor, on the basis of their past trades, determine the relevant percentages R and W. The amount of the gain is calculated as the difference between the purchase price and the sales price. As the above described calculation of the Kelly percentage (K%) gives a rather high result which some risk averse investors might find too aggressive, a more cautious approach is available: it is called "half-Kelly" and as the name suggests it consists in simply dividing the percentage K% by 2.

For readers interested in a more comprehensive description of the Kelly formula please refer to the very readable book of William Poundstone "Fortune's Formula: The Untold Story of the Scientific Betting System That Beat the Casinos and Wall Street."

Entering Positions

A defensive attitude requires entering any position in several steps. Suppose you want to take a position in Berkshire Hathaway corresponding to 10 percent of your total portfolio, the size of which is $500,000. Accordingly, the investor will invest $50,000 in Berkshire B shares (the A shares, basically offering the same economic rights are excluded in this case as their price is too high at the current price of some $300,000 per share). If the investor now decides to buy the B shares at a price of $200 they will be able to buy 250 shares. In order to minimize the entry price, the investor would be well advised to acquire these shares in different small steps, for instance three times some 85 shares. This will allow them to place a second order at a lower price, say at $190 (possibly followed by a third one at a price of $185, for example). In this way the investor will be able to obtain a lower entry price which at the end will boost their profit on the transaction (or reduce the loss thereof) by several percentage points.

When proceeding this way the investor will of course "average down" which many investment advisors strongly advise not to do; for those advisors, averaging down is akin to the proverbial "catching a falling knife." This is not my opinion (and it shouldn't be the one of any thoughtful investor). The reasons are twofold: Firstly, it may be argued that this is not a real averaging-down situation, given that the initially determined position of 10 per cent is not exceeded. The dangers inherent in averaging down could exist in case the initially planned position would be increased, for instance doubled, in our case if the investor did buy not just $50.000 but $100.000 in Berkshire stock. Secondly, the "prohibition" of averaging down reflects the philosophy of investors who consider that the stock market is always right and that after having bought some shares at $200, which then decrease to $190, the investor has made a mistake and should under no circumstances purchase additional shares of that company in order not to double down on that mistake. Obviously, this attitude disregards the fact that markets are often irrational, exaggerating, and off the mark by a long shot. This creates volatility and those investors who are able to profit thereof (because they do not count on the market's wisdom and do not consider that if the share prices move downwards this must represent a bad sign and this move may only be a first step of an evolution leading straight to bankruptcy) are able to considerably reduce their risk by decreasing their entry price *and at the same time increasing their return*. Yes: risk and return are not always inversely related. It is perfectly possible to increase the return and decrease risk (as explained in Chapter 2).

The neophyte investor, pushed by excitement created for instance by an analyst who guided their attention to a stock belonging to a currently faddish area (say hydrogen production, or plant-based meat), unfortunately does not have the patience to time their purchases and by FOMO, the "fear of missing out" the formidable increase of the stock price (which they have been able to see before their very eyes) will purchase right away, perhaps even by a market order.

Dollar-Cost Averaging (DCA)

One frequently recommended technique to be used in order to reduce the cost of stocks purchased is "dollar-cost averaging." The merits of this approach are appreciated differently by practicians and academicians. Let's first explain the essence of this method. "Dollar-cost averaging" consists in investing identical amounts of capital in the same security over a extended period of time with the consequence that for each periodic investment the number of shares purchased will be higher if prices are low and lower if prices are high, and in this way the arithmetic average cost per share will be reduced (and the more so the more volatile those prices are). This method is often recommended as an alternative to the mostly futile attempts to time the market.

For example: investor A, each month, buys shares of Company XYZ for $1,000 which shares currently trade at $20. In January our investor will buy 50 shares. In February the shares trade at 18 and the investor will buy 55.55 shares. In March the shares trade at 25 and A will buy only 40 shares, etc. Although the average share price over the 3 months has been $21 the average price paid by A is lower as it amounts to only $20.61 (50+55.55+40=145.55 shares for a total cost of 3,000).

Academicians have been critical on the merits of this method on the grounds that if dollar-cost averaging is beneficial to the investor in falling markets, it is hurting them in bull markets: in this last case, it is more efficient to go in for the whole amount as soon as possible (lump-sum method). According to this reasoning, as markets are going up most of the time, dollar-cost averaging is not an advisable method.

This being said, dollar-cost averaging is a suitable method to handle the emotional aspects of investing (and its pitfalls) by going on auto-pilot. The investor is protected, even if only slightly, against an investment at the wrong moment, meaning just before the market breaks down. Conversely, investors will also miss the full benefit of an investment at the market bottom if they did not invest the full amount of funds available at that moment.

If you follow Peter Lynch's advice to only buy stocks that make Wall Street yawn the likelihood that your share prices explode over a short period of time is very low. If it is certainly true that markets are more often raising than falling, this effect is clearly visible only over a very long period of time but it does not prevent that over short periods of time this effect is not playing. If you are cost-averaging, and spreading your investment over several weeks' time, the likelihood that stock prices will have substantially increased may safely be discarded.

The argument that cost-averaging is not advantageous is based on the comparison with lump sum investing. It should not be lost out of sight that dollar-cost averaging may apply even if lump sum investing is not an alternative, as is the case if an investor decides to invest monthly the same amount taken from their pay cheque. In addition to getting used to a regular investment discipline this method will guarantee lower average prices than those prevailing if they bought monthly the same number of shares (instead of the same dollar amount).

Some authors consider that DCA finds its followers in the basic loss aversion behavior of humans. By feeling the pain of a financial loss more than twice as much as they enjoy a similar gain, they accept an inferior strategy although it costs them money but it eliminates the risk of one big mistake (with the corresponding load of regret and emotional pain).

Falling Stock Prices

Investors should be flexible and always have an eye on stocks which are falling rapidly because such moves may offer great buying opportunities. The all-important point is to know the reasons for the price decrease: is it due to some widely published news, for instance (very) bad quarterly results? The fear of the markets is always that such bad results (assuming they are not just the continuation of bad previous results) are initiating a negative trend for the company. It may be that the loss in value is due to a downgrade by influential analysts (say Steve Tusa on General Electric) or it may be that there is a one-time issue which appears solvable, the impact of which may just be over-estimated by the markets. For instance, several years ago Wal-Mart was accused of having bribed officials in Mexico which led to a significant decrease of the stock price, or Samsung's Galaxy Note 7 catching fire which led to the recall and exchange against new ones of 2.5 million smartphones in 2016. JP Morgan's stocks took a huge hit when the so-called "London Whale" story became public. Quite often the reaction of the markets to such negative events is clearly excessive and assuming that the stock was not overbought before these events became public, these market drops may represent interesting buying opportunities.

The more tricky situations are those where the share prices dive for no apparent reason. Extreme caution is advisable: the market might "know" something which the investor does not know yet as the news has not yet become public. Over the last years, several of the most severe decreases of the share prices have been due to some so-called activist investors who shorted the shares of some companies which they thought to be either fraudulent, or simply over-valued or both. As a very prominent example of this tendency, the case of Herbalife, which was the target of hedge fund Pershing Square managed by Bill Ackman may be mentioned. Ackman alleged that Herbalife was running a so-called pyramid scheme which would be illegal. This issue has finally been settled in July 2016 when the FTC (Federal Trade Commission) fined Herbalife for an amount of $200.000.000 and requiring to change some of its more aggressive business practices. Another similar example would be the campaign run by another hedge fund, Prescient, against Chicago Bridge & Iron (CBI) a construction firm focused on the energy sector. The hedge fund alleged that CBI, during the 2013 merger with Shaw had followed questionable accounting practices and successfully shorted their CBI's stocks.

These hedge funds, in a first step quietly and secretly are accumulating huge short positions in the stocks they have selected which may lead to a continuous and rather steep declines in stock prices. It's only when they have completed their full position that they will go public with their thesis hoping to convince other investors to follow their move and go also short, in this way running the stock price further down. Once their price target is reached the hedge funds will cover their shorts and cash in their profits. A recent variant of this theme was initiated by forensic accountant Harry Markopolos (often referred to as the "Madoff whistleblower") who on August 15, 2019 alleged in a 175-pages report that GE had committed a $38 billion fraud, "bigger than Enron and Worldcom combined" (his words) allegedly due to under-provisioning in GE's long term care insurance business, forecasting that GE would go bankrupt before the end of 2019. He admitted that he had entered into a deal with a hedge fund (which he refused to name) who had shorted the GE stock and that the fund would pay him an agreed upon percentage of the gain realized on the short sale. The charges made by Markopolos were dismissed not only by GE (which called them "market manipulation pure and simple") but as well by the insurance supervisor responsible for GE, and most analysts, one of them labelled the whole report as "silly." On September 26, 2019 Barron's reported that the website www.gefraud.com had disappeared.

For investors, the lesson to be learned from such situations is that, confronted with an unexplained and sudden decrease in stock prices they should refrain from taking any position. Once the hedge funds have published their investment thesis, it is up to the investor to decide on the merits of the case. Very often however the conclusion for the investor will be to abstain from taking any position in the targeted shares. It may be too late to go short anyway for the reason that when the hedge funds publish their thesis the shares have already most of the downfall behind them. Going long could be an option: however, generally speaking hedge funds, who are specialized in searching for overvalued companies, are doing good research and you may be sure that they will only follow up on the very small number of companies which they consider to be clear cases for shorting.

If the investor wants to go long, they should not be in a hurry at all. They should just wait at least until the shares have bottomed out (or appear to have bottomed out). In other words, they should not buy on an all-time low. Once they consider a bottom is formed and if they are convinced that the short thesis is not justified they may slowly start buying. All things equal it is preferable to be too late than to be too early. By being too late, and by buying on the upside already, the investors reduce their risks of a catastrophic capital loss. Furthermore, the time during which their capital will be invested will be shorter.

In case they have serious doubts on the eventual outcome of the short they should simply abstain from taking any position.

When to Sell?

Most inexperienced investors believe that the hardest thing in investing is to know what shares to buy. Professional investors do know that this is not the case and that the most difficult thing is to know when to sell. In any case, an exit strategy is needed as many investors found out the hard way when the internet bubble burst in 2000-2001. At that time, many investors did not have such exit strategy and they kept their shares all the way down (some of them resisted the idea to sell by fear of having to pay the capital gains taxes on their latent profits… that issue was soon resolved…) often to a level close to zero.

An easy exit strategy consists in going on automated pilot and simply sell the shares if they have lost a fixed percentage of their purchase price (say 5, 8 or 10%) by a stop loss order (a stop loss order consists in instructing the broker to place a market order when a certain price level is hit) or by selling if the price reaches a certain level, for instance if the market price has reached a level of, say, 25 percent or 40 percent higher than the purchase price. This is a mechanical system which will be implemented by the broker without any further intervention by the investor. The principal advantage of this system is its simplicity and of course also that it will avoid any really catastrophic losses (assuming that the stop-loss limit has been fixed sufficiently close to the purchase price). However, such an automatic system has its fair share of disadvantages.

The first disadvantage is that in fact it takes the price movement of the stock as being an efficient guide for investor decisions. For a long time already it can be taken as accepted wisdom that the stock market should never be taken as a guide on the real value of stocks but its value for investors is simply to provide them liquidity, and nothing else. By placing a stop-loss order some 5-10 percent below the stock's purchase price the investor simply admits to have made a mistake by buying those shares. It might well be that the investor has made a mistake by buying those shares but they should not rely on the markets to tell them that truth. Price movements over a short period are erratic and unpredictable and any decrease following the purchase may be due to causes totally unconnected with any reasonable intrinsic value calculation. In such case, it would make a lot more sense for the investor instead of selling their position which has decreased in price to buy more shares. If a stock priced $60 is a buy, the same stock priced $54 is certainly a better buy even (all other things equal).

With respect to sales made automatically once a certain profit margin is reached (or after a certain time period, for instance sale at a 20 percent profit and in any case after a two-year holding period) the appraisal of this method is also all but positive. The first and very obvious point is that if an investor will always sell once a stock has increased by 20 percent or so, the big hits (those which make a difference in the long run), the purchases which allow to double, triple, etc. the invested capital (the X-baggers), will always escape them.

By selling after realizing a small capital gain, taxes become due: it is a lot more efficient to save the amount of taxes (by not selling) and keep the corresponding funds invested in the market.

Finally, the moment to sell a certain stock is certainly when the market price of the stock exceeds intrinsic value of the stock and this by a significant margin. Indeed, when this is the case, you do own a stock which you would not buy: as indicated previously, stocks should only be bought if their price is significantly below their intrinsic value. It is only this difference that creates the margin of safety which is an absolute must for sound investing.

This statement may attract criticism for being too narrow in the sense that it only takes into consideration the stock concerned without reference to alternative investment opportunities. If we do take those other opportunities into consideration as well, we may conclude that a stock should be sold as soon as the margin of safety gets negative or, even if that is not the case, if the market offers alternative opportunities with a higher margin of safety.

In this context, two things should not be lost out of sight: it is not possible to determine the intrinsic value with mathematical certainty; furthermore, tax aspects have to be taken into consideration as well. If a taxable person, selling the shares will trigger the levy of income taxes on the accumulated capital gain. The price to be obtained on the market will have to be decreased by the tax on capital gains which will become due on the disposal of the shares.

Let's consider the following example. An investor has purchased 100 Microsoft shares at the price of $20 many years ago. In 2020 the price has increased to $200, so that on sale of these shares the capital gain will be taxable at the long-term capital gains tax rate of 15%. The taxable capital gain amounts to 100*(200-20) = $18,000 which will trigger the levy of a capital gains tax of $2,700. The tax cost per share will amount to $27 so that the investor will have to count that their sales price in fact does not reach the price of $200 but only $173.

An important element in this situation is to know whether the investor is able to find stocks with an adequate margin of safety. If so, the question of the sale of those stocks which no longer have such margin of safety has probably to be answered positively. Indeed, these alternative options will allow the investor to buy shares with a low risk and with a higher earnings rate over the next several years (as they will be able to repeat the same scenario once again: profit from the normal appreciation of the shares in addition to profiting from the closing of the gap existing between intrinsic value and market price).

Conclusion

When choosing an itinerary on a road map the first thing to do is to find out what is the traveller's present location meaning where they are currently standing. When applied to the field of investing in stocks the "position check" is somewhat more difficult as it consists in assessing what are the present market conditions prevailing on the stock markets where the investors are operating, how expensive are the stocks currently compared to business fundamentals, historical data, etc. Which stocks sectors are currently overbought and which sectors are neglected for one reason or the other? When doing this market positioning at the current time, that is at the end of the 3rd quarter of 2020, the conclusion is that stock prices are very volatile, due to extreme market uncertainty, which is a direct consequence of the Covid-19 pandemic, combatted by so far unheard of $X trillion government financed economic support packages, the effects of which are however currently very difficult to forecast.

In such an environment, it is not easy to figure out what are the durable consequences on the behavior of people induced by the pandemic: what counts are the lasting effects on such behavior, which is a life-or-death question hanging over the future of entire economic sectors, say, the airline industry and airplane construction sector with its suppliers (for instance the aircraft engines), the cruise ship industry, including the construction of these cruise ships, the hotel industry, entertainment parks, professional sports, etc..

For all these sectors there is a very broad range of possible outcomes which make that valuing those stocks has become a high-risk activity and the wisest decision is probably to navigate around those sectors for the time being. Once a reliable vaccine is found (or at least a treatment which allows for healing the disease with a high degree of reliability) a reassessment of these industries will certainly be made by the markets: in all likelihood prices will strongly correct once the announcements of positive reliable results on the sanitary front will be made. One thing is sufficiently sure: the amounts of capital waiting to be invested in the stock markets are considerable which was abundantly proved by the quick rebound of the stocks after March 23, 2020 the day of the market low following the Covid-19 crisis.

Another key question, which is also directly connected to the pandemic, is what will be the incidence on interest rates over the medium and long term of the $X trillion aid packages which have been set up all over the globe. In the short term interest rates will probably not go up significantly but beyond 2 to 5 years it is far from being sure that the same will hold true.

Political uncertainty is not absent either: in the first place, the result of the forthcoming US presidential election will certainly have an impact on fiscal policy (impact which will be heavily influenced by the result of the Congress elections occurring at the same time). Relations with China which will most certainly remain stressed, regardless of the results of the November 2020 elections, will also make that geopolitically the situation will remain highly uncertain.

To the surprise of many people, myself included, stock markets have shown enormous resilience since the pandemic hit outside China and has forced the lockdown of most of the economic activity of Western countries including many of the emerging economies. This lockdown period is behind us and in most of the countries, economic activity continues to recover, although only slowly. Not surprisingly the results of the second quarter 2020 have been bad to disastrous depending on what sector the companies concerned are a part of. On the other hand, there are some winners of the pandemic, in the first place the megacap high-tech companies, Amazon, Apple, Facebook, Google and Microsoft but also other technology companies for which the stock behavior shows increasingly signs for concern. Take the stock split of two prominent companies which have over the past years and especially during the last months increased beyond the wildest hopes of even their most fanatic supporters: reference is made here to Apple (3 new shares for 1 old share) and Tesla (4 new shares for 1 old share) which both proceeded to a stock split on August 31, 2020. From the day of the announcement of this stock split the stock on July, 30 by Apple its stock continued to increase by 30%. Tesla announced the stock split even later, on August 11, 2020 and still its stock price increased by 61% (you read that right) until the date of the split on August 31, 2020, which leads that company to a P/E ratio of only … 1,145. Notwithstanding this already outlandish valuation, both stocks went on to increase the days after the stock split before, together with other companies of their group, they have started to correct severely as of September 4th.

As seen above, stock splits are (or should be) non-events ("nothing to write home about") for the rational investor and if for the herd they are the pretext for a stock market orgy concerning two already fully valuated companies to increase their capitalization by tens and even hundreds of $ billions then time has come to get (very) fearful as many others have already become extremely and excessively greedy. Another preoccupying feature is that the stock market increasingly does double-counting: if favorable news are announced the stock price increases and these good news are now baked into the stock price (which is normal) but when the said event actually unfolds then the stock price increases a second time (which is not justifiable).

Such signs, and others, are ignored by investors at their own peril only.

September 12th, 2020

Index

O

P

S

T

Endnotes

1 Even if no brokerage fees are charged anymore, stock transactions have not become entirey free; the spread between "bid" and "ask" remains a cost factor suffered by the investor.

2 Jeremy Siegel, The Future for Investors: Why the Tried and the True Triumphs Over the Bold and the New.

3 It appears that if these series of figures were prolongated to the year 2019 not much would change except that the relative performance for gold would have improved somewhat, and this mostly due to the relatively strong performance over the years 2004 to 2012.

4 Andrew Craig, Roger Gifford, How to Own the World: A Plain English Guide to Thinking Gobally and Investing Wisely: The New Edition of the Life-changing Personal Finance Bestseller.

5 Julia La Roche, Yahoo Finance of August 17, 2020.

6 Robert Shiller in "Irrational Exuberance: Revised and Expanded Third Edition" (2015).

7 Dimson/Marsh/Staunton, Triumph of the Optimists: 101 Years of Global Investment Returns, Princeton University Press, 2002.

8 William Proctor, Scott Phillips, The Templeton Touch.

9 Financila Times of February 10, 2020, John Dizard, Coronavirus strikes World Bank 'cat' bonds.

10 Robin Wigglesworth, Financial Times of September 12, 2019.

11 Dimson/Marsh/Staunton, Triumph of the Optimists: 101 Years of Global Investment Returns, Princeton University Press, 2002.

12 According to official US CPI data.

13 Research Affiliates, as reported by the Financial Times of July 29, 2019.

[14] Financial Times of July 29, 2019.
[15] "Investing in Japan (English Edition)" by Steven Towns).

[16] Quoted from Dimson/Marsh/Staunton, Triumph of the Optimists: 101 Years of Global Investment Returns, Princeton University Press, 2002.

[17] Aswath Damodaran, Financial Times of June 11, 2019.

[18] The reader may rightfully be surprised to read the phrase "…to generate beta, which is the market return" as beta normally is an expression of risk/volatility. This is Wall Street speak which I follow here for reasons of shortness: to "generate beta" means a risk-adjusted return given beta of the specific stock (or portfolio

[19] It needs to be added that the reality of this "small-cap." effect appears to be somewhat doubtful as it was confirmed only for some relatively short periods in the US and was hardly found in other countries.

[20] Lockett/Hughes, Financial Times of April 11, 2020.

[21] See Wikipedia, S&P 500 Dividend aristocrats.

[22] This quotation is made from the 2019 Annual Report of Nike, p. 45.

[23] Aswath Damodaran, Financial Times of June 11, 2019, p. 20.

[24] Patrick Jenkins, Financial Times of March 27, 2019.

[25] Tom Braitwaite, Financial Times of July 27/28, 2019.

[26] More details on these concepts are given under the next paragraph, Normal Distribution.

[27] Alex Beard, Natural Born Learners: Our Incredible Capacity to Learn and How We Can Harness It.

[28] A similar book title, where the concept of Black Box has a completely different meaning is the one given by Frank Pasquale to his book "The Black Box Society" which deals with the intrasparency of the large technology groups, like Amazon, Apple, Facebook, Google and Microsoft.

[29] Seeking Wisdom: Thoughts on Value Investing, by Thomas G Macpherson.

30 Grossmann and Stiglitz, On the impossibility of informationally efficient markets, American Economic Review, 393-408.

31 Adam Kucharski "The Rules of Contagion: Why Things Spread - and Why They Stop".

32 Nudge: Improving Decisions About Health, Wealth and Happiness (English Edition)" by Richard H Thaler, Cass R Sunstein.

[33] Bethany McLean, Peter Elkind, "The Smartest Guys in the Room: The Amazing Rise and Scandalous Fall of Enron"

[34] John Dizard, Financial Times, November 25, 2019.

[35] The interested reader may find some comments on the peculiarities of this Apple stock split (and the simultaneous Tesla stock split) in the Conclusion.

[36] It has to be mentioned that for non-listed companies, goodwill is still a depreciable asset which is written off over 10 years (in the US).

[37] Due to the reduction of the Corporate tax rate which decreased from 35 to 21% enacted by the TCJA the provisions for future income taxes payable were calculated by the reduced rate of 21% instead of the previously applicable rate to 35%.

[38] Tom Braitwaite, FT, July 27/28 2019.

[39] Rana Foroohar, Don't Be Evil: The Case Against Big Tech

[40] Shoshana Zuboff, The Age of Surveillance Capitalism: The Fight for a Human Future at the New Frontier of Power.

[41] At the time of this writing (August 2020) the stockmarket value of shareholding in Apple is higher by more than $50 bn (!) compared to the one of December 31, 2019.

[42] John Heins/Whitney Tilson, The Art of Value Investing, Wiley, p. 191.

43 Simon Kuper, Financial Times of April 13/14, 2019.

[44] In general one assumes a strong growh rate in earnings for the first 10 years and a lower rate for the following years; one might as well do the opposite (but that might not be cautious…) and both assumptions may lead to the the same valuation. The only point to be aware of is that the growth rate of the second period cannot be identical or higher than the discount rate used.

[45] As Buffett explains in his 2007 chairman's letter to shareholders, p. 6.

[46] Martin Wolf, Financial Times of February 26, 2020.

[47] Financial Times of October 17, 2019.
[48] T. Phelps, 100 to 1 in the Stock Market, p. 221.

49 According to the Financial Times of October 17, 2019.